The Queer Art of Failure

A JOHN HOPE

FRANKLIN CENTER

BOOK

The Queer Art of Failure

Judith Halberstam

DUKE UNIVERSITY PRESS | DURHAM AND LONDON | 2011

Printed in the United States
of America on acid-free paper ∞
Designed by Amy Ruth Buchanan
Typeset in Quadraat and Quadraat Sans
by Tseng Information Systems, Inc.
Library of Congress Cataloging-
in-Publication Data appear on the
last printed page of this book.

Duke University Press gratefully
acknowledges the University of
Southern California, which
provided funds toward the
production of this book.

FOR

ALL OF

HISTORY'S

LOSERS

Figures

ACKNOWLEDGMENTS

Perhaps no one actually wants acknowledgement in relation to a project on failure! Nonetheless, in the spirit of the alternative forms of knowledge production that this book advocates, I must recognize here all the wonderful people who have guided me to failure, stupidity, and negativity, not to mention loss, lack, and SpongeBob SquarePants. Though she may not remember it, Lauren Berlant first introduced me to the wacky art of plot summary when she narrated at length and in hilarious detail the *South Park* episode "Mr. Hankey, the Christmas Poo." The episode stayed with me for many reasons, not least for its themes of exclusion and loneliness in the story line about a Jewish kid at Christmas. But it was in the retelling, at an MLA convention no less, that the Christmas Poo seemed to open up new narrative zones of possibility. There is much plot summary in this book, hopefully of the Berlant entertaining variety. I have performed some of it for audiences at many universities, and I thank all the people who have invited me to speak in the past five years, as this book took shape. I also thank my wonderful colleagues at USC, including Ruthie Gilmore, Sarah Gualtieri, Ange-Marie Hancock, Kara Keeling, Robin Kelley, Josh Kun, Akira Lippit, David Lloyd, Maria Elena Martinez, Teresa McKenna, Tania Modleski, Laura Pulido, Shana Redmond, John Carlos Rowe, George Sanchez, Karen Tongson, and Sherry Velasco.

I thank the many artists whose work has in part inspired this book: Judie Bamber, Nao Bustamante, Cabello/Carceller, LTTR, Monica Majoli, J. A. Nicholls, Collier Schorr, and others. And I thank the students with whom I work, especially Deborah Alkamano, Zach Blas, Matthew Carrillo-Vincent, Jih-Fei Cheng, April Davidauski, Jennifer DeClue, Laura

Fugikawa, Kiana Green, Yetta Howard, Alexis Lothian, Stacy Macias, Alvaro Marquez, Alice-Mihaela Bardan, Gretel Rosas, and Evren Savci, for making their own contributions to my thinking on alternative pedagogies and the pursuit of ignorance.

At a time when, sadly, the idea of subversion has gone out of style, I still want to pitch my tent with a renegade band of persistently subversive intellectuals: Paul Amar, Alicia Arrizon, Carmen Romero Bachiller, Jennifer Brody, Daphne Brooks, Jayna Brown, Judith Butler, Heather Cassils, Mel Chen, T. Cooper, Ann Cvetkovich, Harry Dodge, David Eng, Antke Engel, Kale Fajardo, Roderick Ferguson, Carla Freccero, Rosa-Linda Fregoso, Elena Glasberg, Gayatri Gopinath, Herman Grey, Dominique Grisard, Aeyal Gross, Christina Hanhardt, Gil Hochberg, Sharon Holland, John Howard, Silas Howard, Annamarie Jagose, Keri Kanetsky, Jane Knox, Tim Lawrence, Ariel Levy, Ira Livingston, Renate Lorenz, Heather Love, Lisa Lowe, Martin Manalansan, Angela McRobbie, Robert McRuer, Mara Mills, Nick Mirzoeff, Fred Moten, José Esteban Muñoz, Eileen Myles, Maggie Nelson, Tavia Nyong'o, Marcia Ochoa, Gema Perez-Sanchez, Raquel (Lucas) Platero, Chandan Reddy, Isabel Reiss, Lisa Rofel, Jordana Rosenberg, Tiina Rosenberg, Cherry Smyth, Dean Spade, Anna Joy Springer, Omise'eke Natasha Tinsley, Jürg Tschirren, Deborah Vargas, Del Grace Volcano, Jane Ward, Patricia White, and Julia Bryan Wilson. I thank the UCI Humanities Research Center and David Goldberg in particular for selecting me for the Critical Animal Studies group, and thanks to Mel Chen for her leadership in the group.

Special thanks to Ken Wissoker at Duke University Press and to Lisa Duggan, Elizabeth Freeman, and Lisa Rofel for their astute and encouraging readings of various drafts of the book. Last but not least, I offer thanks and love to my very own quirky little animated family of Ixchel Leni, Renato Leni, and (most important) Macarena Gomez-Barris, all of whom inspire me and encourage me to fail better every day.

Parts of this book have appeared as essays. A piece of chapter 1 appeared as "Beyond Broadway and Main: A Response to the Presidential Address," *American Quarterly* 61, no. 1 (2009), 33–38. A very early version of chapter 2 was published as "Forgetting Family: Queer Alternatives to Oedipal Relations," *Companion to Lesbian, Gay, Bisexual, Transgender and Queer Studies*, ed. Molly McGarry and George Haggerty (London: Blackwell, 2007). An early version of chapter 4 appeared in German as "Notes on Failure," *The Power and Politics of the Aesthetic in American Culture*, ed. Klaus Benesch and Ulla Haselstein (Heidelberg: Universitatsverlag, 2007).

What's the Alternative?

Mr. Krabs: And just when you think you've found the land of milk and honey, they grab ya by the britches, and haul you way up high, and higher, and higher, and HIGHER, until you're hauled up to the surface, flopping and gasping for breath! And then they cook ya, and then they eat ya—or worse!

SpongeBob: [*Terrified*] What could be worse than that?

Mr. Krabs: [*Softly*] Gift shops.

—"Hooky," *SpongeBob SquarePants*

Just when you think you have found the land of milk and honey, Mr. Krabs tells poor old SpongeBob SquarePants, you find yourself on the menu, or worse, in the gift shop as part of the product tie-in for the illusion to which you just waved goodbye. We are all used to having our dreams crushed, our hopes smashed, our illusions shattered, but what comes after hope? And what if, like SpongeBob SquarePants, we don't believe that a trip to the land of milk and honey inevitably ends at the gift shop? What is the alternative, in other words, to cynical resignation on the one hand and naïve optimism on the other? What is the alternative, SpongeBob wants to know, to working all day for Mr. Krabs, or being captured in the net of commodity capitalism while trying to escape? This book, a kind of "SpongeBob SquarePants Guide to Life," loses the idealism of hope in order to gain wisdom and a new, spongy relation to life, culture, knowledge, and pleasure.

So what is the alternative? This simple question announces a political project, begs for a grammar of possibility (here expressed in gerunds and the passive voice, among other grammars of pronouncement), and expresses a basic desire to live life otherwise. Academics, activists, artists, and cartoon characters have long been on a quest to articulate an alternative vision of life, love, and labor and to put such a vision into practice. Through the use of manifestoes, a range of political tactics, and new technologies of representation, radical utopians continue to search for different ways of being in the world and being in relation to one another than those already prescribed for the liberal and consumer subject. This book uses "low theory" (a term I am adapting from Stuart Hall's work) and popular knowledge to explore alternatives and to look for a way out of the usual traps and impasses of binary formulations. Low theory tries to locate all the in-between spaces that save us from being snared by the hooks of hegemony and speared by the seductions of the gift shop. But it also makes its peace with the possibility that alternatives dwell in the murky waters of a counterintuitive, often impossibly dark and negative realm of critique and refusal. And so the book darts back and forth between high and low culture, high and low theory, popular culture and esoteric knowledge, in order to push through the divisions between life and art, practice and theory, thinking and doing, and into a more chaotic realm of knowing and unknowing.

In this book I range from children's animation to avant-garde performance and queer art to think about ways of being and knowing that stand outside of conventional understandings of success. I argue that success in a heteronormative, capitalist society equates too easily to specific forms of reproductive maturity combined with wealth accumulation. But these measures of success have come under serious pressure recently, with the collapse of financial markets on the one hand and the epic rise in divorce rates on the other. If the boom and bust years of the late twentieth century and the early twenty-first have taught us anything, we should at least have a healthy critique of static models of success and failure.

Rather than just arguing for a reevaluation of these standards of passing and failing, *The Queer Art of Failure* dismantles the logics of success and failure with which we currently live. Under certain circumstances failing, losing, forgetting, unmaking, undoing, unbecoming, not knowing may in fact offer more creative, more cooperative, more surprising ways of being in the world. Failing is something queers do and have always done exceptionally well; for queers failure can be a style, to cite Quentin Crisp, or a way of life, to cite Foucault, and it can stand in contrast to the grim scenarios of success that depend upon "trying and trying again." In fact if success requires so much effort, then maybe failure is easier in the long run and offers different rewards.

What kinds of reward can failure offer us? Perhaps most obviously, failure allows us to escape the punishing norms that discipline behavior and manage human development with the goal of delivering us from unruly childhoods to orderly and predictable adulthoods. Failure preserves some of the wondrous anarchy of childhood and disturbs the supposedly clean boundaries between adults and children, winners and losers. And while failure certainly comes accompanied by a host of negative affects, such as disappointment, disillusionment, and despair, it also provides the opportunity to use these negative affects to poke holes in the toxic positivity of contemporary life. As Barbara Ehrenreich reminds us in *Bright-sided*, positive thinking is a North American affliction, "a mass delusion" that emerges out of a combination of American exceptionalism and a desire to believe that success happens to good people and failure is just a consequence of a bad attitude rather than structural conditions (2009: 13). Positive thinking is offered up in the U.S. as a cure for cancer, a path to untold riches, and a surefire way to engineer your own success. Indeed believing that success depends upon one's attitude is far preferable to Americans than recognizing that their success is the outcome of the tilted scales of race, class, and gender. As Ehrenreich puts it, "If optimism is the key to material success, and if you can achieve an optimistic outlook through the discipline of positive thinking, then there is no excuse for failure." But, she continues, "the flip side of positivity is thus a harsh insistence on personal responsibility," meaning that while capitalism produces some people's success through other people's failures, the ideology of positive thinking insists that success depends only upon working hard and failure is always of your own doing (8). We know better of course in an age when the banks that ripped off ordinary people have been deemed "too big to fail" and the people who bought bad mortgages are simply too little to care about.

In *Bright-sided* Ehrenreich uses the example of American women's application of positive thinking to breast cancer to demonstrate how dangerous the belief in optimism can be and how deeply Americans want to believe that health is a matter of attitude rather than environmental

positive thinking, Am. exceptionalism

degradation and that wealth is a matter of visualizing success rather than having the cards stacked in your favor. For the nonbelievers outside the cult of positive thinking, however, the failures and losers, the grouchy, irritable whiners who do not want to "have a nice day" and who do not believe that getting cancer has made them better people, politics offers a better explanatory framework than personal disposition. For these negative thinkers, there are definite advantages to failing. Relieved of the obligation to keep smiling through chemotherapy or bankruptcy, the negative thinker can use the experience of failure to confront the gross inequalities of everyday life in the United States.

From the perspective of feminism, failure has often been a better bet than success. Where feminine success is always measured by male standards, and gender failure often means being relieved of the pressure to measure up to patriarchal ideals, not succeeding at womanhood can offer unexpected pleasures. In many ways this has been the message of many renegade feminists in the past. Monique Wittig (1992) argued in the 1970s that if womanhood depends upon a heterosexual framework, then lesbians are not "women," and if lesbians are not "women," then they fall outside of patriarchal norms and can re-create some of the meaning of their genders. Also in the 1970s Valerie Solanas suggested that if "woman" takes on meaning only in relation to "man," then we need to "cut up men" (2004: 72). Perhaps that is a little drastic, but at any rate these kinds of feminisms, what I call shadow feminisms in chapter 5, have long haunted the more acceptable forms of feminism that are oriented to positivity, reform, and accommodation rather than negativity, rejection, and transformation. Shadow feminisms take the form not of becoming, being, and doing but of shady, murky modes of undoing, unbecoming, and violating.

By way of beginning a discussion of failure, let's think about a popular version of female failure that also proves instructive and entertaining. In Little Miss Sunshine (2006, directed by Jonathan Dayton and Valerie Faris) Abigail Breslin plays Olive Hoover, a young girl with her sights set on winning a Little Miss Sunshine beauty pageant. The road trip that takes her and her dysfunctional family to southern California from Albuquerque makes as eloquent a statement about success and failure as any that I could conjure here. With her porn-obsessed junky grandfather providing her with the choreography for her pageant routine and a cheerleading squad made up of a gay suicidal uncle, a Nietzsche-reading mute brother, an aspiring but flailing motivational speaker father, and an exasperated stay-at-home mom, Olive is destined to fail, and to fail spectacularly. But while her failure could be the source of misery and humiliation, and while it does indeed deliver precisely this, it also leads to a kind of ecstatic exposure of the contradictions of a society obsessed with meaningless competition. By implication it also reveals the precarious models of success by which American families live and die.

Michael Arndt, who won an Oscar as the scriptwriter for the film, said that he was inspired to write the script after hearing Governor Arnold Schwarzenegger of California declare, "If there is one thing in this world that I despise, it's losers!" Obviously the faintly fascistic worldview of winners and losers that Schwarzenegger promotes has contributed in large part to the bankrupting of his state, and *Little Miss Sunshine* is in many ways a view from below, the perspective of the loser in a world that is interested only in winners. While Olive's failure as a beauty pageant contestant plays out against the soundtrack of "Superfreak" on a stage in a bland hotel in Redondo Beach in front of a room full of supermoms and their "JonBenet" daughters, this failure, hilarious in its execution, poignant in its meaning, and exhilarating in its aftermath, is so much better, so much more liberating than any success that could possibly be achieved in the context of a teen beauty contest. By gyrating and stripping to a raunchy song while heavily made-up and coiffed little cowgirls and princesses wait in the wings for their chance to chastely sway in the spotlight, Olive reveals the sexuality that is the real motivation for the preteen pageant. Without retreating to a puritanical attack on sexual pleasure or a moral mode of disapproval, *Little Miss Sunshine* instead relinquishes the Darwinian motto of winners, "May the best girl win," and cleaves to a neo-anarchistic credo of ecstatic losers: "No one gets left behind!" The dysfunctional little family jumps in and out of its battered yellow vw and holds together despite being bruised and abused along the way. And despite or perhaps because of the suicide attempts, the impending bankruptcy, the death of the family patriarch, and the ultimate irrelevancy of the beauty contest, a new kind of optimism is born. Not an optimism that relies on positive thinking as an explanatory engine for social order, nor one that insists upon the bright side at all costs; rather this is a little ray of sunshine that produces shade and light in equal measure and knows that the meaning of one always depends upon the meaning of the other.

Undisciplined

Illegibility, then, has been and remains, a reliable source for political autonomy.
—James C. Scott, *Seeing Like a State*

Any book that begins with a quote from *SpongeBob SquarePants* and is motored by wisdom gleaned from *Fantastic Mr. Fox*, *Chicken Run*, and *Finding Nemo*, among other animated guides to life, runs the risk of not being taken seriously. Yet this is my goal. Being taken seriously means missing out on the chance to be frivolous, promiscuous, and irrelevant. The desire to be taken seriously is precisely what compels people to follow the tried and true paths of knowledge production around which I would like to map a few detours. Indeed terms like *serious* and *rigorous* tend to be code words, in academia as well as other contexts, for disciplinary correctness; they signal a form of training and learning that confirms what is already known according to approved methods of knowing, but they do not allow for visionary insights or flights of fancy. Training of any kind, in fact, is a way of refusing a kind of Benjaminian relation to knowing, a stroll down uncharted streets in the "wrong" direction (Benjamin 1996); it is precisely about staying in well-lit territories and about knowing exactly which way to go before you set out. Like many others before me, I propose that instead the goal is to lose one's way, and indeed to be prepared to lose more than one's way. Losing, we may agree with Elizabeth Bishop, is an art, and one "that is not too hard to master / Though it may look like a disaster" (2008: 166–167).

In the sciences, particularly physics and mathematics, there are many examples of rogue intellectuals, not all of whom are reclusive Unabomber types (although more than a few are just that), who wander off into uncharted territories and refuse the academy because the publish-or-perish pressure of academic life keeps them tethered to conventional knowledge production and its well-traveled byways. Popular mathematics books, for example, revel in stories about unconventional loners who are self-schooled and who make their own way through the world of numbers. For some kooky minds, disciplines actually get in the way of answers and theorems precisely because they offer maps of thought where intuition and blind fumbling might yield better results. In 2008, for example, *The New Yorker* featured a story about an oddball physicist who, like many ambitious physicists and mathematicians, was in hot pursuit of a grand theory, a "theory of everything." This thinker, Garrett Lisi, had dropped out of academic physics because string theory dominated the field at that time and he thought the answers lay elsewhere. As an outsider to the discipline, writes Benjamin Wallace-Wells, Lisi "built his theory as an outsider might, relying on a grab bag of component parts: a hand-built mathematical structure, an unconventional way of describing gravity, and a mysterious mathematical entity known as E8."[1] In the end Lisi's "theory of everything" fell short of expectations, but it nonetheless yielded a whole terrain of new questions and methods. Similarly the computer scientists who pioneered new programs to produce computer-generated imagery (CGI), as many accounts of the rise of Pixar have chronicled, were academic rejects or dropouts who created independent institutes in order to explore their dreams of animated worlds.[2] These alternative cultural and academic realms, the areas beside academia rather than within it, the intellectual worlds conjured by losers, failures, dropouts, and refuseniks, often serve as the launching pad for alternatives precisely when the university cannot.

This is not a bad time to experiment with disciplinary transformation on behalf of the project of generating new forms of knowing, since the fields that were assembled over one hundred years ago to respond to new market economies and the demand for narrow expertise, as Foucault described them, are now losing relevance and failing to respond either to real-world knowledge projects or student interests. As the big disciplines begin to crumble like banks that have invested in bad securities we might ask more broadly, Do we really want to shore up the ragged boundaries of our shared interests and intellectual commitments, or might we rather take this opportunity to rethink the project of learning and thinking altogether? Just as the standardized tests that the U.S. favors as a guide to intellectual advancement in high schools tend to identify people who are good at standardized exams (as opposed to, say, intellectual visionaries), so in universities grades, exams, and knowledge of canons identify scholars with an aptitude for maintaining and conforming to the dictates of the discipline.

This book, a stroll out of the confines of conventional knowledge and into the unregulated territories of failure, loss, and unbecoming, must make a long detour around disciplines and ordinary ways of thinking. Let me explain how universities (and by implication high schools) squash rather than promote quirky and original thought. Disciplinarity, as defined by Foucault (1995), is a technique of modern power: it depends upon and deploys normalization, routines, convention, tradition, and regularity, and it produces experts and administrative forms of governance. The university structure that houses the disciplines and jealously guards their boundaries now stands at a crossroads, not of disciplinarity and interdisciplinarity, past and future, national and transnational; the crossroads at which the rapidly disintegrating bandwagon of disciplines, subfields, and interdisciplines has arrived offer a choice between the university as corporation and investment opportunity and the university as a new kind of public sphere with a different investment in knowledge, in ideas, and in thought and politics.

A radical take on disciplinarity and the university that presumes both the breakdown of the disciplines and the closing of gaps between fields conventionally presumed to be separated can be found in a manifesto published by Fred Moten and Stefano Harney in 2004 in *Social Text* titled "The University and the Undercommons: Seven Theses." Their essay is a searing critique directed at the intellectual and the critical intellectual, the professional scholar and the "critical academic professionals." For Moten and Harney, the critical academic is not the answer to encroaching professionalization but an extension of it, using the very same tools and legitimating strategies to become "an ally of professional education." Moten and Harney prefer to pitch their tent with the "subversive intellectuals," a maroon community of outcast thinkers who refuse, resist, and renege on the demands of "rigor," "excellence," and "productivity." They tell us to "steal from the university," to "steal the enlightenment for others" (112), and to act against "what Foucault called the Conquest, the unspoken war that founded, and with the force of law refounds, society" (113). And what does the undercommons of the university want to be? It wants to constitute an unprofessional force of fugitive knowers, with a set of intellectual practices not bound by examination systems and test scores. The goal for this unprofessionalization is not to abolish; in fact Moten and Harney set the fugitive intellectual against the elimination or abolition of this, the founding or refounding of that: "Not so much the abolition of prisons but the abolition of a society that could have prisons, that could have slavery, that could have the wage, and therefore not abolition as the elimination of anything but abolition as the founding of a new society" (113).

Not the elimination of anything but the founding of a new society. And why not? Why not think in terms of a different kind of society than the one that first created and then abolished slavery? The social worlds we inhabit, after all, as so many thinkers have reminded us, are not inevitable; they were not always bound to turn out this way, and what's more, in the process of producing this reality, many other realities, fields of knowledge, and ways of being have been discarded and, to cite Foucault again, "disqualified." A few visionary books, produced alongside disciplinary knowledge, show us the paths not taken. For example, in a book that itself began as a detour, *Seeing Like a State: How Certain Schemes to Improve the Human Condition Have Failed* (1999), James C. Scott details the ways the modern state has run roughshod over local, customary, and undisciplined forms of knowledge in order to rationalize and simplify social, agricultural, and political practices that have profit as their primary motivation. In the process, says Scott, certain ways of seeing the world are established as normal or natural, as obvious and necessary, even though they are often entirely counterintuitive and socially engineered. *Seeing Like a State* began as a study of "why the state has always seemed to be the enemy of 'people who move around,'" but quickly became a study of the demand by the state for legibility through the imposition of methods of standardization and uniformity (1). While Dean Spade (2008) and other queer scholars use Scott's book to think about how we came to insist upon the documentation of gender identity on all governmental documentation, I want to use his monumental study to pick up some of the discarded local knowledges that are trampled underfoot in the rush to bureaucratize and rationalize an economic order that privileges profit over all kinds of other motivations for being and doing.

In place of the Germanic ordered forest that Scott uses as a potent metaphor for the start of the modern imposition of bureaucratic order upon populations, we might go with the thicket of subjugated knowledge that sprouts like weeds among the disciplinary forms of knowledge, threatening always to overwhelm the cultivation and pruning of the intellect with mad plant life. For Scott, to "see like a state" means to accept the order of things and to internalize them; it means that we begin to deploy and think with the logic of the superiority of orderliness and that we erase and indeed sacrifice other, more local practices of knowledge, practices moreover that may be less efficient, may yield less marketable results, but may also, in the long term, be more sustaining. What is at stake in arguing for the trees and against the forest? Scott identifies "legibility" as the favored technique of high modernism for sorting, organizing, and profiting from land and people and for abstracting systems of knowledge from local knowledge practices. He talks about the garden and gardeners as representative of a new spirit of intervention and order favored within high modernism, and he points to the minimalism and simplicity of Le Corbusier's urban design as part of a new commitment to symmetry and division and planning that complements authoritarian preferences for hierarchies and despises the complex and messy forms of organic profusion and improvised creativity. "Legibility," writes Scott, "is a condition of manipulation" (1999: 183). He favors instead, borrowing from European anarchist thought, more practical forms of knowledge that he calls *metis* and that emphasize mutuality, collectivity, plasticity, diversity, and adaptability. Illegibility may in fact be one way of escaping the political manipulation to which all university fields and disciplines are subject.

While Scott's insight about illegibility has implications for all kinds of subjects who are manipulated precisely when they become legible and visible to the state (undocumented workers, visible queers, racialized minorities), it also points to an argument for antidisciplinarity in the sense that knowledge practices that refuse both the form and the content of traditional canons may lead to unbounded forms of speculation, modes of thinking that ally not with rigor and order but with inspiration and unpredictability. We may in fact want to think about how to see unlike a state; we may want new rationales for knowledge production, different aesthetic standards for ordering or disordering space, other modes of political engagement than those conjured by the liberal imagination. We may, ultimately, want more undisciplined knowledge, more questions and fewer answers.

Disciplines qualify and disqualify, legitimate and delegitimate, reward and punish; most important, they statically reproduce themselves and inhibit dissent. As Foucault writes, "Disciplines will define not a code of law, but a code of normalization" (2003: 38). In a series of lectures on knowledge production given at the College de France and then published posthumously as a collection titled *Society Must Be Defended*, Foucault provides a context for his own antidisciplinary thinking and declares the age of "all-encompassing and global theories" to be over, giving way to the "local character of critique" or "something resembling a sort of autonomous and non-centralized theoretical production, or in other words a theoretical production that does not need a visa from some common regime to establish its validity" (6). These lectures coincide with the writing of *The History of Sexuality* Volume 1, and we find the outline of his critique of repressive power in these pages (Foucault, 1998). I will return to Foucault's insights about the reverse discourse in *The History of Sexuality* later in the book, especially to the places where he implicates sexual minorities in the production of systems of classification, but in *Society Must Be Defended* his target is academic legibility and legitimation, and he describes and analyzes the function of the academic in the circulation and reproduction of hegemonic structures.

In place of the "all-encompassing and global theories" that the university encourages, Foucault exhorts his students to think about and turn to "subjugated knowledges," namely those forms of knowledge production that have been "buried or masked in functional coherences or formal systematizations" (2003: 7). These forms of knowledge have not simply been lost or forgotten; they have been disqualified, rendered nonsensical or nonconceptual or "insufficiently elaborated." Foucault calls them "naïve knowledges, hierarchically inferior knowledges, knowledges that are below the required level of erudition or scientificity" (7)—this is what we mean by *knowledge from below*.

In relation to the identification of "subjugated knowledges," we might ask, How do we participate in the production and circulation of "subjugated knowledge"? How do we keep disciplinary forms of knowledge at bay? How do we avoid precisely the "scientific" forms of knowing that relegate other modes of knowing to the redundant or irrelevant? How do we engage in and teach antidisciplinary knowledge? Foucault proposes this answer: "Truth to tell, if we are to struggle against disciplines, or rather against disciplinary power, in our search for a nondisciplinary power, we should not be turning to the old right of sovereignty; we should be looking to a new right that is both anti-disciplinary and emancipated from the principle of sovereignty" (2003: 40). In some sense we have to untrain ourselves so that we can read the struggles and debates back into questions that seem settled and resolved.

On behalf of such a project, and in the spirit of the "Seven Theses" proposed by Moten and Harney, this book joins forces with their "subversive intellectual" and agrees to steal from the university, to, as they say, "abuse its hospitality" and to be "in but not of it" (101). Moten and Harney's theses exhort the subversive intellectual to, among other things, worry about the university, refuse professionalization, forge a collectivity, and retreat to the external world beyond the ivied walls of the campus. I would add to their theses the following. First, *Resist mastery*. Here we might insist upon a critique of the "all-encompassing and global theories" identified by Foucault. In my book this resistance takes the form of investing in counterintuitive modes of knowing such as failure and stupidity; we might read *failure*, for example, as a refusal of mastery, a critique of the intuitive connections within capitalism between success and profit, and as a counterhegemonic discourse of losing. *Stupidity* could refer not simply to a lack of knowledge but to the limits of certain forms of knowing and certain ways of inhabiting structures of knowing.

Really imaginative ethnographies, for example, depend upon an unknowing relation to the other. To begin an ethnographic project with a goal, with an object of research and a set of presumptions, is already to stymie the process of discovery; it blocks one's ability to learn something that exceeds the frameworks with which one enters. For example, in an ethnography to which I return later in the book, a study of "the Islamic revival and the feminist subject" in contemporary Egypt, Saba Mahmood explains how she had to give up on mastery in order to engage certain forms of Islamism. She writes: "it is through this process of dwelling in the modes of reasoning endemic to a tradition that I once judged abhorrent, by immersing myself within the thick texture of its sensibilities and attachments, that I have been able to dislocate the certitude of my own projections and even begin to comprehend why Islam . . . exerts such a force in people's lives" (2005: 199). She concludes this thought as follows: "This attempt at comprehension offers the slim hope in the embattled and imperious climate, one in which feminist politics runs the risk of being reduced to a rhetorical display of the placard of Islam's abuses, that analysis as a mode of conversation, *rather than mastery*, can yield a vision of co-existence that does not require making others lifeworlds extinct or provisional" (199). Conversation rather than mastery indeed seems to offer one very concrete way of being in relation to another form of being and knowing without seeking to measure that life modality by the standards that are external to it.

Second, *Privilege the naïve or nonsensical* (stupidity). Here we might argue for the nonsensible or nonconceptual over sense-making structures that are often embedded in a common notion of ethics. The naïve or the ignorant may in fact lead to a different set of knowledge practices. It certainly requires what some have called oppositional pedagogies. In pursuit of such pedagogies we must realize that, as Eve Kosofsky Sedgwick once said, ignorance is "as potent and multiple a thing as knowledge" and that learning often takes place completely independently of teaching (1991: 4). In fact, to speak personally for a moment, I am not sure that I myself am teachable! As someone who never aced an exam, who has tried and tried without much success to become fluent in another language, and who can read a book without retaining much at all, I realize that I can

equal rather than hierarchical pedagogy

learn only what I can teach myself, and that much of what I was taught in school left very little impression upon me at all. The question of unteachability arises as a political problem, indeed a national problem, in the extraordinary French documentary about a year in the life of a high school in the suburbs of Paris, The Class (Entre Les Murs, 2008, directed by Laurent Cantet). In the film a white schoolteacher, François Bégaudeau (who wrote the memoir upon which the film is based), tries to reach out to his disinterested and profoundly alienated, mostly African, Asian, and Arab immigrant students. The cultural and racial and class differences between the teacher and his students make effective communication difficult, and his cultural references (The Diary of Ann Frank, Molière, French grammar) leave the students cold, while theirs (soccer, Islam, hip-hop) induce only pained responses from their otherwise personable teacher. The film, like a Frederick Wiseman documentary, tries to just let the action unfold without any voice-of-God narration, so we see close up the rage and frustrations of teacher and students alike. At the end of the film an extraordinary moment occurs. Bégaudeau asks the students to think about what they have learned and write down one thing to take away from the class, one concept, text, or idea that might have made a difference. The class disperses, and one girl shuffles up to the front. The teacher looks at her expectantly and draws out her comment. "I didn't learn anything," she tells him without malice or anger, "nothing. . . . I can't think of anything I learned." The moment is a defeat for the teacher and a disappointment for the viewer, who wants to believe in a narrative of educational uplift, but it is a triumph for alternative pedagogies because it reminds us that learning is a two-way street and you cannot teach without a dialogic relation to the learner.

"I didn't learn anything" could be an endorsement of another French text, a book by Jacques Ranciére on the politics of knowledge. In The Ignorant Schoolmaster Ranciére (1991) examines a form of knowledge sharing that detours around the mission of the university, with its masters and students, its expository methods and its standards of excellence, and instead endorses a form of pedagogy that presumes and indeed demands equality rather than hierarchy. Drawing from the example of an eighteenth-century professor who taught in French to Belgian students who spoke only Flemish, Ranciére claims that conventional, discipline-based pedagogy demands the presence of a master and proposes a mode of learning by which the students are enlightened by the superior knowledge, training, and intellect of the schoolmaster. But in the case of Joseph

Jacotot, his experience with the students in Brussels taught him that his belief in the necessity of explication and exegesis was false and that it simply upheld a university system dependent upon hierarchy. When Jacotot realized that his students were learning to read and speak French and to understand the text *Télémaque* without his assistance, he began to see the narcissistic investment he had made in his own function. He was not a bad teacher who became a "good" teacher; rather he was a "good" teacher who realized that people must be led to learn rather than taught to follow. Ranciére comments ironically, "Like all conscientious professors, he knew that teaching was not in the slightest about cramming students with knowledge and having them repeat it like parrots, but he knew equally well that students had to avoid the chance detours where minds still incapable of distinguishing the essential from the accessory, the principle from the consequence, get lost" (3). While the "good" teacher leads his students along the pathways of rationality, the "ignorant schoolmaster" must actually allow them to get lost in order for them to experience confusion and then find their own way out or back or around.

The *Ignorant Schoolmaster* advocates in an antidisciplinary way for emancipatory forms of knowledge that do not depend upon an overtrained pied piper leading obedient children out of the darkness and into the light. Jacotot summarizes his pedagogy thus: "I must teach you that I have nothing to teach you" (15). In this way he allows others to teach themselves and to learn without learning and internalizing a system of superior and inferior knowledges, superior and inferior intelligences. Like Paulo Freire's *Pedagogy of the Oppressed*, which argues against a "banking" system of teaching and for a dialogic mode of learning that enacts a practice of freedom, Jacotot and then Ranciére see education and social transformation as mutually dependent. When we are taught that we cannot know things unless we are taught by great minds, we submit to a whole suite of unfree practices that take on the form of a colonial relation (Freire 2000). There are several responses possible to colonial knowledge formations: a violent response, on the order of Frantz Fanon's claim that violent impositions of colonial rule must be met with violent resistance; a homeopathic response, within which the knower learns the dominant system better than its advocates and undermines it from within; or a negative response, in which the subject refuses the knowledge offered and refuses to be a knowing subject in the form mandated by Enlightenment philosophies of self and other. This book is in sympathy with the violent and negative forms of anticolonial knowing and builds on Moten's

and Harney's opposition to the university as a site of incar~~cerated knowl~~
edge.

In the project on subjugated knowledge, I propose a th ~~[obscured]~~
pect memorialization. While it seems commonsensical to prod ~~[obscured]~~
of memory about homophobia or racism, many contemp ~~[obscured]~~
erary and theoretical, actually argue against memorializat ~~[obscured]~~
rison's *Beloved* (1987), Saidiya Hartman's memoir, *Lose Your* ~~[obscured]~~
and Avery Gordon's meditation on forgetting and haunting ~~[obscured]~~
ters (1996), all advocate for certain forms of erasure over ~~[obscured]~~
cisely because memorialization has a tendency to tidy up di ~~[obscured]~~
ries (of slavery, the Holocaust, wars, etc.). Memory is itself ~~[obscured]~~
mechanism that Foucault calls "a ritual of power"; it selects for what is
important (the histories of triumph), it reads a continuous narrative into
one full of ruptures and contradictions, and it sets precedents for other
"memorializations." In this book *forgetting* becomes a way of resisting the
heroic and grand logics of recall and unleashes new forms of memory
that relate more to spectrality than to hard evidence, to lost genealogies
than to inheritance, to erasure than to inscription.

Low Theory

We expose ourselves to serious error when we attempt to "read off" concepts that
were designed to operate at a high level of abstraction as if they automatically
produced the same theoretical effects when translated to another, more concrete,
"lower" level of operation.
—Stuart Hall, "Gramsci's Relevance for the Study of Race and Ethnicity"

Building on Ranciére's notion of intellectual emancipation, I want to
propose low theory, or theoretical knowledge that works at many levels
at once, as precisely one of these modes of transmission that revels in
the detours, twists, and turns through knowing and confusion, and that
seeks not to explain but to involve. So what is *low theory*, where does it
take us, and why should we invest in something that seems to confirm
rather than upset the binary formation that situates it as the other to a
high theory? Low theory is a model of thinking that I extract from Stuart
Hall's famous notion that theory is not an end unto itself but "a detour en
route to something else" (1991: 43). Again, we might consider the utility
of getting lost over finding our way, and so we should conjure a Benjaminian stroll or a situationist *derivé*, an ambulatory journey through the

[margin handwritten: detours]

[handwritten note on sticky: seems sus-picious. Not remembering historical events is also a dangerous sanitization.]

[handwritten bottom: low theory]

unplanned, the unexpected, the improvised, and the surprising. I take the term *low theory* from Hall's comment on Gramsci's effectiveness as a thinker. In response to Althusser's suggestion that Gramsci's texts were "insufficiently theorized," Hall notes that Gramsci's abstract principles "were quite explicitly designed to operate at the lower levels of historical concreteness" (413). Hall goes on to argue that Gramsci was "not aiming higher and missing his political target"; instead, like Hall himself, he was aiming low in order to hit a broader target. Here we can think about *low theory* as a mode of accessibility, but we might also think about it as a kind of theoretical model that flies below the radar, that is assembled from eccentric texts and examples and that refuses to confirm the hierarchies of knowing that maintain the *high* in high theory.[3]

As long as there is an entity called *high theory*, even in casual use or as shorthand for a particular tradition of critical thinking, there is an implied field of low theory; indeed Hall circles the issue in his essay "Gramsci's Relevance for the Study of Race and Ethnicity." Hall points out that Gramsci was not a "general theorist," but "a political intellectual and a socialist activist on the Italian political scene" (1996: 411). This is important to Hall because some theory is goal-oriented in a practical and activist way; it is designed to inform political practice rather than to formulate abstract thoughts for the sake of some neutral philosophical project. Gramsci was involved in political parties his whole life and served at various levels of politics over time; ultimately he was imprisoned for his politics and died shortly after his release from a fascist jail.

Building on this image of Gramsci as a political thinker, Hall argues that Gramsci was never a Marxist in a doctrinal, orthodox, or religious sense. Like Benjamin, and indeed like Hall himself, Gramsci understood that one cannot subscribe to the text of Marxism as if it were etched in stone. He draws attention to the historical specificity of political structures and suggests that we adjust to developments that Marx and Marxism could not predict or otherwise account for. For Benjamin, Hall, and Gramsci, orthodoxy is a luxury we cannot afford, even when it means adherence to an orthodox leftist vision. Instead, Hall says, Gramsci practiced a genuinely "open" Marxism, and of course an open Marxism is precisely what Hall advocates in "Marxism without Guarantees." *Open* here means questioning, open to unpredictable outcomes, not fixed on a telos, unsure, adaptable, shifting, flexible, and adjustable. An "open" pedagogy, in the spirit of Ranciére and Freire, also detaches itself from prescriptive methods, fixed logics, and epistemes, and it orients us toward problem-solving knowledge or social visions of radical justice.

Accordingly hegemony, as Gramsci theorized it and as Hall interprets it, is the term for a multilayered system by which a dominant group achieves power not through coercion but through the production of an interlocking system of ideas which persuades people of the rightness of any given set of often contradictory ideas and perspectives. *Common sense* is the term Gramsci uses for this set of beliefs that are persuasive precisely because they do not present themselves as ideology or try to win consent.

For Gramsci and Hall, everyone participates in intellectual activity, just as they cook meals and mend clothes without necessarily being chefs or tailors. The split between the traditional and the organic intellectual is important because it recognizes the tension between intellectuals who participate in the construction of the hegemonic (as much through form as through content) and intellectuals who work with others, with a class of people in Marxist terms, to sort through the contradictions of capitalism and to illuminate the oppressive forms of governance that have infiltrated everyday life.

Today in the university we spend far less time thinking about counterhegemony than about hegemony. What Gramsci seemed to mean by counterhegemony was the production and circulation of another, competing set of ideas which could join in an active struggle to change society. The literature on hegemony has attributed so much power to it that it has seemed impossible to imagine counterhegemonic options. But Hall, like Gramsci, is very interested in the idea of education as a popular practice aimed at the cultivation of counterhegemonic ideas and systems. Hall has spent much of his career in the Open University, and he does what he ascribes to Gramsci in his essay: he manages to operate "at different levels of abstraction."

Both Hall and Gramsci were impatient with economism. This is a general principle ascribed to Marxist thought and describing a too rigid theorization of the relation between base and superstructure. As Althusser makes clear, the "ultimate condition of production is [therefore] the reproduction of the conditions of production"; in other words, in order for a system to work, it has to keep creating and maintaining the structures or the structured relations which allow it to function (2001: 85). But this is not the same as saying that the economic base *determines* the form of every other social force. Economism, for both Gramsci and Hall, leads only to moralizing and cheap insight and does not really allow for a complex understanding of the social relations that both sustain the mode of production and can change it. Low theory might constitute the name for a counterhegemonic form of theorizing, the theorization of alternatives within an undisciplined zone of knowledge production.

Pirate Cultures

What else is criminal activity but the passionate pursuit of alternatives?
—Design Collective Zine, Shahrzad (Zurich and Tehran)

A great example of low theory can be found in Peter Linebaugh's and Marcus Rediker's monumental account of the history of opposition to capitalism in the seventeenth and eighteenth century, *The Many-Headed Hydra: Sailors, Slaves, Commoners, and the Hidden History of the Revolutionary Atlantic*. Their book traces what they call "the struggles for alternative ways of life" that accompanied and opposed the rise of capitalism in the early seventeenth century (2001: 15). In stories about piracy, dispossessed commoners, and urban insurrections they detail the modes of colonial and national violence that brutally stamped out all challenges to middle-class power and that cast proletarian rebellion as disorganized, random, and apolitical. Linebaugh and Rediker refuse the common wisdom about these movements (i.e., that they were random and not focused on any particular political goal); instead they emphasize the power of cooperation within the anticapitalist mob and pay careful attention to the alternatives that this "many-headed hydra" of resistant groups imagined and pursued.

The Many-Headed Hydra is a central text in any genealogy of alternatives because its authors refuse to accede to the masculinist myth of Herculean capitalist heroes who mastered the feminine hydra of unruly anarchy; instead they turn that myth on its many heads to access "a powerful legacy of possibility," heeding Hall's cogent warning, "The more we understand about the development of Capital itself, the more we understand that it is only part of the story" (1997: 180). For Linebaugh and Rediker, capital is always joined to the narratives of the resistance it inspired, even though those resistant movements may ultimately not have been successful in their attempts to block capitalism. And so they describe in detail the wide range of resistance with which capitalism was met in the late sixteenth century: there were levelers and diggers who resisted the enclosure of the public land, or commons; there were sailors and mutineers and would-be slaves who rebelled against the captain's authority on ships to the New World and devised different understandings of group relations; there were religious dissidents who believed in the absence of hierarchies in the eyes of the Lord; there were multinational "motley crews" who engineered mutinies on merchant ships and who sailed around the world bringing news of uprisings to different ports. All of these groups represent lineages of opposition that echo in the present. Linebaugh and Rediker flesh out the alternatives that these resistant groups proposed in terms of how to live, how to think about time and space, how to inhabit space with others, and how to spend time separate from the logic of work.

The history of alternative political formations is important because it contests social relations as given and allows us to access traditions of political action that, while not necessarily successful in the sense of becoming dominant, do offer models of contestation, rupture, and discontinuity for the political present. These histories also identify potent avenues of failure, failures that we might build upon in order to counter the logics of success that have emerged from the triumphs of global capitalism. In *The Many-Headed Hydra* failure is the map of political paths not taken, though it does not chart a completely separate land; failure's byways are all the spaces in between the superhighways of capital. Indeed Linebaugh and Rediker do not find new routes to resistance built upon *new* archives; they use the same historical accounts that have propped up dominant narratives of pirates as criminals and levelers as violent thugs, and they read different narratives of race and resistance in these same records of church sermons and the memoirs of religious figures. Their point is that dominant history teems with the remnants of alternative possibilities, and the job of the subversive intellectual is to trace the lines of the worlds they conjured and left behind.

My archive is not labor history or subaltern movements. Instead I want to look for low theory and counterknowledge in the realm of popular culture and in relation to queer lives, gender, and sexuality. Gender and sexuality are, after all, too often dropped from most large-scale accounts of alternative worlds (including Linebaugh's and Rediker's). In *The Queer Art of Failure* I turn repeatedly but not exclusively to the "silly" archives of animated film. While many readers may object to the idea that we can locate alternatives in a genre engineered by huge corporations for massive profits and with multiple product tie-ins, I have found that new forms of animation, CGI in particular, have opened up new narrative doors and led to unexpected encounters between the childish and the transformative and the queer. I am not the first to find eccentric allegories for queer knowledge production in animated film. Elizabeth Freeman (2005) has used the Pixar feature *Monsters, Inc.* to expose the exploitive reality of the neoliberal vision of education and the absence of gender and sexuality in the radical opposition to the neoliberal university. Describing *Monsters, Inc.* as a film about desire, class, and the classroom, Freeman joins forces with Bill Readings's (1997) scathing indictment of neoliberal university reform and argues that the film, an allegory of corporate extractions of labor, "illuminates the social relations of production" even as it mediates them (Freeman, 2005: 90). In the repeated staging of an encounter between the monster and the child in the bedroom—which in the film is designed to generate screams, which in turn are funneled into energy to power Monstropolis—*Monsters, Inc.* implies but does not address, according to Freeman, an erotic exchange. For Freeman, the queerness of this encounter must be acknowledged in order for the film to move beyond its own humanist solution of substituting one form of exploitation (the extraction of screams) for another (the extraction of children's laughter). The libidinal energy of the exchange between monster and child, like the libidinally charged relations between teachers and students, should be able to shock the system out of its complacency. Freeman writes, "The humanities are the shock to common sense, the estranging move that will always make what we do unintelligible and incalculable and that may release or catalyze enough energy to blow out a few institutional fuses" (93). She advocates for teachers to create monsters of their students and to sustain in the process "unruly forms of relationality" (94).

I am less interested than Freeman in the libidinal exchange between teacher and student, which I believe remains invested in the very narcissistic structure of education that Ranciére critiques. But like her, I do believe deeply in the pedagogical project of creating monsters; also like her, I turn to the silly archive for information on how to do so. Not everything in this book falls under the headings of frivolity, silliness, or jocularity, but the "silly archive," to adapt Lauren Berlant's priceless phrase about "the counter-politics of the silly object," allows me to make claims for alternatives that are markedly different from the claims that are made in relation to high cultural archives (1997: 12). The texts that I prefer here do not make us better people or liberate us from the culture industry, but they might offer strange and anticapitalist logics of being and acting and knowing, and they will harbor covert and overt queer worlds. I do believe that if you watch *Dude, Where's My Car?* slowly and repeatedly and while perfectly sober, the mysteries of the universe may be revealed to you. I also believe that *Finding Nemo* contains a secret plan for world revolution and that *Chicken Run* charts an outline of feminist utopia for those who can see beyond the feathers and eggs. I believe in low theory in popular places, in the small, the inconsequential, the antimonumental, the micro, the irrelevant; I believe in making a difference by thinking little thoughts and sharing them widely. I seek to provoke, annoy, bother, irritate, and amuse; I am chasing small projects, micropolitics, hunches, whims, fancies. Like Jesse and Chester in *Dude, Where's My Car?*, I don't really care whether I remember where the hell I parked; instead I merely hope, like the dudes, to conjure some potentially world-saving, wholly improbable fantasies of life on Uranus and elsewhere. At which point you may well ask, as Evey asks Gordon in *V for Vendetta*, "Is everything a joke to you?" To which the very queer and very subversive TV maestro responds, "Only the things that matter."

The animated films that make up the main part of the archive for my book all draw upon the humorous and the politically wild implications of species diversity, and they deploy chickens, rats, penguins, woodland creatures, more penguins, fish, bees, dogs, and zoo animals. Pixar and DreamWorks films in particular have created an animated world rich in political allegory, stuffed to the gills with queerness and rife with analogies between humans and animals. While these films desperately try to package their messages in the usual clichéd forms ("Be yourself," "Follow your dreams," "Find your soul mate"), they also, as Freeman implies in her piece on *Monsters, Inc.*, deliver queer and socialist messages often packaged in relation to one another: Work together, Revel in difference, Fight exploitation, Decode ideology, Invest in resistance.

In the process of studying animation—a knowledge path that might track through popular culture, computer graphics, animation histories and technologies, and cellular biology—we study, as Benjamin knew so well, classed modes of pleasure and technologies of cultural transmission. In an early version of "The Work of Art in the Age of Mechanical Reproduction" Benjamin reserved a special place for the new animation art of Walt Disney that, for him, unleashed a kind of magical consciousness upon its mass audiences and conjured utopic spaces and worlds. In "Mickey Mouse and Utopia" in her inspired book *Hollywood Flatlands*, Esther Leslie writes, "For Walter Benjamin . . . the cartoons depict a realist—though not naturalist—expression of the circumstances of modern daily life; the cartoons make clear that even our bodies do not belong to us—we have alienated them in exchange for money, or have given parts of them up in war. The cartoons expose the fact that what parades as civilization is actually barbarism. And the animal-human beasts and spirited things insinuate that humanism is nothing more than an ideology" (2004: 83). According to Leslie, Benjamin saw cartoons as a pedagogical opportunity, a chance for children to see the evil that lies behind the façade of bourgeois respectability and for adults to recapture the visions of magical possibilities that were so palpable in childhood: "Disney's cartoon world is a world of impoverished experience, sadism and violence. That is to say, it is our world" (2004: 83).

The early Disney cartoons, in tandem with Chaplin's films, built narrative around baggy caricatures and eschewed mimetic realism. The characters themselves fell apart and then reassembled; they engaged in transformative violence and they took humor rather than tragedy as their preferred medium for engaging the audience. But as Benjamin recognized and as Leslie emphasizes, the Disney cartoons all too quickly resolved into a bourgeois medium; they quickly bowed to the force of *Bildung* and began to present moral fables with gender-normative and class-appropriate characterizations, and in the 1930s they became a favorite tool of the Nazi propaganda machine.

Contemporary animations in CGI also contain disruptive narrative arcs, magical worlds of revolution and transformation, counterintuitive groupings of children, animals, and dolls that rise up against adults and unprincipled machines. Like the early Disney cartoons that Benjamin found so charming and engaging, early Pixar and DreamWorks films join a form of collective art making to a narrative world of anarchy and antifamilial bands of characters. But, like late Disney, late Pixar, in *Wall-e*, for example, joins a narrative of hope to narratives of humanity and entertains a critique of bourgeois humanism only long enough to assure its return. Wall-e's romance with the iPod-like Stepford wife Eva, for example, and his quest to bring a bloated humanity back to earth overturn the fantastic rejection of commodity fetishism early in the film in which he combs the trash heaps on earth for priceless objects, casually throwing away diamond rings while cherishing the velvet boxes in which they sit.

Very few mainstream films made for adults and consumed by large audiences have the audacity and the nerve anymore to tread on the dangerous territory of revolutionary activity; in the contemporary climate of crude literalism even social satire seems risky. And in a world of romantic comedies and action adventure films there are very few places to turn in search of the alternative. I would be bold enough to argue that it is only in the realm of animation that we actually find the alternative hiding. Nonanimated films that trade in the mise-en-scène of revolution and transformation, films like *V for Vendetta* and *The X Men*, are based on comic books and animated graphic novels. What is the relationship between new forms of animation and alternative politics today? Can animation sustain a utopic project now, whereas, as Benjamin mourned, it could not in the past?

Failure As a Way of Life

Practice More Failure!
—Title of LTTR event, 2004

In this book on failure I hold on to what have been characterized as child-ish and immature notions of possibility and look for alternatives in the form of what Foucault calls "subjugated knowledge" across the culture: in subcultures, countercultures, and even popular cultures. I also turn the meaning of failure in another direction, at the cluster of affective modes that have been associated with failure and that now characterize new di-rections in queer theory. I begin by addressing the dark heart of the nega-tivity that failure conjures, and I turn from the happy and productive fail-ures explored in animation to darker territories of failure associated with futility, sterility, emptiness, loss, negative affect in general, and modes of unbecoming. So while the early chapters chart the meaning of failure as a way of being in the world, the later chapters allow for the fact that failure is also unbeing, and that these modes of unbeing and unbecom-ing propose a different relation to knowledge. In chapter 4 I explore the meaning of masochism and passivity in relation to failure and femininity, and in chapter 6 I refuse triumphalist accounts of gay, lesbian, and trans-gender history that necessarily reinvest in robust notions of success and succession. In order to inhabit the bleak territory of failure we sometimes have to write and acknowledge dark histories, histories within which the subject collaborates with rather than always opposes oppressive regimes and dominant ideology. And so in chapter 6 I explore the vexed question of the relationship between homosexuality and fascism and argue that we cannot completely dismiss all of the accounts of Nazism that link it to gay male masculinism of the early twentieth century. While chapters 4 and 5 therefore mark very different forms of failure than the chapters on animation, art, stupidity, and forgetfulness earlier in the book, still the early chapters flirt with darker forms of failure, particularly chapter 2 on losing and forgetfulness, and the later chapters on negativity continue to engage more alternative renderings of the meaning of loss, masochism, and passivity.

All in all, this is a book about alternative ways of knowing and being that are not unduly optimistic, but nor are they mired in nihilistic critical dead ends. It is a book about failing well, failing often, and learning, in the words of Samuel Beckett, how to fail better. Indeed the whole notion of failure as a practice was introduced to me by the legendary lesbian performance group LTTR. In 2004 they asked me to participate in two events, one in Los Angeles and one in New York, called "Practice More Failure," which brought together queer and feminist thinkers and performers to inhabit, act out, and circulate new meanings of failure. Chapter 3, "The Queer Art of Failure," began as my presentation for this event, and I remain grateful to LTTR for shoving me down the dark path of failure and its follies. That event reminded me that some of the most important intellectual leaps take place independently of university training or in its aftermath or as a detour around and away from the lessons that disciplined thinking metes out. It reminded me to take more chances, more risks in thinking, to turn away from the quarrels that seem so important to the discipline and to engage the ideas that circulate widely in other communities. To that end I hope this book is readable by and accessible to a wider audience even if some nonacademic readers find my formulations too convoluted and some academics find my arguments too obvious. There is no happy medium between academic and popular audiences, but I hope my many examples of failure provide a map for the murky, dark, and dangerous terrains of failure we are about to explore.

By exploring and mapping, I also mean detouring and getting lost. We might do well to heed the motto of yet another peppily alternative Dream-Works film, *Madagascar*: "Get lost, stay lost!" In the sequel, *Madagascar: Escape 2 Africa* (whose byline is "Still lost!"), the zoo escapees from *Madagascar 1*—Marty the zebra, Melman the giraffe, Gloria the hippo, and Alex the lion—try to get home to New York with the help of some crazed penguins and a loopy lemur. Why the animals want to get back to captivity is only the first of many existential questions raised by and smartly not answered by the film. (Why the lemur wants to throw Melman into the volcano is another, but we will leave that one alone too.) At any rate, the zoo animals head home in a plane that, since it is piloted by penguins, predictably crashes. The crash landing places the animals back in "Africa," where they are reunited with their prides and herds and strikes in the "wild." What could have been a deeply annoying parable about family and sameness and nature becomes a whacky shaggy lion tale about collectivity, species diversity, theatricality, and the discomfort of home. Perversely it is also an allegorical take on antidisciplinary life in the university: while some of us who have escaped our cages may start looking for ways back into the zoo, others may try to rebuild a sanctuary in the wild, and a few fugitive types will actually insist on staying lost. Speaking personally, I didn't even manage to pass my university entrance exams, as my aged father recently reminded me, and I am still trying hard to master the art of staying lost. On behalf of such a detour around "proper" knowledge, each chapter that follows will lose its way in the territories of failure, forgetfulness, stupidity, and negation. We will wander, improvise, fall short, and move in circles. We will lose our way, our cars, our agenda, and possibly our minds, but in losing we will find another way of making meaning in which, to return to the battered vw van of Little Miss Sunshine, no one gets left behind.

CHAPTER ONE

Animating Revolt and Revolting *Animation*

The chickens are revolting!
—Mr. Tweedy in *Chicken Run*

Animated films for children revel in the domain of failure. To captivate the child audience, an animated film cannot deal only in the realms of success and triumph and perfection. Childhood, as many queers in particular recall, is a long lesson in humility, awkwardness, limitation, and what Kathryn Bond Stockton has called "growing sideways." Stockton proposes that childhood is an essentially queer experience in a society that acknowledges through its extensive training programs for children that hetero-sexuality is not born but made. If we were all already normative and heterosexual to begin with in our desires, orientations, and modes of being, then presumably we would not need such strict parental guidance to deliver us all to our common destinies of marriage, child rearing, and hetero-reproduction. If you believe that children need training, you assume and allow for the fact that they are always already anarchic and rebellious, out of order and out of time. Animated films nowadays succeed, I think, to the extent to which they are able to address the disorderly child, the child who sees his or her family and parents as the problem, the child who knows there is a bigger world out there beyond the family, if only he or she could reach it. Animated films are for children who believe that "things" (toys, nonhuman animals, rocks, sponges) are as lively as humans and who can

1. *Chicken Run*, directed by Peter Lord and Nick Park, 2000.
"The chickens are organized!"

glimpse other worlds underlying and overwriting this one. Of course this notion of other worlds has long been a conceit of children's literature; the Narnia stories, for example, enchant the child reader by offering access to a new world through the back of the wardrobe. While much children's literature simply offers a new world too closely matched to the old one it left behind, recent animated films actually revel in innovation and make ample use of the wonderfully childish territory of revolt.

In the opening sequence in the classic claymation feature *Chicken Run* (2000, directed by Peter Lord and Nick Park), Mr. Tweedy, a bumbling farmer, informs his much more efficient wife that the chickens are "organized." Mrs. Tweedy dismisses his outrageous notion and tells him to focus more on profits, explaining to him that they are not getting enough out of their chickens and need to move on from egg harvesting to the chicken potpie industry. As Mrs. Tweedy ponders new modes of production, Mr. Tweedy keeps an eye on the chicken coop, scanning for signs of activity and escape. The scene is now set for a battle between production and labor, human and animal, management and employees, containment and escape. *Chicken Run* and other animated feature films draw much of their dramatic intensity from the struggle between human and nonhuman creatures. Most animated features are allegorical in form and adhere to a fairly formulaic narrative scheme. But as even this short scene indicates, the allegory and the formula do not simply line up with the conventional generic schemes of Hollywood cinema. Rather animation pits two groups against each other in settings that closely resemble what used to be called "class struggle," and they offer numerous scenarios of revolt and alternatives to the grim, mechanical, industrial cycles of production and consumption. In this first clip Mr. Tweedy's intuitive sense that the chickens on his farm "are organized" competes with Mrs. Tweedy's assertion that the only thing more stupid than chickens is Mr. Tweedy himself. His paranoid suspicions lose out to her exploitive zeal until the moment when the two finally agree that "the chickens are revolting."

What are we to make of this Marxist allegory in the form of a children's film, this animal farm narrative of resistance, revolt, and utopia pitted against new waves of industrialization and featuring claymation birds in the role of the revolutionary subject? How do neo-anarchistic narrative forms find their way into children's entertainment, and what do adult viewers make of them? More important, what does animation have to do with revolution? And how do revolutionary themes in animated film connect to queer notions of self?

I want to offer a thesis about a new genre of animated feature films that use CGI technology instead of standard linear animation techniques and that surprisingly foreground the themes of revolution and transformation. I call this genre "Pixarvolt" in order to link the technology to the thematic focus. In the new animation films certain topics that would never appear in adult-themed films are central to the success and emotional impact of these narratives. Furthermore, and perhaps even more surprisingly, the Pixarvolt films make subtle as well as overt connections between communitarian revolt and queer embodiment and thereby articulate, in ways that theory and popular narrative have not, the sometimes counterintuitive links between queerness and socialist struggle. While many Marxist scholars have characterized and dismissed queer politics as "body politics" or as simply superficial, these films recognize that alternative forms of embodiment and desire are central to the struggle against corporate domination. The queer is not represented as a singularity but as part of an assemblage of resistant technologies that include collectivity, imagination, and a kind of situationist commitment to surprise and shock.

Let's begin by asking some questions about the process of animation, its generic potential, and the ways the Pixarvolts imagine the human and the nonhuman and rethink embodiment and social relations. Beginning with Toy Story in 1995 (directed by John Lasseter), animation entered a new era. As is well known, Toy Story, the first Pixar film, was the first animation to be wholly generated by a computer; it changed animation from a two-dimensional set of images to a three-dimensional space within which point-of-view shots and perspective were rendered with startling liveness. Telling an archetypal story about a world of toys who awaken when the children are away, Toy Story managed to engage child audiences with the fantasy of live toys and adults with the nostalgic narrative of a cowboy, Woody, whose primacy in the toy kingdom is being challenged by a new model, the futuristic space doll Buzz Lightyear. While kids delighted in the spectacle of a toy box teeming with life, reminiscent of "Nutcracker Suite," adults were treated to a smart drama about toys that exploit their own *toyness* and other toys that do not realize they are not humans. The whole complex narrative about past and present, adult and child, live and machinic is a metacommentary on the set of narrative possibilities that this new wave of animation enables and exploits. It also seemed to establish the parameters of the new genre of CGI: Toy Story marks the genre as irrevocably male (the boy child and his relation to the prosthetic and phallic capabilities of his male toys), centered on the domestic (the playroom) and unchangeably Oedipal (always father-son dynamics as the motor or, in a few cases, a mother-daughter rivalry, as in Coraline). But the new wave of animated features is also deeply interested in social hierarchies (parent-child but also owner-owned), quite curious about the relations between an outside and an inside world (the real world and the world of the bedroom), and powered by a vigorous desire for revolution, transformation, and rebellion (toy versus child, toy versus toy, child versus adult, child versus child). Finally, like many of the films that followed, Toy Story betrays a high level of self-consciousness about its own relation to innovation, transformation, and tradition.

Most of the CGI films that followed Toy Story map their dramatic territory in remarkably similar ways, and most retain certain key features (such as the Oedipal theme) while changing the mise-en-scène—from bedroom to seabed or barnyard, from toys to chickens or rats or fish or penguins, from the cycle of toy production to other industrial settings. Most remain entranced by the plot of captivity followed by dramatic escape and culminating in a utopian dream of freedom. A cynical critic might find this narrative to be a blueprint for the normative rites

2. *Toy Story*, directed by John Lasseter, 1995.
"The first CGI Feature Film for Pixar."

of passage in the human life cycle, showing the child viewer the journey from childhood captivity to adolescent escape and adult freedom. A more radical reading allows the narrative to be utopian, to tell of the real change that children may still believe is possible and desirable. The queer reading also refuses to allow the radical thematics of animated film to be dismissed as "childish" by questioning the temporal order that assigns dreams of transformation to pre-adulthood and that claims the accommodation of dysfunctional presents as part and parcel of normative adulthood.

How does *Chicken Run*, a film about "revolting chickens," imagine a utopian alternative? In a meeting in the chicken coop the lead chicken, Ginger, proposes to her sisterhood that there must be more to life than sitting around and producing eggs for the Tweedys or not producing eggs and ending up on the chopping block. She then outlines a utopian future in a green meadow (an image of which appears on an orange crate in the coop), where there are no farmers and no production schedule and no one is in charge. The future that Ginger outlines for her claymation friends relies very much on the utopian concept of escape as exodus, conjured variously by Paolo Virno in *A Grammar of the Multitude* and by Hardt and Negri in *Multitude*, but here escape is not the war camp model that most people project onto *Chicken Run*'s narrative. The film is indeed quoting *The Great Escape*, *Colditz*, *Stalag 17*, and other films whose setting is the Second World War, but war is not the mise-en-scène; rather, remarkably, the transition from feudalism to industrial capitalism frames a life-and-death story about rising up, flying the coop, and creating the conditions for escape from the materials already available. *Chicken Run* is different from *Toy Story* in that the Oedipal falls away as a point of reference in favor of a Gramscian structure of counterhegemony engineered by organic (chicken) intellectuals. In this film an anarchist's utopia is actually realized as a stateless place without a farmer, an unfenced territory with no owners, a diverse (sort of, they are mostly female) collective motivated by survival, pleasure, and the control of one's own labor. The chickens dream up and inhabit this utopian field, which we glimpse briefly at the film's conclusion, and they find their way there by eschewing a "natural" solution to their imprisonment (flying out of the coop using their wings) and engineering an ideological one (they must all pull together to power the plane they build). *Chicken Run* also rejects the individualistic solution offered by Rocky the Rooster (voiced by Mel Gibson) in favor of group logics. As for the queer element, well, they are chickens, and so, at least in *Chicken Run*, utopia is a green field full of female birds with just the occasional rooster strutting around. The revolution in this instance is feminist and animated.

Penguin Love

Building new worlds by accessing new forms of sociality through animals turns around the usual equation in literature that makes the animal an allegorical stand-in in a moral fable about human folly (*Animal Farm* by Orwell, for example). Most often we project human worlds onto the supposedly blank slate of animality, and then we create the animals we need in order to locate our own human behaviors in "nature" or "the wild" or "civilization." As the Chicken Run example shows, however, animated animals allow us to explore ideas about humanness, alterity, and alternative imaginaries in relation to new forms of representation.

But what is the status of the "animal" in animation? Animation, animal sociality, and biodiversity can be considered in relation to the notion of transbiology developed by Sarah Franklin and Donna Haraway. For Haraway, and for Franklin, the transbiological refers to the new conceptions of the self, the body, nature, and the human within waves of new technological advancement, such as cloning and cell regeneration. Franklin uses the history of Dolly the cloned sheep to explore the ways kinship, genealogy, and reproduction are remade, resituated by the birth and death of the cloned subject. She elaborates a transbiological field by building on Haraway's theorization of the cyborg in her infamous "Cyborg Manifesto," and she returns to earlier work by Haraway that concerned itself with biogenetic extensions of the body and of the experience of embodiment. Franklin explains, "I want to suggest that in the same way that the cyborg was useful to learn to see an altered landscape of the biological, the technical, and the informatic, similarly Haraway's 'kinding' semiotics of trans can help identify features of the postgenomic turn in the biosciences and biomedicine toward the idioms of immortalization, regeneration, and totipotency. However, by reversing Haraway's introduction of trans- as the exception or rogue element (as in the transuranic elements) I suggest that transbiology—a biology that is not only born and bred, or born and made, but made and born—is indeed today more the norm than the exception" (2006: 171). The transbiological conjures hybrid entities or in-between states of being that represent subtle or even glaring shifts in our understandings of the body and of bodily transformation. The female cyborg, the transgenic mouse, the cloned sheep that Franklin researches, in which reproduction is "reassembled and rearranged," the Tamagotchi toys studied by Sherrie Turkle, and the new forms of animation I consider here, all question and shift the location, the terms, and the meanings of the artificial boundaries between humans, animals, machines, states of life and death, animation and reanimation, living, evolving, becoming, and transforming. They also refuse the idea of human exceptionalism and place the human firmly within a universe of multiple modes of being.

Human exceptionalism comes in many forms. It might manifest as a simple belief in the uniqueness and centrality of humanness within a world shared with other kinds of life, but it might also show itself through gross and crude forms of anthropomorphism; in this case the human projects all of his or her uninspired and unexamined conceptions about life and living onto animals, who may actually foster far more creative or at least more surprising modes of living and sharing space. For example, in one of the most popular of the "Modern Love" columns—a popular weekly column in the *New York Times* dedicated to charting and narrating the strange fictions of contemporary desire and romance— titled "What Shamu Taught Me about a Happy Marriage," Amy Sutherland describes how she adapted animal training techniques that she learned at Sea World for use at home on her husband.[1] While the column purports to offer a location for the diverse musings of postmodern lovers on the peculiarities of modern love, it is actually a primer for adult heterosexuality. Occasionally a gay man or a lesbian will write about his or her normative liaison, its ups and downs, and will plea for the right to become "mature" through marriage, but mostly the column is dedicated to detailing, in mundane and banal intricacy, the roller-coaster ride of bourgeois heterosexuality and its supposed infinite variety and elasticity. The typical "Modern Love" essay will begin with a complaint, usually and predictably a female complaint about male implacability, but as we approach the end of the piece resolution will fall from the sky in the manner of a divine vision, and the disgruntled partner will quickly see that the very thing that she found irritating about her partner is also the very thing that makes him, well, him! That is, unique, flawed, human, and lovable.

Sutherland's essay is true to form. After complaints about her beloved husband's execrable domestic habits, she settles on a series of training techniques by placing him within a male taxonomy: "The exotic animal known as Scott is a loner, but an alpha male. So hierarchy matters, but being in a group doesn't so much. He has the balance of a gymnast, but moves slowly, especially when getting dressed. Skiing comes naturally, but being on time does not. He's an omnivore, and what a trainer would call food-driven." The resolution of the problem of Scott depends upon the hilarious scenario within which Sutherland brings her animal training techniques home and puts them to work on her recalcitrant mate. Using methods that are effective on exotic animals, she manages her husband with techniques ranging from a reward system for good behavior to a studied indifference to bad behavior. Amazingly the techniques work, and, what's more, she learns along the way that not only is she training her husband, but her husband, being not only adaptable and malleable but also intelligent and capable of learning, has started to use animal training techniques on her. Modern marriage, the essay concludes, in line with the "modern love" ideology, is an exercise in simultaneous evolution, each mate adjusting slightly to the quirks and foibles of the other, never blaming the structure, trying not to turn on each other, and ultimately triumphing by staying together no matter what the cost.

Amusing as Sutherland's essay may be, it is also a stunning example of how, as Laura Kipnis puts it in *Against Love*, we maneuver around "the large, festering contradictions at the epicenter of love in our time" (2004: 13). Kipnis argues that we tend to blame each other or ourselves for the failures of the social structures we inhabit, rather than critiquing the structures (like marriage) themselves. Indeed so committed are we to these cumbersome structures and so lazy are we about coming up with alternatives to them that we bolster our sense of the rightness of heteronormative coupledom by drawing on animal narratives in order to place ourselves back in some primal and "natural" world. Sutherland, for example, happily casts herself and Scott as exotic animals in a world of exotic animals and their trainers; of course the very idea of the exotic, as we know from all kinds of postcolonial theories of tourism and orientalism, depends upon an increasingly outdated notion of the domestic, the familiar, and the known, all of which come into being by positing a relation to the foreign, the alien, and the indecipherable. Not only does Sutherland domesticate the fabulous variation of the animals she is studying by making common cause with them, but she also exoticizes the all too banal setting of her own domestic dramas, and in the process she reimposes the boundary between human and nonhuman. Her humorous adaptation of animal husbandry into husband training might require a footnote now, given the death in 2010 of a Sea World trainer who was dragged into deep waters and drowned by the whale she had been training and working with for years. While Sutherland lavished her regard on the metaphor of gentle mutual training techniques, the death of the trainer reminds us of the violence that inheres in all attempts to alter the behavior of another being.

The essay as a whole contributes to the ongoing manic project of the renaturalization of heterosexuality and the stabilization of relations between men and women. And yet Sutherland's piece, humor and all, for all of its commitments to the human, remains in creative debt to the intellectually imaginative work of Donna Haraway in *Primate Visions*. Haraway reversed the relations of looking between primatologists and the animals they studied and argued that, first, the primates look back, and second, the stories we tell are much more about humans than about animals. She wrote, "Especially western people produce stories about primates while simultaneously telling stories about the relations of nature and culture, animal and human, body and mind, origin and future" (1990: 5). Similarly people who write the "Modern Love" column, these vernacular anthropologists of romance, produce stories about animals in order to locate heterosexuality in its supposedly natural setting. In Sutherland's essay the casting of women and men in the roles of trainers and animals also refers indirectly to Haraway's reconceptualization of the relationship between humans and dogs in her *Companion Species Manifesto: Dogs, People and Significant Otherness* (2003). While the earlier cyborg manifesto productively questioned the centrality of the notion of a soft and bodily, anti-technological "womanhood" to an idealized construction of the human, the later manifesto decentralizes the human altogether in its account of the relationship between dogs and humans — and refuses to accept the common wisdom about the dog-human relationship. For Haraway, the dog is not a representation of something about the human but an equal player in the drama of evolution and a site of "significant otherness." The problem with Haraway's vivid and original rewriting of the evolutionary process from the perspective of the dog is that it seems to reinvest in the idea of nature per se and leaves certain myths about evolution itself intact.

In fact Haraway herself seems to be invested in the "modern love" paradigm of seeing animals as either extensions of humans or their moral superiors. As Heidi J. Nast comments in a polemical call for "critical pet studies," a new disposition toward "pet love" has largely gone unnoticed in social theory and "where pet lives are addressed directly, most studies shun a critical international perspective, instead charting the cultural histories of pet-human relationships or, like Haraway, showing how true pet love might invoke a superior ethical stance" (2006: 896). Nast proposes that we examine the investments we are making in pets and in a pet industry in the twenty-first century and calls for a "scholarly geographical elaboration" of who owns pets, where they live, what kinds of affective and financial investments they have made in pet love, and who lies outside the orbit of pet love. She writes, "Those with no affinity for pets or those who are afraid of them are today deemed social or psychological misfits and cranks, while those who love them are situated as morally and even spiritually superior, such judgments having become hegemonic in the last two decades" (896). Like adults who choose not to reproduce, people with no interest in pets occupy a very specific spot in contemporary sexual hierarchies. In her anatomy of pet love Nast asks, "Why, for example, are women and queers such central purveyors of the language and institutions of pet love? And why are the most commodified forms of pet love and the most organized pets-rights movements emanating primarily out of elite (and in the U.S., Canada and Europe) 'white' contexts?" (898). Her account of pet love registers the need for new graphs and pyramids of sexual oppression and privilege, new models to replace the ones Gayle Rubin produced nearly two decades ago in "Thinking Sex" to complicate the relations between heterosexual privilege and gay oppression. In a postindustrial landscape where the size of white families has plummeted, where the nuclear family itself has become something of an anachronism, and where a majority of women live outside of conventional marriages, the elevation of pets to the status of love objects certainly demands attention. In a recent song by the radical rapper Common, he asks, "Why white folks focus on dogs and yoga? / While people on the low end tryin to ball and get over?" Why indeed? It's all for modern love.

While the relationship between sexuality and reproduction has never been much more than a theological fantasy, new technologies of reproduction and new rationales for nonreproductive behavior call for new languages of desire, embodiment, and the social relations between reproductive and nonreproductive bodies. At the very moment of its impending redundancy, some newly popular animal documentaries seek to map reproductive heterosexuality onto space; they particularly seek to "discover" it in nature by telling tales about awesomely creative animal societies. But a powerfully queer counterdiscourse in areas as diverse as evolutionary biology, avant-garde art productions, animated feature films, and horror films unwrites resistant strains of heterosexuality and recasts them in an improbably but persistently queer universe.

So let's turn to a popular text about the spectacular strangeness of animals to see how documentary-style features tend to humanize animal life. While animal documentaries use voice-overs and invisible cameras to try to provide a God's-eye view of "nature" and to explain every type of animal behavior in ways that reduce animals to human-like creatures, we might think of animation as a way of maintaining the animality of animal social worlds. I will return to the question of animation later in the chapter, but here I want to discuss *The March of the Penguins* (2005) as an egregious form of anthropomorphism on the one hand and the source of alternative forms of family, parenting, and sociality on the other.

In his absorbing documentary about the astonishing life cycle of Antarctica's emperor penguins, Luc Jacquet framed the spectacle of the penguins' long and brutal journey to their ancestral breeding grounds as a story about love, survival, resilience, determination, and the hetero-reproductive family unit. Emperor penguins, for those who missed the film (or the Christian Right's perverse readings of it), are the only remaining inhabitants of a particularly brutal Antarctic landscape that was once covered in verdant forests but is now a bleak and icy wilderness. Due to global warming, however, the ice is melting, and the survival of the penguins depends on a long trek that they must make once a year, in March, from the ocean to a plateau seventy miles inland, where the ice is thick and fast enough to support them through their breeding cycle. The journey out to the breeding grounds is awkward for the penguins, which swim much faster than they waddle, and yet the trek is only the first leg of a punishing shuttle they will make in the next few months, back and forth between the inland nesting area and the ocean, where they feed. This may not sound like a riveting narrative, but the film was a huge success around the world.

The film's success depends upon several factors: first, it plays to a basic human curiosity about how and why the penguins undertake such a brutal circuit; second, it provides intimate footage of these animals that seems almost magical given the unforgiving landscape and that has a titillating effect given the access the director provides to these creatures; and third, it cements the visual and the natural with a sticky and sentimental voice-over (provided by Morgan Freeman in the version released in the U.S.) about the transcendence of love and the power of family that supposedly motivate the penguins to pursue reproduction in such inhospitable conditions. Despite the astonishing footage, the glorious beauty of the setting and of the birds themselves, *The March of the Penguins* ultimately trains its attention on only a fraction of the story of penguin communities because its gaze remains so obstinately trained upon the comforting spectacle of "the couple," "the family unit," "love," "loss," heterosexual reproduction, and the emotional architecture that supposedly welds all these moving parts together. However, the focus on heterosexual reproduction is misleading and mistaken, and ultimately it blots out a far more compelling story about cooperation, collectivity, and nonheterosexual, nonreproductive behaviors.

Several skeptical critics remarked that, amazing as the story might be, this was not evidence of romantic love among penguins, and "love" was targeted as the most telling symptom of the film's annoying anthropomorphism.[2] But heterosexual reproduction, the most insistent framing device in the film, is never questioned either by the filmmakers or the critics. Indeed Christian fundamentalists promoted the film as a moving text about monogamy, sacrifice, and child rearing. And this despite the fact that the penguins are monogamous for only one year, and that they promptly abandon all responsibility for their offspring once the small penguins have survived the first few months of arctic life. While conventional animal documentaries like *The March of the Penguins* continue to insist on the heterosexuality of nature, the evolutionary biologist Joan Roughgarden insists that we examine nature anew for evidence of the odd and nonreproductive and nonheterosexual and non-gender-stable phenomena that characterize most animal life. Roughgarden's wonderful study of evolutionary diversity, *Evolution's Rainbow* (2004), explains that most biologists observe "nature" through a narrow and biased lens of socionormativity and therefore misinterpret all kinds of biodiversity. And so, although transsexual fish, hermaphroditic hyenas, nonmonogamous birds, and homosexual lizards all play a role in the survival and evolution of the species, their function has been mostly misunderstood and folded into rigid and unimaginative hetero-familial schemes of reproductive zeal and the survival of the fittest. Roughgarden explains that human observers misread (capitalist) competition into (nonmonetary) cooperative animal societies and activities; they also misunderstand the relations between strength and dominance and overestimate the primacy of reproductive dynamics.

In an essay in the *New York Times* magazine published in 2010 humorously titled "The Love That Dare Not Squawk Its Name," Jon Mooallem asks, "Can animals be gay?"[3] Using the example of mating pairs of albatrosses who were assumed to be paired up in male-female configurations but actually were mostly female-female bonded pairs, Mooallem interviews some biologists about the phenomenon. Noting that the biologists Marlene Zuk and Lindsay C. Young assiduously avoid using anthropomorphizing language about the birds they study, Mooallem reports that when Young did slip up and call the colony of albatrosses "the largest proportion of—I don't know what the correct term is: 'homosexual animals'?— in the world," the media response was massive. Young found herself in the middle of a national debate about whether homosexuality among animals proved the rightness and naturalness of gay and lesbian proclivities among humans! Predictably North American Christians were outraged that this is the research their "tax dollars" were funding. Other media found the story irresistible; on Comedy Central, for example, Stephen Colbert warned that "albatresbians were threatening American family values with a Sappho-avian agenda"!

The more interesting story in this essay, however—more interesting than the discussion of what to call same-sex animal couples, that is—concerns the blind spots of animal researchers themselves. Mooallem rightly notes that researchers constantly provide alibis and excuses for the same-sex sexual behavior they observe, but he also discovers that most researchers do not actually know the sex of the animal they are observing, and so they infer sex based on behavior and relational sets. This has led to all kinds of misreporting on heterosexual courtship because the sex of the creatures in question is not actually scrutinized, and mixed-sex couples, as with the albatrosses and certainly with penguins, very often end up being same-sex couples. In the case of the albatrosses, researchers thought they were finding evidence of a "super-normal clutch" when they found two eggs in a nest rather than one; it never occurred to them that the two birds incubating the eggs were both female and each had an egg. The narrative of male superfertility was more comforting and appealing. Thus intuitive evidence that contradicts the contorted narratives that scientists put together is ignored because heterosexuality is the "human" lens through which all animal behavior is studied.

How should we think about so-called homosexual behavior among animals? Well, as the *New York Times* essay suggests by way of Joan Roughgarden, anything that falls outside of heterosexual behavior is not necessarily homosexual, and anything that conforms to human understandings of heterosexual behavior may not be heterosexual. In fact Roughgarden prefers to think about animals as creatures who may "multitask" with their private parts: some of what we call sexual contact between animals may be basic communication, some of the behavior may be adaptive, some survival-oriented, some reproductive, much of it improvised.

Which brings us back to the penguins and their long march into the snowy, icy, and devastating landscape of Antarctica. It is easy, especially given the voice-over, to see the penguin world as made up of little heroic families striving to complete their natural and pregiven need to reproduce. The voice-over provides a beautiful but nonsensical narrative that remains resolutely human and refuses to ever see the "penguin logics" that structure their frigid quest. When the penguins mass on the ice to find partners, we are asked to see a school prom with rejected and spurned partners on the edges of the dance floor and true romance and soul mates in its center. When the mating rituals begin, we are told of elegant and balletic dances, though we see awkward, difficult, and undignified couplings. When the female penguin finally produces the valuable egg and must now pass the egg from her feet to the male's feet in order to free herself to go and feed, the voice-over reaches hysteria pitch and sees sorrow and heartbreak in every unsuccessful transfer. We are never told how many penguins are successful in passing their egg, how many might decide not to be successful in order to save themselves the effort of a hard winter, how much of the transfer ritual might be accidental, and so on. The narrative ascribes stigma and envy to nonreproductive penguins, sacrifice and a Protestant work ethic to the reproducers, and sees a capitalist hetero-reproductive family rather than the larger group.

Ultimately the voice-over and the Christian attribution of "intelligent design" to the penguins' activity must ignore many inconvenient facts. The penguins are not monogamous; they mate for one year and then move on. The partners find each other after returning from feeding by recognizing each other's call, not by some innate and mysterious coupling instinct. Perhaps most important, the nonreproductive penguins are not merely extras in the drama of hetero-reproduction; in fact the homo or nonrepro queer penguins are totally necessary to the temporary reproductive unit. They provide warmth in the huddle and probably extra food, and they do not leave for warmer climes but accept a part in the penguin collective in order to enable reproduction and to survive. Survival in this penguin world has little to do with fitness and everything to do with collective will. And once the reproductive cycle draws to a close, what happens then? The parent penguins do protect their young in terms of warmth, but the parents do nothing to stave off attacks by aerial predators; there the young penguins are on their own. And once the baby penguins reach the age when they too can take to the water, the parent penguins slip gratefully into another element with not even a backward glance to see if the next generation follows. The young penguins now have five years of freedom, five glorious, nonreproductive, family-free years before they too must undertake the long march. The long march of the penguins is proof neither of heterosexuality in nature nor of the reproductive imperative nor of intelligent design. It is a resolutely animal narrative about cooperation, affiliation, and the anachronism of the homo-hetero divide. The indifference in the film to all nonreproductive behaviors obscures the more complex narratives of penguin life: we learn in the first five minutes of the film that female penguins far outnumber their male counterparts, and yet repercussions of this gender ratio are never explored; we see with our own eyes that only a few of the penguins continue to carry eggs through the winter, but the film provides no narrative at all for the birds who don't carry eggs; we can presume that all kinds of odd and adaptive behaviors take place in order to enhance the penguins' chances for survival (for example, the adoption of orphaned penguins), but the film tells us nothing about this. In fact while the visual narrative reveals a wild world of non-human kinship and affiliation, the voice-over relegates this world to the realm of the unimaginable and unnatural.

The March of the Penguins has created a whole genre of penguin animation, beginning with Warner Brothers' Happy Feet in 2006, soon followed by Sony Pictures' Surf's Up and Bob Saget's animated spoof The Farce of the Penguins for Thinkfilms. The primary appeal of the penguins, based on the success of Happy Feet anyway, seems to be the heart-rending narratives of family and survival that contemporary viewers are projecting onto the austere images of these odd birds. On account of the voice-over, however, we could say that The March of the Penguins is already animated, already an animated feature film, and in fact in the French and German versions the penguins are given individual voices rather than narrated by a "voice of god" trick. Here the animation works not to emphasize the difference between humans and nonhumans, as it does in so many Pixar features, but instead makes the penguins into virtual puppets for the drama of human, modern love that cinema is so eager to tell.

Queer Creatures, Monstrous Animation

May the best monster win!
—Sully in Monsters, Inc.

Pixarvolt films often link the animals to new forms of being and offer us different ways of thinking about being, relation, reproduction, and ideology. The animation lab grows odd human-like creatures and reimagines the human not as animal but as animation—as a set of selves that must appeal to human modes of identification not through simple visual tricks of recognition but through voice cues and facial expressions and actions. Gromit, in Wallace and Gromit, for example, has no mouth and does not speak, yet he conveys infinite reservoirs of resourcefulness and intelligence in his eyes and in the smallest movements of his eyes

3. *Monsters, Inc.*, directed by Pete Doctor and David Silverman, 2001. "May the best monster win!"

within his face (which A. O. Scott in the *New York Times* compares to the face of Garbo). Dory, in *Finding Nemo*, has no memory but represents a kind of eccentric form of knowing which allows her to swim circles around the rather tame and conservative Marlin. How do modes of identification with animated creatures work? Does the child viewer actually feel a kinship with the ahistorical Dory and the speechless Gromit and with the repetition that characterizes all of the narratives? Why do spectators (conservative parents, for instance) endorse these queer and monstrous narratives despite their radical messages, and how does the whimsical nature of the animated world allow for the smuggling of radical narratives into otherwise clichéd interactions about friendship, loyalty, and family values?

As we saw with *Toy Story*, the Pixarvolt films often proceed by way of fairly conventional narratives about individual struggle against the automated process of innovation, and they often pit an individual, independent, and original character against the conformist sensibilities of the masses. But this summary is somewhat misleading, because more often than not the individual character actually serves as a gateway to intricate stories of collective action, anticapitalist critique, group bonding, and alternative imaginings of community, space, embodiment, and responsibility. Often the animal or creature that stands apart from the community is not a heroic individual but a symbol of selfishness who must be taught how to think collectively. For example, in *Over the Hedge* (2006, directed by Tim Johnson) by DreamWorks the film stages a dramatic standoff between some woodland creatures and their new junk-food-consuming, pollution-spewing, SUV-driving, trash-producing, water-wasting, anti-environmentalist human neighbors. When the creatures awake from their winter hibernation they discover that while they were sleeping, a soulless suburban development stole their woodland space and the humans have erected a huge partition, a hedge, to fence them out. At first it seems as if the narrative will be motored by our interest in a plucky raccoon called RJ, but ultimately RJ must join forces with the other creatures—squirrels, porcupines, skunks, turtles, and bears—in a cross-species alliance to destroy the colonizers, tear down the partition, and upend the suburbanites' depiction of them as "vermin." Similarly in *Finding Nemo* the most valuable lesson that Nemo learns is not to "be himself" or "follow his dreams," but, more like Ginger in *Chicken Run*, he learns to think with others and to work for a more collective futurity. In *Monsters, Inc.* (directed by Pete Doctor and David Silverman, 2001) monsters hired to scare children find an affinity with them that wins out over a corporate alliance with the adults who run the scream factory.

Fairy tales have always occupied the ambiguous territory between childhood and adulthood, home and away, harm and safety. They also tend to be as populated by monsters as by "normal" or even ideal people; in fact the relations between monsters and princesses, dragons and knights, scary creatures and human saviors open doors to alternative worlds and allow children to confront archetypal fears, engage in prepubescent fantasy, and indulge infantile desires about being scared, eaten, chased, and demolished. *Monsters, Inc.* makes monstrosity into a commodity and imagines what happens when the child victim of monstrous bogeymen speaks back to her demons and in the process both scares them and creates bonds of affection, affiliation, identification, and desire between her and the monsters. This bond between child and monster, as we know from looking at other texts, is unusual because it allows for the crossing of the divide between the fantasy world and the human world, but also because it imagines a girl child as the vehicle for the transgression of boundaries. The human-monster bond is queer in its

4. *Over the Hedge*, directed by Tim Johnson, 2006. "Collective thinking."

reorganization of family and affinity and in the way it interrupts and disrupts more conventional romantic bonds in the film.

The antihumanist discourse in Pixarvolts is confirmed by the black-and-white depiction of actual humans in these films. We see the humans only through the eyes of the animated creatures, and in *Over the Hedge*, *Finding Nemo*, and *Chicken Run* they look empty, lifeless, and inert—in fact, unanimated. The Pixarvolt genre makes animation itself into a feature of kinetic political action rather than just an elaborate form of puppetry. The human and nonhuman are featured as animated and unanimated but also as constructed and unreconstructed. In a telling moment in *Robots* (2005, directed by Chris Wedge), for example, a male robot announces to the world that he will soon be a father. What follows is a fascinating origin story that locates construction at the heart of the animated self. When he gets home, his wife informs him that he has "missed the delivery," and the camera pans to an unopened box of baby robot parts. The mother and father then begin to assemble their child using both the new parts and some salvaged parts (a grandfather's eyes, for example). The labor of producing the baby is queer in that it is shared and improvised, of culture rather than nature, an act of construction rather than reproduction. In a final hilarious note of punctuation, the mother robot asks the father robot what he thinks the "spare part" that came with the kit might be. The father responds, "We did want a boy, didn't we?" and proceeds to hammer the phallus into place. Like some parody of social construction,

5. *Robots*, directed by Chris Wedge, 2005. "Making babies!"

this children's film imagines embodiment as an assemblage of parts and sees some as optional, some as interchangeable; indeed later in the film the little boy robot wears some of his sister's clothes.

An animated self allows for the deconstruction of ideas of a timeless and natural humanity. The idea of the human does tend to return in some form or another over the course of the animated film, usually as a desire for uniqueness, or an unalienated relation to work and to others, or as a fantasy of liberty, but the notion of a robotic and engineered self takes the animated feature well into the genealogical territory of Harawayesque cyborgs. In *Robots* the cyborgean metaphor is extended into a fabulous political allegory of recycling and transformation. When a big corporation, powered by a nefarious Oedipal triangle of a dominant mother, a wicked son, and an ineffectual father (a common triangle in both fairy tales and animated features), tries to phase out some robots in order to introduce new models, Rodney Coppertop goes to the big city to argue that older models are salvageable and transformable. While Rodney is also part of an Oedipal triangle (good mother, courageous son, expiring father), he becomes powerful, like Nemo, only when he abandons the family and makes common cause with a larger collectivity. This notion of the assembled self and its relation to an ever-shifting and improvised multitude ultimately rests upon and recirculates an antihumanist understanding of sociality.

Not all animated films manage to resist the lure of humanism, and so not all animated films fit comfortably into what I am calling the Pixarvolt genre. What separates the Pixarvolt from the merely pixilated? One answer turns upon the difference between collective revolutionary selves and a more conventional notion of a fully realized individuality. The non-Pixarvolt animated features prefer family to collectivity, human individuality to social bonding, extraordinary individuals to diverse communities. For example, *The Incredibles* builds its story around the supposedly heroic drama of male midlife crisis and invests in an Ayn Randian or scientologist notion of the special people who must resist social pressures to suppress their superpowers in order to fit in with the drab masses. *Happy Feet* similarly casts its lot with individualism and makes a heroic figure out of the dancing penguin who cannot fit in with his community . . . at first. Eventually of course the community expands to incorporate him, but sadly they learn valuable lessons along the way about the importance of every single one of the rather uniform penguins learning to "be themselves." Of course if the penguins really were being themselves, that is, penguins, they would not be singing Earth, Wind & Fire songs in blackface, as they do in the movie, and searching for soul mates; they would be making odd squawking noises and settling down for one year with one mate and then moving on.

In *Over the Hedge*, *Robots*, *Finding Nemo*, and other Pixarvolts desire for difference is not connected to a neoliberal "Be yourself" mentality or to special individualism for "incredible" people; rather the Pixarvolt films connect individualism to selfishness, to untrammeled consumption, and they oppose it with a collective mentality. Two thematics can transform a potential Pixarvolt film into a tame and conventional cartoon: an overemphasis on nuclear *family* and a normative investment in coupled *romance*. The Pixarvolt films, unlike their unrevolting conventional animation counterparts, seem to know that their main audience is children, and they seem to also know that children do not invest in the same things that adults invest in: children are not coupled, they are not romantic, they do not have a religious morality, they are not afraid of death or failure, they are collective creatures, they are in a constant state of rebellion against their parents, and they are not the masters of their domain. Children stumble, bumble, fail, fall, hurt; they are mired in difference, not in control of their bodies, not in charge of their lives, and they live according to schedules not of their own making. The Pixarvolt films offer an animated world of triumph for the little guys, a revolution against the business world of the father and the domestic sphere of the mother—in fact very often the mother is simply dead and the father is enfeebled (as in *Robots*, *Monsters, Inc.*, *Finding Nemo*, and *Over the Hedge*). Gender in these films is shifty and ambiguous (transsexual fish in Finding Nemo, other-species-identified pig in Babe); sexualities are amorphous and polymorphous (the homoerotics of SpongeBob's and Patrick's relationship and of Wallace's and Gromit's domesticity); class is clearly marked in terms of labor and species diversity; bodily ability is quite often at issue (Nemo's small fin, Shrek's giganticism); and only race falls all too often in familiar and stereotyped patterns of characterization (the overly sexual "African American" skunk in Over the Hedge, the "African American" donkey in Shrek). I believe that despite the inability of these films to reimagine race, the Pixarvolt features have animated a new space for the imagining of alternatives.

As Sianne Ngai comments in an excellent chapter on race and "animatedness" in her book Ugly Feelings, "animatedness" is an ambivalent mode of representation, especially when it comes to race, because it reveals the ideological conditions of "speech" and ventriloquism but it also threatens to reassert grotesque stereotypes by fixing on caricature and excess in its attempts to make its nonhuman subjects come alive. Ngai grapples with the contradictions in the TV animated series The PJ's, a "foamation" production featuring Eddie Murphy and focusing on a black, non-middle-class community. In her meticulous analysis of the show's genesis, genealogy, and reception, Ngai describes the array of responses the puppets provoked, many of them negative and many focused on the ugliness of the puppetry and the racial caricatures that the critics felt the show revived. Ngai responds to the charge of the ugliness of the images by arguing that the show actually "introduced a new possibility for racial representation in the medium of television: one that ambitiously sought to reclaim the grotesque and/or ugly, as a powerful aesthetic of exaggeration, crudeness, and distortion" (2005: 105). She examines The PJ's scathing social critique and its intertextual web of references to black popular culture in relation to its technology, the stop-motion process, which, she claims, exploits the relationship between rigidity and elasticity both literally and figuratively: "The PJ's reminds us that there can be ways of inhabiting a social role that actually distort its boundaries, changing the status of 'role' from that which purely confines or constricts to the site at which new possibilities for human agency might be explored" (117). Obviously Happy Feet does not exploit the tension between rigidity and elasticity in the same ways that The PJ's does in Ngai's reading of the show.

The Pixarvolt films show how important it is to recognize the weirdness of bodies, sexualities, and genders in other animal life worlds, not to

6. *Bee Movie*, directed by Steve Hickner and Simon J. Smith, 2007.
"Drones and queens"

mention other animated universes. The fish in *Finding Nemo* and the chickens in *Chicken Run* actually manage to produce new meanings of male and female; in the former, Marlin is a parent but not a father, for example, and in the latter, Ginger is a romantic but not willing to sacrifice politics for romance. The all-female society of chickens allows for unforeseen feminist implications to this utopian fantasy. *Chicken Run*, however, is one of the few animated films to exploit its animal world symbolics. Other features about ants and bees, also all-female worlds, fall short when using these social insect worlds to tell human stories.

Take the Pixar production *Bee Movie* (2007, directed by Steve Hickner and Simon J. Smith), starring Jerry Seinfeld. The film certainly lives up to our expectations of finding narratives about collective resistance to capitalist exploitation. Even as liberal a critic as Roger Ebert noticed that *Bee Movie* contains some rather odd Marxist elements. He writes in his review of the film, "What Barry [the bee voiced by Seinfeld] mostly discovers from human society is, gasp!, that humans rob the bees of all their honey and eat it. He and Adam, his best pal, even visit a bee farm, which looks like forced labor of the worst sort. Their instant analysis of the human-bee economic relationship is pure Marxism, if only they knew it." And indeed it is: Barry is not satisfied with working in the hive doing the same thing everyday, and so he decides to become a pollinator instead of a worker bee. But when he explores the outside world he finds out that all the labor in his hive is for naught, given that the honey the bees are making is being harvested, packaged, and sold by humans. Taking a very non-Marxist approach to remedying this exploitive situation, Barry sues humankind and along the way romances and befriends a human. Now while the romance between Barry and the human could have produced a fascinating trans-biological scenario of interspecies sex, instead it just becomes a vehicle for the heterosexualization of the homoerotic hive.

While it unintentionally skirts communist critiques of work, profit, and the alienation of the labor force, *Bee Movie* forcefully and deliberately replaces the queerly gendered nature of the hive with a masculinist plot about macho pollinators, dogged male workers, and domestic female home keepers. But as Natalie Angier points out in the science section of the *New York Times*:

> By bowdlerizing the basic complexion of a great insect society, Mr. Sein-feld's "Bee Movie" follows in the well-pheromoned path of Woody Allen as a whiny worker ant in *Antz* and Dave Foley playing a klutzy forager ant in *A Bug's Life*. Maybe it's silly to fault cartoons for biological inaccuracies when the insects are already talking like Chris Rock and wearing Phyllis Diller hats. But isn't it bad enough that in Hollywood's animated family fare about rats, clownfish, penguins, lions, hyenas and other relatively large animals, the overwhelming majority of characters are male, despite nature's preferred sex ratio of roughly 50–50? Must even obligately female creatures like worker bees and soldier ants be given sex change surgery, too? Besides, there's no need to go with the faux: the life of an authentic male social insect is thrilling, poignant and cartoonish enough.[4]

She goes on to detail the absurd life cycle of the male drone, noting that only .05 percent of the hive is male:

> The male honeybee's form bespeaks his sole function. He has large eyes to help find queens and extra antenna segments to help smell queens, but he is otherwise ill equipped to survive. On reaching adulthood, he must linger in the hive for a few days until his exoskeleton dries and his wing muscles mature, all the while begging food from his sisters and thus living up to his tainted name, drone. . . . After a male deposits sperm in the queen, his little "endophallus" snaps off, and he falls to the ground. In her single nuptial flight, the queen will collect and store in her body the sperm offerings of some 20 doomed males, more than enough to fertilize a long life's worth of eggs.

Angier concludes dramatically, "A successful male is a dead male, a failure staggers home and begs to be fed and to try again tomorrow." Sounding more like a Valerie Solanas handbook for social change than a popular science meditation on insect life, Angier's essay captures the essentially strange variations of gender, sex, labor, and pleasure in other animal life worlds, variations that often appear in Pixarvolt animation but are skirted in other, less revolting films like *Bee Movie*.

I want to conclude this chapter by turning back to the queerness of the bees and the potential queerness of all allegorical narratives of animal sociality and by advocating for "creative anthropomorphism" over and against endless narratives of human exceptionalism that deploy ordinary and banal forms of anthropomorphism when much more creative versions would lead us in unexpected directions. Hardt's and Negri's notion of the swarm in *Multitude* (2005), like Linebaugh's and Rediker's model of the hydra in *Many-Headed Hydra* (2001), imagines oppositional groups in terms of real or fantasized beasts that rise up to subvert the singularity of the human with the multiplicity of the unruly mob. In practicing creative anthropomorphism we invent the models of resistance we need and lack in reference to other lifeworlds, animal and monstrous. Bees, as many political commentators over the years have noted, signify a model for collective behavior (Preston 2005), the social animal par excellence. A common proverb posits, *Ulla apis, nulla apis*, "One bee is no bee," marking the essentially "political" and "collective" identity of the bee. Bees have long been used to signify political community; they have been represented as examples of the benevolence of state power (Vergil), the power of the monarchy (Shakespeare), the effectiveness of a Protestant work ethic, the orderliness of government, and more (Preston 2005). But bees have also represented the menacing power of the mob, the buzzing beast of anarchism, the mindless conformity of fascism, the organized and soulless labor structures proposed by communism, and the potential ruthlessness of matriarchal power (the ejection of the male drones by the female worker bees). Most recently the bees have served as an analogy for the kinds of movements that oppose global capitalism. Using the analogy of bees or ants, Hardt and Negri combine organic with inorganic to come up with a "networked swarm" of resistance that the system of a "sovereign state of security" contends with. The swarm presents as a mass rather than a unitary enemy and offers no obvious target; thinking as a single superorganism, the swarm is elusive, ephemeral, in flight. Like ants, the bee, a social animal, offers a highly sophisticated, multifunctional model of political life. In movies, too, the bees have been cast as friend and foe, and in some fabulations the bee is Africanized and aggressive (*Deadly Swarm*, directed by Paul Andresen 2003), communist and swarming (*The Swarm*, 1978, directed by Irwin Allen), intelligent and deadly (*The Bees*, 1978, directed by Alfredo Zacharias); bees as ecoterrorists attack humans and swarm in the UN building in New York until defused by a human-made virus that makes them homosexual, female, and dangerous (*Queen Bee*, 1955, directed by Ranald Macdougall and starring Joan Crawford). In *Invasion of the Bee Girls* (1973, directed by Denis Sanders) apian women kill men after sex. Above all, the bee is female and queer and given to the production not of babies but of an addictive nectar, honey. The transbiological element here has to do with the alternative meanings of gender when biology is not in the service of reproduction and patriarchy.

The dream of an alternative way of being is often confused with utopian thinking and then dismissed as naïve, simplistic, or a blatant misunderstanding of the nature of power in modernity. And yet the possibility of other forms of being, other forms of knowing, a world with different sites for justice and injustice, a mode of being where the emphasis falls less on money and work and competition and more on cooperation, trade, and sharing animates all kinds of knowledge projects and should not be dismissed as irrelevant or naïve. In *Monsters, Inc.*, for example, fear generates revenue for corporate barons, and the screams of children actually power the city of Monstropolis. The film offers a kind of prophetic vision of post-9/11 life in the U.S., where the production of monsters allows the governing elites to scare a population into quietude while generating profits for their own dastardly schemes. This direct link between fear and profit is more pointed in this children's feature than in most adult films produced in the era of postmodern anxiety. Again, a cynical reading of the world of animation will always return to the notion that difficult topics are raised and contained in children's films precisely so that they do not have to be discussed elsewhere and also so that the politics of rebellion can be cast as immature, pre-Oedipal, childish, foolish, fantastical, and rooted in a commitment to failure. But a more dynamic and radical engagement with animation understands that the rebellion is ongoing and that the new technologies of children's fantasy do much more than produce revolting animation. They also offer us the real and compelling possibility of animating revolt.

PLATE 1. Tracey Moffat, *Fourth #2*, 2001. Color print on canvas, 36 cm × 46 cm, series of 26. Courtesy of the artist and Roslyn Oxley9 Gallery, Sydney.

PLATE 2. Tracey Moffat, *Fourth #3*, 2001. Color print on canvas, 36 cm × 46 cm, series of 26. Courtesy of the artist and Roslyn Oxley9 Gallery, Sydney.

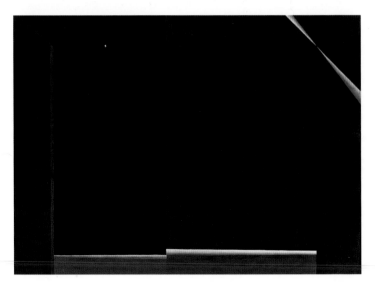

PLATE 3. Monica Majoli, *Kate*, 2009. Oil on panel, 16 in.× 20 in.× 1 in.

PLATE 4. Monica Majoli, *Black Mirror 2 (Kate)*, 2009. Acrylic, acrylic ink, and gouache, 24 in. × 30 in.

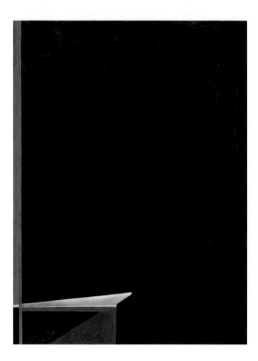

PLATE 5. Monica Majoli, *Jarrett*, 2009. Oil on panel, 9 in. × 12 in. × 1 in.

PLATE 6. Monica Majoli, *Black Mirror 1 (Jarrett)* 2009. Acrylic, acrylic ink, and gouache, 30 in. × 24 in.

PLATE 7. Judie Bamber, *July 22, 2004, 6:15 PM*, 2004. Oil on canvas on board, 30 in. × 36 in. Copyright Judie Bamber. Used by permission.

PLATE 8. Judie Bamber, *June 24, 2004, 8:45 PM*, 2004. Oil on canvas on board, 30 in. × 36 in. Copyright Judie Bamber. Used by permission.

PLATE 9. Judie Bamber *I'll Give You Something to Cry About (Dead Baby Finch)*, 1990.
Oil on canvas, 29 in. × 29 in. Copyright Judie Bamber. Used by permission.

PLATE 10. J. A. Nicholls, *Here and Now*, 2006. Oil and acrylic on canvas, 137 cm × 183 cm. Printed with permission of J. A. Nicholls.

PLATE 11. J. A. Nicholls, *Higher Ground*, 2006. Oil and acrylic on canvas, 120 cm × 180 cm. Printed with permission of J. A. Nicholls.

PLATE 12. J. A. Nicholls, *New Story*, 2006. Oil and acrylic on canvas. 160 cm × 147 cm. Printed with permission of J. A. Nicholls.

PLATE 13. Attila Richard Lukacs, *Love in Union: Amorous Meeting*, 1992. Oil on canvas, 118.8 in. × 79 in. Courtesy of the artist.

Flea Market version

study for Sanders traitor

3

Booby Trap talking about your enemies is another form of narcissism

PLATE 14. Collier Schorr, "Booby Trap," 2000. Pen and pencil on pigment ink print and silver gelatin print, 148.6 cm × 111.8 cm. CS 726. Courtesy of 303 Gallery, New York.

CHAPTER TWO

Dude, Where's My *Phallus?*

It will be immediately obvious how there can be no happiness, no cheerfulness, no hope, no pride, no present, without forgetfulness.
— Nietzsche, *On the Genealogy of Morals*

Stupidity exceeds and undercuts materiality, runs loose, wins a few rounds, recedes, gets carried home in the clutch of denial — and returns. Essentially linked to the inexhaustible, stupidity is also that which fatigues knowledge and wears down history.
— Avital Ronell, *Stupidity*

Patrick: Knowledge can never replace friendship! I PREFER TO BE AN IDIOT!
SpongeBob: You're not just an idiot, Patrick, you're also my pal!
— *SpongeBob SquarePants*, Season 4, Episode 68, "Patrick Smartpants"

As the rather hysterical clownfish Marlin swims frantically in search of his son, Nemo, in *Finding Nemo* (directed by Andrew Stanton, 2003) he encounters a seemingly helpful blue fish named Dory. Voiced by Ellen DeGeneres in the classic Pixar feature, Dory tells Marlin she knows where Nemo is and promptly swims off purposively with Marlin in tow. After a few minutes, however, she seems to lose her vim and begins to loop around in circles, looking back over her shoulder every now and then in a quizzical way at Marlin. Finally she circles around to confront him and asks him why he is following her. Marlin, confused now and angry, reminds her that she had promised to lead him to

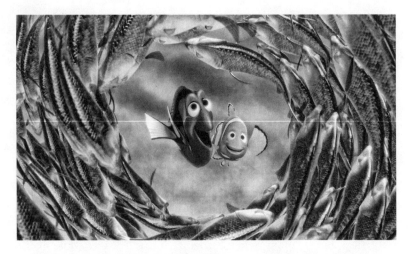

7. *Finding Nemo*, directed by Andrew Stanton, 2003. "Queer fish."

Nemo. But Dory remembers nothing and explains that she suffers from short-term memory loss. From this point on, Dory and Marlin are a queer temporal mode governed by the ephemeral, the temporary, and the elusive—forms of knowing, in other words, that lie at the very edge of memory. Dory, for whom the most recent experience is always a distant shadow, a name on the tip of her tongue, recalls events not as a continuous narrative leading from a past to a present; rather she experiences memory only in flashes and fragments. Those flashes and fragments still allow her to lead her hysterical friend across the ocean, through pods of jellyfish, sharks, and turtles, to Sydney Harbor and the dentist's office where Nemo lives in captivity. Dory represents a different, a queer and fluid form of knowing, that operates independently of coherence or linear narrative or progression. By some standards she might be read as stupid or unknowing, foolish or silly, but ultimately her silliness leads her to new and different forms of relation and action. In this chapter I discuss acts of loopy stupidity associated with forgetfulness and modes of active and passive forgetting often misread as stupidity. In each scenario a certain kind of absence—the absence of memory or the absence of wisdom—leads to a new form of knowing.

Stupidity conventionally means different things in relation to different subject positions; for example, stupidity in white men can signify new modes of domination, but stupidity in women of all ethnicities inevitably symbolizes their status as, in psychoanalytic terms, "castrated" or impaired. In relation to the theme of productive failure, stupidity and forgetfulness work hand in hand to open up new and different ways of being in relation to time, truth, being, living, and dying. I will return to Dory and her fishy forms of forgetting later, but I will start with some basic premises about stupidity.

Stupidity

Stupidity is as profoundly gendered as knowledge formations in general; thus while unknowing in a man is sometimes rendered as part of masculine charm, unknowing in a woman indicates a lack and a justification of a social order that anyway privileges men. Though we both punish and naturalize female stupidity, we not only forgive stupidity in white men, but we often cannot recognize it as such since white maleness is the identity construct most often associated with mastery, wisdom, and grand narratives. In other words, when a white male character in a film or novel is characterized as stupid or unknowing, this is quickly folded back into his general appeal as a winning form of vulnerability. (Think of Jack Nicholson's character in *As Good As It Gets* [1997, directed by James L. Brooks], for example.) An elaborate example of the mastery of white male unknowing occurs in Zadie Smith's hilarious novel, *On Beauty* (2006), which illuminates the ways we naturalize knowledge in relation to the white man. While her novel never does resolve into a racial polemic, it certainly punishes its white male hero for his unquestioned sense of his own mastery. *On Beauty* addresses questions about life, race, and politics by exploring the dramas of life in a New England university named Wellington, a barely disguised version of Harvard. In a critical move at the novel's conclusion, Smith brings her unknowing but masterful white male protagonist, Howard, to an ignominious end. Reviewers make much of Smith's citation of Elaine Scarry's book *On Beauty and Justice* in her title and E. M. Forster's *Howard's End* in her plot, and generally Smith's novel has been read as a tribute to the humanistic impulses behind both Scarry's belief that beauty and justice are related, indeed that one leads to the other, and Forster's celebration of some vague notion of truth and human connection. However, the thrust of *On Beauty* leads readers in a rather different direction than the nods to Scarry and Forster imply. In fact *On Beauty* actually upends all the transparent alibis that dominant groups (in the case of Wellington, white male academics) give themselves in academia and elsewhere to justify their investments in anachronistic forms of knowledge. And so, while Howard is ostensibly writing a book that deconstructs the notion of genius with reference to Rembrandt, he continues to behave as if genius really does exist and as if it exists specifically in him. Howard himself believes that he does not need to write a book to showcase his own intellect because his intelligence is so self-evident and self-authorizing.

Smith leads Howard through a series of comical humiliations in the course of the narrative, none of which humbles him or shakes his belief in his own greatness and his own appeal; then, at the conclusion of the novel, she shows him standing before an audience to present his great work, the centerpiece of his tenure case and the proof of his undying genius. The audience, which includes his estranged African American wife, Kiki, and their children, becomes increasingly uncomfortable as it becomes quite clear that Howard has nothing much to say. In fact he has no talk to give, having left his brief and unfinished manuscript on the backseat of his car, and he finds himself simply flipping through a PowerPoint presentation on Rembrandt's paintings while the audience sits and watches. Some shift in their seats in embarrassment, but others read his brilliance into the mere "ordering" of the slides he shows. Ultimately Howard's end is just that: it signifies the end to a particular model of knowing and being that is organized around the white male principle of genius and that has been institutionalized within a racially specific model of the university that believes in the direct links between beauty and justice. Howard's end is also the end of the authorizing gestures of taste and valuation, in fact is the end of disciplinarity itself and the beginning of the multiple forms of subjugated knowledge that have already, steadily and definitively, replaced it.

The spectacle of Howard clicking through a slideshow with nothing to say while still seducing a few admiring fans in the audience brings to mind countless other millennial dimbos. Since at least the year 2000 and the election of George W. Bush, Americans have shown themselves to be increasingly enamored with the heroic couplet of men and stupidity. As the election in 2004 proved, playing dumb means playing to "the people," who, apparently, find intellectual acumen to be a sign of overeducation, elitism, and Washington insider status. As many critics have pointed out, no one could be more of a Washington insider than George W. Bush, the son of a former president and the brother of the governor of Florida. Even so, in both of his election campaigns Bush made a populist version of stupidity into a trademark and sold himself to the public as a down-home guy, a fun BBQ pal, a man's man, a student privileged enough to go to Yale but "real" enough to only get Cs — in other words, an inarticulate, monolingual buffoon who was a safe bet for the White House because he was not trying to befuddle an increasingly uneducated populace with facts, figures, or, god forbid, ideas. His opponent in the election, John Kerry, was fluent in French, well educated, well spoken, and highly suspicious on all counts.

Stupidity in women, as we know, is often expected in this male-dominated culture, and some women cultivate it because they see it rewarded in popular icons, from Goldie Hawn to Jessica Simpson. Stupid women make men feel bigger, better, smarter. But what is the appeal in North America of the stupid man, and why does the representation of male stupidity not lead to male disempowerment? Stupidity in men is represented as, well, disarming (Adam Sandler), charming (Jerry Lewis), comforting (George W.), or innocent (Will Farrell in Elf, Tom Hanks in everything). Male stupidity masks the will to power that lies just behind the goofy grin, and it masquerades as some kind of internalization of feminist critiques. The clueless male in movies usually requires a spunky and intelligent woman to pull him along, educate and civilize him, and this masks the gender inequality that structures their relationship.

Male stupidity is in fact a new form of macho, and it comes at a time when alternative masculinities have achieved some small measure of currency. It matters little whether we are discussing avant-garde film or popular film, because, in both, male unknowing facilitates male power. Pedro Almodovar's critically acclaimed masterpiece of misogyny, Talk to Her (2004), is an aesthetically complex piece of work in which male stupidity allows for the complete decimation of two talented women. First, a ballet dancer and a female bullfighter are involved in separate accidents that render them comatose. Next, their comatose bodies become wallpaper while two unappealing and unremarkable male admirers flirt and coo across their mute and prone bodies. While the male leads are exposed as flawed, criminal even, deceptive, and conniving, the film still focuses on them while leaving the women inert, simple, silent. Stupidity, in other words, passes as complexity, and male complexity requires, again, female simplicity.

While one could argue that Talk to Her is charting rather than investing in the kinds of misogyny that rescue male stupidity by projecting it onto women, other films with a similar theme confirm the fatal links between male bonding and a form of male pathos (pathetic stupidity) designed to tug at the heartstrings of the women who "love too much."

To give a prime example of this last kind of "male stupidity" film, the universally acclaimed Oscar contender *Sideways* pairs up nebbish, overly intellectual loser Miles (Paul Giamatti) with the patently stupid faded macho actor Jack (Thomas Haden Church) and turns their wine country odyssey into an exploration of wine, women, and wisdom, with the women providing access to first the wine and then the wisdom. The movie seems to be exposing male vulnerability, or making a spectacle of male stupidity, or anatomizing male arrogance, but in the end it is no different from any other buddy movie, recalling the dumb cute guy and smart ugly guy couples of Dean Martin and Jerry Lewis, Butch Cassidy and Sundance, even the much more appealing Jesse and Chester in *Dude, Where's My Car?* But *Sideways* masquerades as a film about alternative masculinity by making male stupidity stand in for male vulnerability and then producing male vulnerability as irresistible to smart women.

In fact popular and seemingly "dumb" films like *Dude, Where's My Car?* (2000, directed by Danny Leiner) actually present far more elaborate understandings of the relations between male stupidity, social power, race, class, and gender than their intelligent counterparts. Male stupidity films like *Dude, Where's My Car?*, *Me, Myself and Irene* (2000, directed by Bobby and Peter Farrelly), *Bill and Ted's Excellent Adventure* (1989, directed by Stephen Herek), *Austin Powers* (1997, directed by Jay Roach), *Dumb and Dumber* (1994, directed by Peter Farrelly), *Dumb and Dumberer* (2003, directed by Troy Miller), *Zoolander* (2001, directed by Ben Stiller), and anything with Jim Carey or Adam Sandler, particularly Jim Carey, precisely because they are not trying to rescue male stupidity, manage to provide a pretty accurate map of the social webs that tie male unknowing to new forms of power. By mapping stupidity in this way we render it useful, provocative, and suggestive of precisely those temporally dissonant forms of knowing that Dory in *Finding Nemo* points to in her ephemeral loops of learning. In the close (too close?) reading of *Dude, Where's My Car?* that follows, I try to grapple with stupidity on its own terms in order to open up other routes to transformative knowing; here I am not diagnosing male stupidity in the way I have so far, but exposing the logic of stupidity as a map of male power.

I have chosen *Dude, Where's My Car?* as a counterexample to the more artsy "male stupidity" films like *Talk to Her* and *Sideways* precisely because *Dude* takes itself less seriously and yet, through its complex time-loop narrative structure, actually reveals the architectures of white male stupidity and the kinds of social relations that it both blocks and makes possible. I start with a plot summary, since saying what happens in *Dude* is actually a lot harder than it may seem; in fact "what happens" and "what does not happen" are a big part of the theory of stupidity and forgetting that the film advances. The plot summary, usually a rejected methodology in literary studies, reveals the stakes in repeating, looping, summarizing, forgetting, and knowing again. I attempt to inhabit the genre of *Dude*, the lexicon of *Dude*, the inspirational idiom of *Dude* in order to *not* know what it does *not* know, in order to forget what it forgets, in order to lose myself in its avenues of charming ignorance and spectacular silliness.

Interlude: Seriously, Dude, Where Is My Car?

In a key moment in the "witless white males" classic, *Dude, Where's My Car?* Jesse and Chester, having been threatened by a male-to-female transsexual and her drag king boyfriend, chased by a troupe of large-breasted hot female aliens, and kidnapped by a religious cult wearing bubble suits, stand before a pair of space travelers and request information about the universe. What do you want to know? ask the space aliens disguised as Swedish gay men. Jesse and Chester smirk and say, "Have you been to Uranus?" We have not heard such a preponderance of anus jokes since *Wayne's World* (1992, directed by Penelope Spheeris), but in a comedy where the bumbling male buddies share many a nude moment, and even a little open-mouth kissing, the Uranus jokes register a new casualness about the permeability of the homosocial-homoerotic divide. They also locate the stupid white male buddies at the very center of an "anything goes" (as long as everything stays the same) kind of world in which race, place, space, and gender are all scrambled and reorganized through a series of complex (?) time loops. Before the space aliens disguised as Swedish gay men leave planet Hollywood for a quick tour around Uranus, they force Jesse and Chester to forget everything that has happened and return to the state of oblivion from whence they came. Jesse and Chester return home only to awake the next morning, still amnesiac, still as befuddled as the day before, still confused about why their fridge is packed with chocolate pudding. The exchange that began this picaresque journey across the landscape of mini malls and miniature golf courses—"Dude, where's my car?" "Where's your car, dude?" "Dude, where's my car?"— begins again, and the lessons the pair learned the night before are lost and remain to be relearned. This Nietzschean act or nonact of forgetting on which the loopy narrative depends arrests the developmental and progress narratives of heteronormativity and strands our feckless heroes in the no-man's land of lost knowledge and scatological humor. While the deliberate forgetting of the George W. kind can and does threaten the very survival of the universe, the benign forgetting of the dude variety seems to allow for a free space of reinvention, a new narrative of self and other, and, for Jesse and Chester, the chance to revisit the hot chicks from the night before as if meeting them for the very first time.

What can a film about two idiot stoners who lose their car and then have to reconstruct the events of the night before in order to find the car, pay back money they owe, and win back the love of the twins they are dating while saving the universe from certain destruction and in the process kicking the ass of moronic jocks, pissing off Fabio, escaping from a fifty-foot hot space alien woman, and receiving as presents from the space aliens some necklaces that make their girlfriends develop huge "hoo-hoos," and receiving in return not sex but only some dumb berets with their names embroidered on them tell us about the relationships between forgetting, stupidity, masculinity, and temporality? More precisely, is this going to be a ridiculous attempt to queer a fourth-rate adolescent comedy with a few laugh lines, lots of butt jokes, a weak heterosexual resolution, and no political consciousness whatsoever? The answer to the first question will engage us for the rest of this chapter; the answer to the second question is *perhaps*.

My quick summary of *Dude* does not immediately suggest that the film offers much in the way of redemptive narratives for a lost generation. And yet if we must live with the logic of white male stupidity, and it seems we must, then understanding its form, its seductions, and its power are mandatory. *Dude* offers a surprisingly complete allegorical map of what Raymond Williams calls "lived hegemony." Williams, commenting on the tendency of definitions of hegemony to reduce it to a singular mode of class domination, suggests, "A lived hegemony is always a process. . . . It is a realized complex of experiences, relationships and activities" (1977: 112). In order to grasp the flux of hegemony, its constellation of "pressures and limits," the seemingly banal pop cultural text, with its direct connection to mass culturally shared assumptions, is far more likely to reveal the key terms and conditions of the dominant than an earnest and "knowing" text. (Here we might juxtapose *Dude* with films like Neil LaBute's *In the Company of Men* in addition to the serious films by Almodovar and others mentioned earlier.) As Peggy Phelan writes, "Representation follows two laws: it always conveys more than it intends and it is never totalizing" (Phelan, 1993: 2). To which Jesse and Chester might add, "Shibby."

The time loop that structures *Dude* appears, on the surface, to be quite simple, but in fact in its eternally spiraling form it provides a fairly complicated understanding of self as a repeated combination of performance, drag, otherness, and memory. The film's ending suggests that Jesse and Chester begin every new day with no memory of what happened the night before and each day their retracing becomes a new performance of forgetting and a new (and failed) attempt to advance, progress, and accumulate knowledge. In these temporal loops that bring the antiheroic but happy losers back to the same spot at the end of every day, white masculinity is engaged in both a world-saving mission courtesy of the Swedish gay aliens from Uranus and a de-creation of their own world courtesy of a pot-smoking guru and his small dog. The seeming irrelevance of the time loops masks a highly charged narrative in which cause and effect constantly switch places until causality ceases to produce the logic for narrative movement. If the moronic Jesse and Chester do save the world, it is not as a consequence of their heroic actions; in fact their bumbling ineptitude first places the world in jeopardy and then saves it. If you save the world and no one remembers, can you really be a hero?

In his beautiful book *Cities of the Dead* Joseph Roach calls forgetting "an opportunistic tactic of whiteness" and quotes a Yoruba proverb: "The white man who made the pencil also made the eraser" (1996: 6). *Dude* is an extended meditation on the precise terms of the relationship between whiteness, labor, and amnesia. Significantly, as a new day begins at the film's conclusion, pieces of the day before erupt into the interactions between the two amnesiac dudes, but in new forms. A racist joke about a Chinese drive-through where the disembodied voice at the entrance says "And then . . . and then . . . and then" after each new order of "Chinese" food now becomes the rhetorical form of Jesse's and Chester's opening/closing dialogue. Again they try to reconstruct the night before and again they fail; as Jesse retrieves bits and pieces from his memory vault, Chester mimics the Chinese food lady saying "And then . . . and then . . . and then." While this could be read as the incorporation of the other, and while it is certainly evidence of the "opportunistic tactic of whiteness," we realize at the film's end that the Chinese takeout lady's "And then . . . and then . . . and then" is the defining principle for the narrative form of *Dude*, a long shaggy dog tale with a supplemental, or simply mental, rather than developmental logic. Whiteness is thus the pencil and the eraser, and racialized labor is the story it both tells and rubs out.

Indeed otherness in this film is distributed evenly across a range of white queers and working-class people of color: the black pizza shop owner who berates the dudes for their shoddy work ethic, the Chinese takeout lady, the Asian American tailor who sews the boys some Adidas suits, the racially ambiguous group of jocks, the transsexual stripper, the gay Swedes, the gay former male model. Certainly the idle pleasures of life as a dude are afforded by the hard labor of the people who employ them, clothe them, feed them, and sexually service them, and yet it turns out that in the land of bland blondes and dumb jocks otherness is not such a bad place to be. The fact that Chester ventriloquizes the Chinese food lady the next day and yet forgets that his speech is citational means that she speaks through him; he is the effect of her narrative logic. Chester and Jesse may forget their own meanderings through the racialized spaces of southern California, but in their belated reconstruction the narratives they have suppressed and forgotten cycle back through the stories they tell; the dudes are undone and unraveled by their amnesia, doomed to replay the shuffled sequences over and over again, becoming more and more unknowing, and in their unknowing they are potentially more open to the knowledge that comes from elsewhere.

In her brilliant extended meditation on stupidity Avital Ronell writes, "Stupidity exceeds and undercuts materiality, runs loose, wins a few rounds, recedes, gets carried home in the clutch of denial—and returns. Essentially linked to the inexhaustible, stupidity is also that which fatigues knowledge and wears down history" (2002: 3). Refusing to simply oppose stupidity or map its destructive path, Ronell takes stupidity seriously as a form of unknowing, which nonetheless does not "stand in the way of wisdom" (5), and turns it into a productive category. Stupidity, she says, is "a political problem hailing from the father" (2002: 16); it combines with conservative desires for stability, comfort, and authenticity, but it also opens up other spaces of knowing. In films like *Dude, Where's My Car?* white guys perform modes of unknowing that sometimes reflect and reinforce the dominant but at other times actually make possible new forms of relation between the white guys, between the white guys and the white girls they love, and between the white guys and girls and "everybody else." That this cluster of "everybody else" remains horribly amorphous and imprecise suggests that we do not leave the realm of white male dominance for long, and yet the small openings provided by white male ignorance must be exploited.

Dude, I think (I hope?), presents viewers with an allegorical frame for understanding present-day geopolitical events, since it casts an improbable duo of dumb dudes as at once the earth's ruin and its salvation: Jesse's and Chester's alien-imposed amnesia prevents them from understanding why they are under attack in the first place ("Dude, why do they hate us?") and permits them to forget and ignore the fact that their "freedom" comes at the expense of other people's unfreedom, but it also allows them to immerse themselves in perversion and fantasy without either disgust or judgment. Their tolerance is revealed to be part and parcel of their stupidity, and their stupidity is represented as a likeable absence of critical judgment which relieves them of being either politically sensitive (aware of their own biases) or politically biased (homophobic). The amnesiac circularity within which the dudes coexist casts them as bound to forget what others around them remember all too well.

Stupidity in Dude is a kind of relaxed relation to knowing which paradoxically makes Jesse and Chester manipulable and permeable, receptive to the narratives of others, precisely because their own stories are so uncertain and irretrievable. Another scene of racialized labor, in which an Asian American tailor provides the way out of one of the film's most enduring and infuriating loops, illustrates how representations of white male stupidity can potentially unlock other modes of knowing. When changing into the Adidas suits that Jesse and Chester no longer remember purchasing from the night before, each discovers that the other has a tattoo on his upper back. Chester's tattoo says "Sweet," and Jesse's "Dude." Jesse says, "Dude you have a tattoo." Chester responds, "You do too." Jesse says, "What does mine say?" Chester responds, "'Dude.' What does mine say?" Jesse says, "'Sweet.' What does mine say?" Chester responds, "'Dude.' What does mine say?" Jesse says, "'Sweet.' What does mine say?" Each dude becomes more and more infuriated at the speech loop as they turn their backs to each other, repeating "What does mine say?" When they come to blows, the tailor finally intervenes, yelling, "Idiots! His says 'Sweet' and yours says 'Dude.'" The tailor sees the whole picture, while each dude can see only his buddy's back. Suture, we could say, is in the position of the tailor; he sews meaning into the narrative and stands in for the patriarchal voice of reason and sense that the film seems to resist and that the stupid white male is unable to supply. For a moment everything makes sense; the dudes embrace, and the Asian American tailor smiles knowingly at the dudes, who for once are marked by their gender, their whiteness, their stupidity. But as quickly as knowledge comes, it disappears, like the car (Dude, where's my car?), like a Freudian lost object (Dude, where's my mother's breast?), like the thread of this argument (Dude, what's my point?).

And then? And then, as quickly as this scene of racial reversal arrives, it seems to dissolve back into a white male gaze. Just as the gaze transfers to the tailor, Mr. Lee, Jesse finds a kaleidoscope in his Adidas suit's secret pocket and turns the gaze back onto the tailor. The kaleidoscope becomes the metaphor for the twists and turns of performance, which alter meaning with each repetition by refracting an image. But it also becomes a very literal representation of the cinematic apparatus, marshaled now for the white male gaze. Just as the scene has revealed what Jesse and Chester cannot see (their own backs, their own marks of gender and race), it quickly reasserts the magic of the white male gaze by aligning it with the kaleidoscope. The kaleidoscope has no other function in the film; it simply serves as a supplement to Jesse's impaired vision and as a way out of the untenable arrangement of power and vision that places the white male in the line of sight and the Asian American male in the place of vision, power, and knowledge.

In the case of the Chinese food lady, as I mentioned, her narrative framework of "And then . . . and then . . . and then" both mimics the supplemental logic of most inquiries into otherness (race . . . and then? . . . . class . . . and then? . . . sexuality . . . and then?) and also calls attention to the physical labor that the drive-through food order effaces. In this scene the representation of the Asian American tailor both mimics the Orientalizing representation of the Asian other as omniscient and exceeds its own racist framework by naming the white males ("Idiots!") and by showing that the white male gaze can be centered only with blatantly artificial and magical "special effects." When the Chinese food lady forces Jesse to repeat his order over and over, she makes him feel the labor hidden by his request. When Mr. Lee intervenes in the dudes' dance of stupidity, he makes them see that he sees their unknowing. On both occasions Jesse tries to bash back against the other's gaze. When he becomes frustrated with the never satiated voice asking "And then?" Jesse smashes the box; when he feels fixed by the gaze of Mr. Lee, he looks back at him with the kaleidoscope, multiplying and splitting the image of Mr. Lee's laughing visage. In his analysis of the performances of whiteness by the black drag queen Vaginal Crème Davis, José Esteban Muñoz remarks on the way "a figure that is potentially threatening to people of color is revealed as a joke" (1999: 109). Dude tells the story of white male stupidity in a way that solicits laughter at the dudes, and as we laugh we disarm the dude and we know, finally, that he is clueless.

When watching the transsexual stripper smooch her transsexual boyfriend, Chester asks Jesse, "Are we supposed to be grossed out or turned on by this?" This scene alone raises the questions Is Dude a queer narrative, and why should we care? In the DVD version the two main actors, Ashton Kutcher and Seann William Scott, and the director, Danny Leiner, all comment on how "gay" the movie is. At one point in the DVD chat Kutcher and Scott say to one another, "Dude, we were so gay in this film, so gay!" While it is comforting to know that the dudes understand that they were participating in a queer universe, the DVD makes clear that this was a temporary state of affairs and that both dudes are now safely secured for and by the heterosexual matrix. So while the film's queerness cannot be located at the level of identity, we can argue for queerness as a set of spatialized relations that are permitted through the white male's stupidity, his disorientation in time and space.[1] This is not news, of course, for, as Eve Kosofsky Sedgwick pointed out in the Epistemology of the Closet, "in relations around the closet . . . ignorance is as potent and as multiple a thing there as is knowledge" (1990: 4).

In his attempt to describe and theorize the kind of memories that adhere to place and survive "the transformation or the relocation of the spaces in which they first flourished," Joseph Roach uses the terms "kinesthetic imagination" and "vortices of behavior." Places remember, he claims, and these memories are "canalized" through certain performances in order to create connections between times and spaces: "The behavioral vortex of the cityscape, the 'ludic space' in Roland Barthes's propitious term, constitutes the collective, social version of the psychological paradox that masquerade is the most powerful form of self-expression" (1996: 28). The dudes' ritualized retracing of the inane actions from the night before, which they are perpetually doomed to forget and bound to remember, allows place-bound memories to inscribe themselves upon and through the bodies of those amnesiac selves who wander through in search of truth. In the ludic space between remembering and forgetting a certain queer affect is created which disrupts, momentarily, the fortification of the white hetero male body and opens it up to other forms of desire.

Transsexualism often makes an appearance in stupid white male films. In *The Hot Chick* (2002, directed by Tom Brady), for example, transsexualism is the framework for the entire film. (Don't ask.) Often it is the inability of the dude to distinguish between an MTF transsexual and a hot female-born chick that constitutes the litmus test for his stupidity. *Dude* goes this trope one better by letting Jesse know that he has had a lap dance from a tranny but by also forgoing the requisite horror and disgust that such knowledge is supposed to inspire. Jesse is simply too stupid to know what is off-limits to a white hetero dude like himself. But while each dude lacks self-knowledge and fails to internalize social biases appropriate to his subject position, each finds himself reflected in and completed by the other. Doubling repeatedly functions in *Dude* to stave off disruptions to the fortress of white manhood. Facing castration and humiliation at the hands of various policemen and policewomen, and later from the beaks of some mean ostriches, Jesse and Chester face menacing obstacles as a team, a unit, a collective, and each functions as the other's phallus, or weenie. Their doubleness is mirrored all around them in the twins they date, the gay Swedish aliens who advise them, the tranny couple who chase them, and the hetero couple who goad them into a homosexual act. The doubleness of white male stupidity here and in all the dimbo films shows white male subjectivity as powerfully singular, even when it is represented as double, precisely because it is mirrored in the ordinary relations between men; patriarchal power, in some sense, takes two: one to be the man and the other to reflect his being the man. But the doubling also draws the dudes down into the swirl and eddy of homoerotic attraction which heterosexual patriarchy inevitably leaves in its wake. In this film white patriarchy comes in the rather questionable form of Fabio!

When Jesse and Chester pull up in their new car alongside the coiffed and buffed Fabio and his girl, they enact a queer mirror scene that could have been scripted by Jacques Lacan and edited by Judith Butler. I will let the gay alternative filmmaker and reviewer Bruce LaBruce describe what happens in the infamous kiss scene. In a Toronto weekly paper, *The Eye*, LaBruce added *Dude* to his top-ten movie list and described the scene in question by way of explanation for the ranking he gave the film:

Fabio looks over contemptuously and revs his engine; Kutcher, behind the wheel, does the same. Fabio responds by putting his arm around his vixen; Kutcher rises to the challenge by placing his arm emphatically around Scott. Fabio then leans over and gives his girl a long, deep tongue kiss. The movie could have gone in infinite directions at this point, but amazingly Kutcher leans over and, gently yet convincingly, delivers the lingering tongue to Scott. The actors neither overplay nor underplay the moment and show no visible trace of disgust or regret afterward. I was almost in tears. This one scene does more to advance the cause of homosexuality than 25 years of gay activism.[2]

How does this scene "advance the cause of homosexuality"? Doesn't it represent homosexuality as an inauthentic representation of heterosexuality? Doesn't it reveal the resilience and mastery of white male heterosexuality that can prevail over even overtly gay encounters? Or does it show competitive male heterosexuality to be the result of homoerotic mimicry? Who leads, who follows, who sucks, who blows, who catches, who pitches, who watches, who learns, who cares? LaBruce's exuberant response to the kiss is a way of resisting the earnestness of so many gay and lesbian texts. Armed with the ammunition of a startlingly queer and sexy encounter between two resolutely straight dudes, LaBruce can rejoice, cry almost, at the dudes' nonchalance, their heady indifference to the sexual codes of dudedom, their gormless plunge into manly gay sex, their knowing mimicry of not Fabio's performed hetero make-out session but of the barely submerged homosexuality of, to quote Zoolander, "really, really, really good-looking male models."

The opening scene of Dude shows Chester watching a show about apes on the Discovery channel and absentmindedly copying the moves of the chimp on the screen. In Primate Visions Donna Haraway suggests that the human study of apes allows for the human to center himself in the story of evolution by projecting human behavior onto the ape and then learning it back from the ape culture we imagine and create. Chester and Jesse are not part of any such complex order of cultural transmission; like the mechanics of dominant culture itself, they absorb whatever they see and make it part of themselves. But the beauty of Dude is that it acknowledges the borrowed and imitative forms of white male subjectivity and traces for us the temporal order of dominant culture that forgets what it has borrowed and never pays back. Dude also acknowledges the banality that history repeats itself but that we fail to learn from the repetition. We survived the era of Bush Senior only to be hit by the era of Bush Junior; we lived through the Gulf War only to witness its deadly replay in Iraq. The amnesiac cycle that solidifies U.S. hegemony, spreads the era of empire, and authorizes the return of the stupid white male is written in *Dude* as the triumph of the few, the brave, the "relentlessly moronic."

Dude, Where's My Car? does manage to rise above its generic limitations (ridiculous premise, stupid white dude protagonists, rampant racism, sexism, and homophobia) and is able to exploit the potential of its mise-en-scène (lots of transgender characters and quite a few hot chicks with big "hoo-hoos," to use the film's own vernacular). In so doing it offers a potent allegory of memory, forgetting, remembering, and forgetting again. We can use this allegory to describe and invent this moment in the university, poised as it is and as we are between offering a distinct "negative" strand of critical consciousness to a public that would rather not know and using more common idioms to engage those who don't know why they should care. I actually intended for this brief summary of *Dude, Where's My Car?* to expand upon the topic of white male stupidity today, to link it to the worsening crisis in knowledge production, to develop a thesis on the relations between stupidity and forgetting. But then I watched the film again and I realized that only a very special kind of unknowing can confront the dangers of white hetero manhood (Dude, where are Saddam Hussein's weapons of mass destruction?) and all of its specialized knowledges, expertise, security plans, high alerts, and hawkish propaganda. There really are lessons to be learned from *Dude* about the place of stupid white males in the new racial landscape of southern California, about gender flexibility and the white male hetero body, about sexual openness and the buddy movie, about the shadow of sodomy and the politics of capital. But I will save those for another time. For now, dude, seriously: forgetting, unknowing, losing, lacking, bumbling, stumbling, these all seem like hopeful developments in the location of the white male. As we watched Bush the Sequel play out its sad, scary, and humorless scenarios, its Wild West fantasies and Top Gun realities, we all hoped for, nay began to beg for a little humor, a little irony, a little ray of self-consciousness to illuminate the path from dumb to dumber. I am not saying that *Dude, Where's My Car?* is a fitting alternative to grim militaristic scenarios of crusading North Americans, but I am wishing that we could all be a little less self-important and a little more stupid. If only we were all like Jesse and Chester, who, in the process of searching for a ray of hope in a landscape of eternal sunshine and cheerleaders, were able to grab the space aliens' "continuum transfunctioner," make friends with a fabulous MTF and her FTM boyfriend, kick some jock ass, get a look up the skirt of the fifty-foot hot alien space invader, end up with a fridge full of chocolate pudding, and save the universe from total destruction, perhaps stupidity might seem like a reasonable path out of the wilderness of theocratic, corporate madness.

Forgetting

I suffer from short-term memory loss. It runs in my family . . .
or at least I think it does. . . . Where are they?
—Dory in *Finding Nemo* (2003)

Jesse and Chester forgot where they parked their car, did not remember saving the world from mass destruction, and found themselves alone again with a fridge full of chocolate pudding. Forgetting apparently has its benefits. It also has world-saving potential, or maybe the point of *Dude* is more that forgetfulness stalls the enactment of a heroic aftermath to salvation because the heroes have forgotten their own messianic mission and have returned to life in Dudesville. But if we learned anything from Jesse and Chester, and I sincerely hope we did not, we learned not to look for grand gestures, we learned that ignorance is bliss, and we learned that resistance lurks in the performance of forgetfulness itself, hiding out in oblivion and waiting for a new erasure to inspire a new beginning. Not all dimbo films loop endlessly in the holding pattern *Dude* creates; sadly, all too many dumb and dumberer comedies teach their stupid white heroes to be better men and to be worthy of their morally superior women. So while we revel in the unknowing practices produced by *Dude* we might also inquire after the function of forgetting when it occurs in a dudette. Does forgetfulness in women produce the same desirable effect of stalling the heroic narrative; steering clear of love, marriage, and romance; and creating each day anew as a blank slate upon which to write a new narrative of forgetting? The answer is, predictably, yes and no. In *Dude, Where's My Car?* forgetfulness and stupidity combine to produce an alternative mode of knowing, one that resists the positivism of memory projects and refuses a straight and Oedipal logic for understanding the transmission of ideas. The dudes are infantile (peeing and shitting everywhere, needing to be fed and cared for) but parentless, and in the absence of wisdom passed down from father or mother (but probably father) to son they are enlightened by peer relations that predictably preclude advancement, progress, and learning. The dudes learn through imitation, often of a TV image (as when Chester mimics the ape from the nature show he is watching and learns to use a stick as a tool), and they accumulate information without ever putting that information together in a coherent or temporally logical sequence. This lack of sequence that stalls knowledge and makes discovery into a function of chance and random timing also disrupts many other temporal logics, primarily generational ones, in the film, stranding the dudes in the no-man's land of adolescence.

For women and queer people, forgetfulness can be a useful tool for jamming the smooth operations of the normal and the ordinary. These operations, generally speaking, take on an air of inevitability and naturalness simply by virtue of being passed on from one generation to another. Women are most often the repositories for generational logics of being and becoming, and then become the transmitters of that logic to the next generation. Aided by a few more plot summaries and some animated films, we will see how forgetfulness becomes a rupture with the eternally self-generating present, a break with a self-authorizing past, and an opportunity for a non-hetero-reproductive future. But why should women and queer people learn to forget? Generational logic underpins our investments in the dialectic of memory and forgetting;[3] we tend to organize the chaotic process of historical change by anchoring it to an idea of generational shifts (from father to son), and we obscure questions about the arbitrariness of memory and the necessity of forgetting by falling back on some notion of the inevitable force of progression and succession. De-linking the process of generation from the force of historical process is a queer kind of project: queer lives seek to uncouple change from the supposedly organic and immutable forms of family and inheritance; queer lives exploit some potential for a *difference in form* that lies dormant in queer collectivity not as an essential attribute of sexual otherness but as a possibility embedded in the break from heterosexual life narratives. We may want to forget family and forget lineage and forget tradition in order to start from a new place, not the place where the old engenders the new, where the old makes a place for the new, but where the new begins afresh, unfettered by memory, tradition, and usable pasts.

To say that we might want to think about memory and forgetting differently is in fact to ask that we start seeing alternatives to the inevitable and seemingly organic models we use for marking progress and achievement; it also asks us to notice how and whether change has happened: How do we see change? How do we recognize it? Can we be aware of change without saying that change has ended everything (the death of . . .) or that change has meant nothing (plus ça change . . .)? Can we recognize the new without discarding the old? Can we hold on to multiple frameworks of time and transformation at once? I think the answer to these latter questions is yes, and yet there is plenty of evidence in queer culture that we simply allow the rhythms of Oedipal modes of development to regulate the disorderliness of queer culture. The deployment of the concept of *family*, whether in hetero or homo contexts, almost always introduces normative understandings of time and transmission. Family as a concept is deployed in contemporary popular culture as well as in academic cultures to gloss a deeply reactionary understanding of human interaction; it may be the case that we must *forget* family in our theorizations of gender, sexuality, community, and politics and adopt forgetting as a strategy for the disruption of the regularity of Oedipal transmission.

As a kind of false narrative of continuity, as a construction that makes connection and succession seem organic and natural, family also gets in the way of all sorts of other alliances and coalitions. An ideology of family pushes gays and lesbians toward marriage politics and erases other modes of kinship in the process. In an article in *The Nation* Lisa Duggan and Richard Kim argue that contemporary marriage politics manages to unite conservatives by consolidating support for the nuclear and conjugal family through marital support programs and a revival of covenant marriage while dividing progressive groups by creating anxiety and conflict about the status of same-sex marriage rights. According to Duggan and Kim, the pro-marriage and pro-family campaigns have had to counter rocketing divorce rates and the reality of diverse household forms in the U.S., and they have done so by anchoring the conventional family to financial security in the absence of a welfare state:

> The net effect of the neo-liberal economic policies imposed in recent decades has been to push economic and social responsibility away from employers and government and onto private households. The stress on households is intensifying, as people try to do more with less. Care for children and the elderly, for the ill and disabled, has been shifted toward unpaid women at home or to low-paid, privately employed female domestic workers. In this context, household stability becomes a life-and-death issue. On whom do we depend when we can't take care of ourselves? If Social Security shrinks or disappears and your company sheds your pen-

sion fund, what happens to you when you can no longer work? In more and more cases, the sole remaining resource is the cooperative, mutually supporting household or kinship network.[4]

The family takes on new significance in this scenario as it becomes a sole source of support in the shift away from public and toward private networks of economic relief. In this context, Duggan and Kim propose, gay and lesbian activists should not be pushing for marriage but arguing along with other progressives for the recognition of household diversity.

Alternative kinship has long been a cause célèbre among gay and lesbian groups and queer scholars, and while anthropologists such as Kath Weston, Gayle Rubin, and Esther Newton have applauded the effort and creativity that go into making new kinship bonds in queer communities, other scholars, mostly psychoanalytic theorists such as Judith Butler and David Eng, have examined the family as a disciplinary matrix and have linked its particular forms of social control to colonialism and globalization.[5] Why, many of these scholars have asked, does the nuclear family continue to dominate kinship relations when in reality people are enmeshed in multiple and complex systems of relation? In her work Kath Weston examines how kinship discourses invest in normative temporalities which privilege longevity over temporariness and permanence over contingency. These normative conceptions of time and relation give permanent (even if estranged) connections precedence over random (even if intense) associations. So an authenticating notion of longevity renders all other relations meaningless and superficial, and family ties, by virtue of being early bonds, seem more important than friendships. In the realm of kinship, terms like *casual* signify time as well as mood, and terms like *enduring* signify relevance as an effect of temporality.

Queer interventions into kinship studies have taken many forms: some call for new models of family (Butler's Antigone as a substitute for Oedipus, Weston's chosen families as a substitute for blood bonds); others call for the recognition of friendship ties as kinship; and still others ask that we recognize the difference that gay and lesbian parents make to the very meaning of family. But few scholars call for a de-emphasis on family or a rejection of the family as *the* form of social organization par excellence. In what follows I examine what happens in popular narrative when characters like Dory do forget their families and in the process access other modes of relating, belonging, and caring.

What family promises and what marriage-chasing gays and lesbians desire is not simply acceptance and belonging but a form of belonging that binds the past to the present and the present to the future by securing what Lee Edelman has called "heterofuturity" through the figure of the child. As Edelman argues in *No Future* and as Kathryn Bond Stockton demonstrates in her book on the queer child, *Growing Sideways*, the child is always already queer and must therefore quickly be converted to a proto-heterosexual by being pushed through a series of maturational models of growth that project the child as the future and the future as heterosexual. Queer culture, with its emphasis on repetition (Butler), horizontality (Muñoz, Stockton), immaturity and a refusal of adulthood (me), where adulthood rhymes with heterosexual parenting, resists a developmental model of substitution and instead invests in what Stockton calls "sideways" relations, relations that grow along parallel lines rather than upward and onward. This queer form of antidevelopment requires healthy doses of forgetting and disavowal and proceeds by way of a series of substitutions. Of course all of culture, as Joseph Roach argues, emerges from the kinetic and even frantic process of what he calls "surrogation": forms constantly supplant each other while holding on to a vestige of the performance they replace in the form of a gesture here, a use of language there. Roach's work in *Cities of the Dead* teaches us to find the evidence of long-gone subterranean cultures by reading the traces they leave behind within canonical cultural forms—the other is always buried in the dominant. Queer culture enacts rupture as substitution as the queer child steps out of the assembly line of heterosexual production and turns toward a new project. This new project holds on to vestiges of the old but distorts the old beyond recognition; for example, a relation to the father dedicated to social stability in straight culture becomes a daddy-boy relationship in queer contexts dedicated to the sexualization of generational difference.

Eve Kosofsky Sedgwick proposes one way queer cultures have managed to sidestep the stifling reproductive logics of Oedipal temporality. In an essay on the perils of paranoid knowledge production she calls attention to the temporal frame within which paranoid reasoning takes place, arguing that paranoia is anticipatory, that it is a reading practice "closely tied to a notion of the inevitable." Sedgwick tells us that paranoid readings and relations are "characterized by a distinctly Oedipal regularity and repetitiveness: it happened to my father's father, it happened to my father, it is happening to me, and it will happen to my son, and it will happen to my son's son" (2003: 147). By contrast, Sedgwick claims, queer life unfolds differently: "But isn't it a feature of queer possibility . . . that our generational relations don't always proceed in this lockstep?" (2003: 26). Obviously heterosexual relations are not essentially bound to "regularity and repetitiveness," yet the bourgeois family matrix, with its emphasis on lineage, inheritance, and generation, does tend to cast temporal flux in terms of either seamless continuity or total rupture.

The stability of heteronormative models of time and transformation impacts many different models of social change; as J. K. Gibson-Graham point out in her feminist critique of political economy, if we represent capitalism, heteropatriarchy, and racist economies as totalizing and inevitable, as seamless and impermeable, then we have "little possibility of escape" from those systems and few ways of accessing a "non-capitalist imaginary" (1996: 21). And as Roderick Ferguson argues in his book *Aberrations in Black* (2005), the normative temporal and spatial frames of historical materialism have ironically forced a congruence between Marxist and bourgeois definitions of *civilization*, both of which cast racialized nonnormative sexualities as anterior and as signs of disorder and social chaos within an otherwise stable social system. The contingency of queer relations, their uncertainty, irregularity, and even perversity, disregards the so-called natural bonds between memory and futurity, and in the process make an implicit argument for forgetfulness, albeit one that is rarely reflected in mainstream texts about memory and forgetting.

Forgetfulness is not always queer, of course; indeed in the early twenty-first century it has become a major trope of mainstream cinema. But while most forms of forgetting in mainstream cinema operate according to a simple mapping of memory onto identity and memory loss onto the loss of history, location, and even politics, a few films, often unintentionally, set forgetting in motion in such a way as to undermine dominant modes of historicizing. While a glut of films in the early twenty-first century, such as *Memento* (2000, directed by Christopher Nolan), *The Eternal Sunshine of the Spotless Mind* (2004, directed by Michel Gondry), the remake of *The Manchurian Candidate* (2004, directed by Jonathan Demme), and *Code 46* (2003, directed by Michael Winterbottom), all equate memory manipulation with brainwashing, loss of humanity, and state intrusions on privacy, some comedic films in the same period tackle the same topic with different and wildly unpredictable results. It is these films that open up to queer readings of memory loss. *Finding Nemo* (2003) and *50 First Dates* (2004, directed by Peter Segal) are the examples I have chosen because both deploy forgetting to represent a disordering of social bonds, both deploy transgender motifs to represent a kind of queer disruption in the logic of the normal, and both understand queer time as somehow operating against the logics of succession, progress, development, and tradition proper to hetero-familial development. These films revolve around characters who forget their families, with radically different results.

While *Finding Nemo* has been generally received as a groundbreaking and innovative film for adults and children, it is easy and tempting to dismiss *50 First Dates* out of hand as just another moronic Adam Sandler vehicle (especially given its racist depictions of native Hawaiians, its colonial depiction of Island culture, and its transphobic use of queer characters). However, precisely because the film stages its drama of memory loss against the backdrop of Hawaii and its narrative of heteronormativity against the seeming perversity of transgenderism, the trope of forgetting in this film becomes interesting and potentially disruptive of the dominant narrative. Let's begin with a little more plot summary: *50 First Dates* features Drew Barrymore as Lucy, a woman afflicted by short-term memory loss due to an injury to her temporal lobe. Adam Sandler is Henry Roth, a zoo veterinarian by day who romances tourists by night. Hawaii operates as the setting for Roth's promiscuity, as the island seems to offer an endless supply of single women looking for a few nights of fun. Hawaii is thus cast as the place of pleasure without responsibility, a paradise of course, but one that must be left behind during the white male's quest for responsible adulthood. Henry's dating exploits are watched with voyeuristic glee by his native Hawaiian friend Ula (played by Rod Schneider in brownface), who has kids and a wife; far from representing an alternative Hawaii or an alternative model of kinship, Ula is cast as a buffoon whom marriage has reduced to a kind of infantile state. Other native Hawaiians serve as friendly onlookers to the scene of white romance, but all are subtly hostile and contemptuous of the unfolding spectacle of romance in a vacuum. For example, one immigrant Chinese man is cast as a crazy guy in a local restaurant, but he watches Henry's and Lucy's romance and makes wry and pointedly critical comments about Henry ("stupid idiot" being the most frequent). Hawaii is also analogized to a zoo, a controlled environment where the spectacle of wildness is showcased, and, since Henry is a zoo veterinarian, a menagerie of animals play minor roles in the romantic comedy of a man who fails to leave a lasting impression on his first date and must begin again the next day.

Like the looping amnesia that powered *Dude, Where's My Car?* and made it impossible for anyone to learn anything or to move on or to understand basic causal relations, 50 First Dates depends on a drama within which heterosexual romance cannot proceed as usual because the heroine has no recollection of her suitor from one date to the next. While this is a potentially disabling narrative that might put a dent in the most iron-clad masculinity, the manifest narrative strand in the film pushes to one side the implications of a truly forgettable hero and instead focuses on the comic situation of a guy who must treat every date as a first date and therefore must continue to make a good first impression. Lucy's memory loop forces her to relive the same day, the day of her accident, over and over again; her father and brother (the mother, representing normative time, is dead both in this film and in Finding Nemo) try to re-create the ordinariness of that day every day by removing from view all temporal markers that would reveal the real date to Lucy. Stuck in her cocoon with her father and brother and looping mindlessly from one day to the next, Lucy has a certain charm and ingenuousness, and her fresh start gives her the appearance of innocence and purity. It also engages Henry's desire by inspiring him to attempt to interrupt that loop by using her interest in him to start a new loop, with him at its center. This new loop would re-place the stasis of her family of birth with the supposed dynamism of a new nuclear family. It would oust the time of the father and replace it with the time of marriage and husband and children. While the new future looks remarkably similar to the old past, the heterosexual conceit of all romantic comedies is revealed here as the misguided belief that in passing from father to husband the woman starts life anew.

Unlike other recent films set in Hawaii, such as the cartoon Lilo and Stitch (2002, directed by Dean Deblois), 50 First Dates has no particular interest in the geopolitical significance of its Island setting. Lilo and Stitch at least weaves its narrative of family and kinship through complex subplots about native hostility to tourists, the influence of U.S. popular culture on colonized locations, and the paternalistic function of the state. In contrast, 50 First Dates utilizes Hawaii as a kind of blank slate, a place emptied of political turmoil and a perfect metaphor for the state of mind produced by the erasure of memory. Unwittingly the film's emphasis on short-term memory loss does raise issues about national memory and histories of colonization, and the film allows the discerning viewer to understand the status of Hawaii in relation to state-authorized forms of forgetting. Tensions between Hawaii and the mainland, between native

Hawaiians and white Americans, between the history of colonization and the narrative of statehood are all wiped away like the damaged memory of the film's romantic heroine. Yet those tensions linger on and cannot be resolved as easily as the romantic obstacles.[6]

Henry's solution to Lucy's memory loss problem is to create a video-tape for her to watch every morning, which gives her a quick account of world news (including 9/11) and then reminds her of the traumatic accident that robbed her of her memories and its aftermath, her afflicted state. At certain moments in the film Lucy tries to replace the video record with her own diary in order to "tell herself" the narrative and to steer clear of the "Stepford wives" implication of the image of the woman being programmed every morning to perform her familial duties. Yet the narrative cannot pull itself clear of the "brainwashing" motif, and so ultimately it reveals heterosexual romance to be nothing more than the violent enforcement of normative forms of sociality and sexuality: heterosexuality is literally reduced to a visual text which installs the national narrative as a basis for the personal narrative of marriage and childbearing. Within such a structure, where the heroine forgets to get married and have kids (as a Barbara Krueger cartoon would have it), forgetting surprisingly stalls the implantation of heteronormativity and creates a barrier to the conventional progress narrative of heterosexual romance. The film unconsciously analogizes U.S. imperialism to heterosexuality and casts memory as the motor of national belonging. By implication, forgetting, when directed at a dominant narrative rather than at subaltern knowledges, could become a tactic for resisting the imposition of colonial rule.

In her book about Hawaiian resistance to American colonialism Noenoe Silva studies the erasure of local histories through the imposition of English-language histories and interpretations of indigenous culture. Of the struggle between English texts about Hawaii and oral accounts she writes, "When the stories told at home do not match up with the texts at school, students are taught to doubt the oral versions" (2004: 3). Obviously forgetting has been a colonial tactic in the past and has produced a hierarchical relationship between foreign and native knowledge, but in order to remember and recognize the anticolonial struggles, other narratives do have to be forgotten and unlearned. I am suggesting that a "stupid" film like 50 First Dates unconsciously reinforces the power of forgetting and disrupts the seamless production of white settlers as native Hawaiians by demonstrating how national memory constructs those locals as natives. When Lucy forgets Henry, she forgets patriarchy, hetero-sexuality, gender hierarchies; despite itself the film allows us to think about forgetting as a tactic of anticolonial resistance.

The host of transgender characters in the film also reveals how de-pendent normative heterosexuality is on the production of nonnorma-tive subjects. From Alexa, Henry's androgynous and sexually ambiguous assistant at the zoo, to Doug, Lucy's steroid-pumping brother, and John/Jennifer, a female-to-male transsexual from Lucy's past, the transgender characters represent the dangers of life outside of the nuclear family. In order for Lucy's and Henry's bizarre and even disturbing courtship to seem authentic and chosen, these other characters must model a kind of freakish excess which is then associated with too much freedom (the single and predatory Alexa), not enough maternal guidance (Doug), and adolescent angst (Jennifer/John). The native Hawaiian characters are similarly cast as sexually depraved (Ula), fetishistically phallic (Nick), and physically repugnant (Ula's wife). Hence Henry and Lucy, despite their potentially perverse arrangement, can occupy the place of the ideal family by turning short-term memory loss less into a metaphor for the constant training that women endure in order to become mothers and wives and more into the necessary preamble to white national and familial stability. That the new family sails off at the end of the film to another utopian state, Alaska, suggests that they go in search of new blank landscapes upon which they hope to write their persistent tales of whiteness, be-nevolence, and the inevitable reproduction of the same.

The transgender body in 50 First Dates seems to represent anxiety and ambivalence about change and transformation in general. If Lucy is stuck in one temporal frame through memory loss, Henry creates another for her within domestic heterosexuality. The trans characters that surround the semisinister romantic narrative imply that change can mean loss of tradition, family, history. But can memory loss actually go beyond the mere temporary disruption of heteronormativity, and can forgetting actu-ally create distinctly queer and alternative futures? Finding Nemo suggests that it can, and the film uses many of the same tropes as 50 First Dates to do so, turning those tropes away from the construction of and narrativi-zation of family and toward the creation of a long, gerund-laden story of dying, reuniting, growing, learning, unlearning, losing, searching, for-getting, rising, uniting, singing, swimming, threatening, doing, being, finding, and becoming.

In the opening sequence of Finding Nemo a hungry shark decimates a clownfish family. The mother fish and almost all of her eggs are consumed, leaving a very anxious adult male fish, Marlin, with one slightly disabled offspring (he has a small fin on one side), Nemo. Marlin, whose voice is supplied by Albert Brooks, becomes understandably paranoid about the safety of his only son, and he nervously and even hysterically tries to guard him from all of the dangers of the deep. Inevitably Nemo grows tired of his father's ministrations and, in a fit of Oedipal rebellion, tells his father he hates him and swims off recklessly into the open sea, only to be netted by a diver and placed in an aquarium in a dentist's office. Marlin, his paranoid fears now realized, begins a mad search for his missing son and swims his way to Sydney, Australia. When he finally finds him, he and Nemo orchestrate a fish uprising against their human jailors and work out a different, non-Oedipal, nonparanoid mode of relation.

In chapter 1 I argued that new CGI animation is preoccupied with revolt, change, cooperation, and transformation. The chickens in Chicken Run aspire to fly over the fences in the farm and to break free of the fences "in their minds" in order to find a better place far from the murderous machines of the Tweedys and the soul-destroying logic of profit margins. The fish in Finding Nemo also aspire to a better world, and the seabed becomes a sanctuary from the open ocean, where fishermen patrol the waters and wage war on ocean life. Indeed the climactic scene from the seemingly tame film features not simply the recovery of the lost Nemo but a fish revolt led by the forgetful blue fish, Dory (voiced by the very queer Ellen DeGeneres). After Nemo is captured by a diver he learns about escape and revolt from an old-timer in the aquarium, Gill, who stresses the importance of banding together with other species in the fight against man. The climactic scene reunites Nemo and Marlin but also shows Dory being swept up into the fishing nets. Nemo exhorts Dory and all the other fish "Swim down!" (the advice he had received from Gill), and when they do, the nets break and the fish swim free. In the midst of this muscular scene of proletarian revolt (the other fish are represented as black and white masses!) Dory, the forgetful fish, sings the song "Keep Swimming, Keep Swimming." Earlier in the film the song signaled her blissful inattentiveness to the important business of the ocean; here it becomes a queer anthem of revolt.

There are some key features to this film that change the Toy Story archetype I identified earlier as part of the new Pixar revolution in animation. First, the father-son dynamic is dependent upon the queer "helper" fish, Dory, and can never simply resolve into a patriarchal bond. Second,

Dory is not relegated to the margins of the story but ends up "knowing" all kinds of things that go against received wisdom but that facilitate Marlin's quest to find his son. So while Dory suffers from short-term memory loss, she also reads human texts, speaks whale, charms sharks, and understands the primacy of friends over family. Third, while the film presents itself as an Oedipal narrative, the son learns how to be a leader from the jaded and wise old fish in the prison aquarium, and not from his biological father. Fourth, the film features a virtual ocean menagerie of cooperative species—birds, fish, turtles, mammals—and casts humans as careless and crude, unable to share space and resources.

Dory's forgetfulness does more than simply interrupt the Oedipal re-lationship. She actually signals a new version of selfhood, a queer version that depends upon disconnection from the family and contingent rela-tions to friends and improvised relations to community. In fact, because of her short-term memory loss she actively blocks the transformation of Marlin, Nemo, and herself into nuclearity; she is not Nemo's mother sub-stitute nor Marlin's new wife, she cannot remember her relation to either fish, and so she is forced, and happily so, to create relation anew every five minutes or so. Forgetfulness has long been associated with radical action and a revolutionary relation to the now. The situationists under-stood themselves to be "partisans of forgetting," allowing them to "for-get the past" and "live in the present." Furthermore situationists saw for-getting as the weapon of the proletariat, who have no past and for whom the choice is only and always "now or never." Dory links this radical for-getting as a break with history to a notion of queer forgetting within which the forgetful subject, among other things, forgets family and tra-dition and lineage and biological relation and lives to create relationality anew in each moment and for each context and without a teleology and on behalf of the chaotic potentiality of the random action.

Like *Chicken Run*, the Gramscian cartoon about organic chicken intel-lectuals, *Finding Nemo* weds its story of family to a tale of successful collec-tive opposition to enslavement, forced labor, and commodification. And like "stupid white guy films" such as *50 First Dates* and *Dude, Where's My Car?*, *Finding Nemo* both thematizes the limits to masculinist forms of knowing and posits forgetting as a powerful obstacle to capitalist and patriarchal modes of transmission. (Forgetfulness actually stalls the reproduction of the dominant in these films.) *Finding Nemo* also makes queer coali-tion, here represented by Dory, into a major component of the quest for freedom and the attempts to reinvent kinship, identity, and collectivity.

Dory's short-term memory loss and her odd sense of time introduce absurdity into an otherwise rather straight narrative and scramble all temporal interactions. When explaining her memory problem to Marlin, she says that she thinks she must have inherited it from her family, but then again, she cannot remember her family so she is not sure how she came to be afflicted. In her lack of family memory, her exile in the present tense, her ephemeral sense of knowledge, and her continuous sense of a lack of context, Dory offers fascinating models of queer time (short-term memory), queer knowledge practices (ephemeral insights), and antifamilial kinship. By aiding Marlin without desiring him, finding Nemo without mothering him, and going on a journey without a telos, Dory offers us a model of cooperation which is not dependent on payment or remunerative alliance. Dory literally swims alongside the broken family without becoming part of it and helps to repair familial bonds without being invested in knowing specifically what the relations between Marlin and Nemo might be. The fact that they are father and son is of no more interest to her than if they were lovers or brothers, strangers or friends.

Furthermore *Finding Nemo* covertly harbors a transgender narrative about transformation. Clownfish, we learn from the work of the transgender theoretical ecologist Joan Roughgarden, are one of many species of fish who can and often do change sex. Roughgarden's *Evolution's Rainbow* (2004) explains the role that sexual diversity might play in different forms of animal sociality and reinterprets all kinds of sexual behaviors that other researchers have interpreted as exceptional or unusual among fish, birds, and lizards as actually a crucial part of species evolution and survival. In the case of the clownfish, according to Roughgarden, the mating couple does tend to be monogamous, so much so that if the female partner should perish (as she does in *Finding Nemo*), the male fish will transsex and become female. She will then mate with one of her offspring to re-create a kinship circuit. Roughgarden explains clownfish behavior, along with all kinds of other such morphing and shifting, less as evidence of the dominance of the reproductive circuit than as an adaptive affiliative process that creates a stable community rather than familial structures. Her models of animal community deliberately break with Darwinian readings of animal behavior that have coded human values like competition, restraint, and physical superiority into interpretations of eclectic and diverse animal behaviors.

It is significant that in both *Finding Nemo* and *50 First Dates* the drama of short-term memory loss plays out against the backdrop of the missing mother and in relation to a host of transgender characters. The mother in both films represents the relation to the past, and when she dies memory dies with her. The transsexual and transgender characters in each film represent the disorder that the death of the mother introduces into the system. The conservative reading of such films might lead us to conclude that popular culture is remembering nostalgically a mythical time of continuity and stability which is associated with the mother and which has to be energetically re-created in her absence. The more hopeful reading of the genre and of the notion of generationality which it provokes might see the forgetful blue fish in Finding Nemo and the temporally challenged chick in 50 First Dates as opportunities to reject the historical or Oedipal fix and to resist the impulse to retrace a definitive past and map a prescriptive future. The example of Dory in Finding Nemo in fact encourages us to rest a while in the weird but hopeful temporal space of the lost, the ephemeral, and the forgetful.

Conclusion

Forgetting as a practice is already a necessary part of all kinds of political and cultural projects. At the end of Toni Morrison's novel Beloved (1987), for example, the ghost of Sethe's child and of all the "disremembered and unaccounted for" people lost to slavery disappears and allows Sethe and Denver to enter a space of forgetfulness, a space where the horrors of slavery do not have to haunt them at every turn, where life can fill up the spaces that previously were saturated with loss, violation, dehumanization, and memory. Morrison describes the effect of Beloved's departure on those who remained: "They forgot her like a bad dream. After they made up their tales, shaped and decorated them, those that saw her that day on the porch quickly and deliberately forgot her. . . . Remembering seemed unwise" (274). Morrison's embrace of the act of forgetting has a very specific function and is not intended as a wholesale endorsement of forgetting as a strategy for survival. Rather she situates forgetting as contingent, necessary, impermanent, but also as a rupture in the logic of remembering (the conventional slave narrative, for example) that shapes memories into acceptable and palatable forms of knowing the past. Forgetting is also what allows for a new way of remembering, so while the survivors of slavery in Morrison's novel forget the ghost that has haunted them, they also learn how to live with the traces she leaves behind.

Morrison's novel reminds us that forgetting can easily be used as a tool of dominant culture to push the past aside in order to maintain the fantasy and fiction of a just and tolerant present. While we live every day with the evidence of the damage done by forgetting—the desire in American society to "put slavery behind us," for example—it is still worth assessing the power of forgetfulness in creating new futures not tied to old traditions. While they do not specifically mention forgetfulness both José Muñoz and Elizabeth Freeman in books on queer temporality construct queer futurity as a break with heteronormative notions of time and history. For Muñoz, queer futurity is a "realm of potential that must be called upon" and that is "not quite here" (2010: 21), for Freeman, queer relations to time are accessed through new arrangements of bodies, pleasure, history, and time, arrangements that she names as "erotohistoriography" or "counterhistory of history itself," one linked to queerness and accessed through pleasure (2010: 95).[7]

Forgetting allows for a release from the weight of the past and the menace of the future. In *The History of Forgetting* Norman Klein links the uncertainty of memory to the fragility of place in ever-changing urban landscapes. He rejects an empiricist project of salvaging memory and instead turns to a method he mines from Borges, namely "selective forgetting": "Selective forgetting is a literary tool for describing a social imaginary: how fictions are turned into facts, while in turn erasing facts into fictions" (1997: 16). Nietzsche tells us that forgetting can be "active," and that in its active mode it serves as a "preserver of psychic order." Indeed for Nietzsche, there can be no "happiness, no cheerfulness, no hope, no pride, no present, without forgetfulness" (1969: 58).

Nietzsche's notion that happiness requires forgetfulness echoes the psychoanalytic notion of repression; indeed Freud once characterized the hysteric as someone who "suffers from reminiscences." Memory can be painful, for it actively and passively keeps alive the experience of events that one may do better to blot out. And while the hysteric is an unsuccessful repressor, one whose repression of unacceptable material in one instance has just created a new symptom in another, there are characters who are capable of radical forgetting, total forgetting, willful forgetting. Of course we all engage in willful forgetting all the time; sometimes we have to simply erase something on our brain's hard drive in order to allow for new information to take its place. If we get a new phone number, for example, the old phone number must be forgotten or else its retention will keep rewriting the new one. Learning in fact is part memorization and part forgetting, part accumulation and part erasure. But forgetting is not simply a pragmatic strategy to open up more space for new things; it is also a gate-keeping mechanism, a way of protecting the self from unbearable memories. And so shock and trauma, as so many scholars have noted, engender a form of forgetting, a cocooning of the self in order to allow the self to grow separate from the knowledge that might destroy it.

Not surprisingly, given its role in trauma, forgetting also occupies a central position in Holocaust studies. The phrase "Never forget," which serves as a moral imperative for all knowledge work on the Holocaust, tends to obliterate the complex web of relations between memory and forgetting that actually function in Holocaust memoirs. Anyone who has ever been around a survivor of the Holocaust will easily recognize the kind of active forgetting practiced by many survivors. Claude Lanzman's film Shoah (1985) is perhaps the most nuanced representation of a forgetting that is not a denial. His film is punctuated with pauses and silences, interrupted narratives and broken memories; people begin to tell and then break off, they start to speak and then fall back on gestures. Complicit Polish witnesses of the Shoah as well as former concentration camp victims all engage in this form of narrative and unwrite as much as they write of the story of destruction.

The desire for oblivion and the experience of not being able to remember traumatic experiences from which one has been rescued make up much of the narrative in W. G. Sebald's Austerlitz. This novel about a former Kindertransport boy dramatizes the plight of being plucked out of harm's way and, as a consequence, out of memory. The title character, the ethereal Jacques Austerlitz, has been named for a railway station; he finds the fragments of his childhood scattered across Europe, along the lines of the railroads that moved some bodies to freedom and others to certain doom in the Nazi death camps. Austerlitz is haunted by spatial perceptions that never resolve into memory, and he studies railway architecture in order to discover and detail "the marks of pain which trace countless fine lines through history" (2002: 14). In his studies he finds that he can never "quite shake off thoughts of the agony of leave-taking and the fear of foreign places, although such ideas were not part of architectural history proper." For Austerlitz, the railway station, in all its austerity, its monumentalism, its commitment to the temporality of the schedule, its rhythmic comfort, offers him an architecture of forgetting, a history of leave-taking, and he follows the trace of lost memories through empty streets devoid of commerce, quiet stations lost to time, and natural vistas redolent with the shapes of loss and the outlines of what remains out of memory's reach. Austerlitz cannot remember the Holocaust because he was removed from its violent orbit, and yet it haunts him as an absence and as a childhood he never had, a death he missed, a menacing abyss in the center of his autobiography.

Sebald's novel is remarkable for its ability to conjure up a character who remains unknowable both to himself and to the reader. Jacques Austerlitz is doubled in the persona of the narrator, who frames Austerlitz's narrative for the reader but who also hints at his own problems, his own failing health and career disappointments. The mood of the novel hovers perpetually between light and dark in a kind of twilight state of consciousness that the narrator compares to the artificial light produced at a zoo to keep nocturnal animals awake during the day, the nocturama. But he also evokes the half-light of the dungeon, with its small window-less cells or oubliettes, places in medieval fortresses where prisoners were thrown and then forgotten. For Sebald and his nameless narrator, what is lost can never be retrieved, what disappears leaves no trace, and he who leaves may never return. Austerlitz never can recover the pieces of his childhood that he left behind when he took a train from Czechoslovakia to England; when he does finally return to Czechoslovakia and goes to Terezienstadt to wander around the town that now sits in the spot of the former concentration camp, he finds himself staring at a plaster-cast squirrel in a small antique shop. The squirrel, he realizes, has more value to the shopkeeper or antique collector than any of the human specimens (mostly women and children) who found their way to Terezienstadt before going on to Auschwitz. The squirrel represents the banality of continuity, longevity, and survival when it is set against the casual wasting of millions of people. When Austerlitz begins to remember, he collapses. When he learns to forget, he can go on, even as "going on" means never going back.

In fact we can never really put the past back together again in the way that memory promises. In a haunting memoir that is in part a meditation on the impossibility of making the connections between past wrongs and present conditions, Saidiya Hartman asks, "What is it we choose to remember about the past and what is it we will to forget? Did my great-great-grandmother believe that forgetting provided the possibility of a new life?" (2007: 15). Noting her great-great-grandmother's reluctance to talk about slavery even though Hartman had discovered her name in a volume of slave testimony from Alabama, Hartman wonders about the contemporary tendency to restore memory and recognizes that to connect to a traumatic past is also to connect to shame and guilt. She writes, "Alongside the terrible things one had survived was also the shame of having survived it. Remembering warred with the will to forget" (16). Later she returns to this theme: "No doubt there were those who chose to 'murder the memory' because it was easier that way. Forgetting might have made it less painful to bear the hardships of slavery and easier to accept a new life in a world of strangers" (96). Survival, Hartman implies, requires a certain amount of forgetting, repressing, moving on.

In "Archive Fever" Derrida links the death drive to forgetfulness and remarks that the death drive "operates in silence, it never leaves any archives of its own" (1998: 10). The anti-archive of death, the anarchic space of forgetting, spurs an "archive fever," a will to memory, which, according to Derrida, has both conservative (literally) and revolutionary potential. In its most traditional forms archive fever "verges on radical evil" (1998: 20). In the next three chapters I try to link queerness and femininity and feminism to the radical evil conjured by failing, losing, stumbling, remembering, and forgetting.

CHAPTER THREE

The Queer Art of *Failure*

If at first you don't succeed, failure may be your style.
—Quentin Crisp, *The Naked Civil Servant*

The value of some aspects of historical gay identity—deeply ideological
though they may be—have been diminished or dismissed with succes-
sive waves of liberation. Central among these is the association between
homosexual love and loss—a link that, historically, has given queers
insight into love's failures and impossibilities (as well as, of course, wild
hopes for its future). Claiming such an association rather than disavow-
ing it, I see the art of losing as a particularly queer art.
—Heather Love, *Feeling Backwards: Loss and the Politics of Queer History*

Queer failure . . . is more nearly about escape and a certain virtuosity.
—José E. Muñoz, *Cruising Utopia: The There and Then of Queer Utopia*

Toward the end of the first decade of the twenty-first century, as
the United States slipped into one of the worst financial crises
since the Great Depression and as economists everywhere threw
up their hands and said that they had not seen the financial collapse coming, as working people lost their homes due to bad
mortgages and the middle class watched their retirement accounts dwindle to nothing because of bad investments, as rich
people pocketed ever bigger bailouts and sought shelters for
their wealth, as casino capitalism showed its true face as a game
played by banks with someone else's money, it was clearly time
to talk about failure.

Failure, of course, goes hand in hand with capitalism. A market economy must have winners and losers, gamblers and risk takers, con men and dupes; capitalism, as Scott Sandage argues in his book *Born Losers: A History of Failure in America* (2005), requires that everyone live in a system that equates success with profit and links failure to the inability to accumulate wealth even as profit for some means certain losses for others. As Sandage narrates in his compelling study, losers leave no records, while winners cannot stop talking about it, and so the record of failure is "a hidden history of pessimism in a culture of optimism" (9). This hidden history of pessimism, a history moreover that lies quietly behind every story of success, can be told in a number of different ways; while Sandage tells it as a shadow history of U.S. capitalism, I tell it here as a tale of anticapitalist, queer struggle. I tell it also as a narrative about anticolonial struggle, the refusal of legibility, and an art of unbecoming. This is a story of art without markets, drama without a script, narrative without progress. The queer art of failure turns on the impossible, the improbable, the unlikely, and the unremarkable. It quietly loses, and in losing it imagines other goals for life, for love, for art, and for being.

Failure can be counted within that set of oppositional tools that James C. Scott called "the weapons of the weak" (1987: 29). Describing peasant resistance in Southeast Asia, Scott identified certain activities that looked like indifference or acquiescence as "hidden transcripts" of resistance to the dominant order. Many theorists have used Scott's reading of resistance to describe different political projects and to rethink the dynamics of power; some scholars, such as Saidiya Hartman (1997), have used Scott's work to describe subtle resistances to slavery like working slowly or feigning incompetence. The concept of "weapons of the weak" can be used to recategorize what looks like inaction, passivity, and lack of resistance in terms of the practice of stalling the business of the dominant. We can also recognize failure as a way of refusing to acquiesce to dominant logics of power and discipline and as a form of critique. As a practice, failure recognizes that alternatives are embedded already in the dominant and that power is never total or consistent; indeed failure can exploit the unpredictability of ideology and its indeterminate qualities.

In his refusal of economic determinism Gramsci writes, "Mechanical historical materialism does not allow for the possibility of error, but assumes that every political act is determined, immediately, by the structure, and therefore as a real and permanent (in the sense of achieved) modification of the structure" (2000: 191). For Gramsci, ideology has as much to do with error or failure as with perfect predictability; therefore a radical political response would have to deploy an improvisational mode to keep pace with the constantly shifting relations between dominant and subordinate within the chaotic flow of political life. Gramsci views the intellectual function as a mode of self-awareness and an applied knowledge of the structures that constrain meaning to the demands of a class-bound understanding of "common sense."

Queer studies offer us one method for imagining, not some fantasy of an elsewhere, but existing alternatives to hegemonic systems. What Gramsci terms "common sense" depends heavily on the production of norms, and so the critique of dominant forms of common sense is also, in some sense, a critique of norms. Heteronormative common sense leads to the equation of success with advancement, capital accumulation, family, ethical conduct, and hope. Other subordinate, queer, or counter-hegemonic modes of common sense lead to the association of failure with nonconformity, anticapitalist practices, nonreproductive life styles, negativity, and critique. José Muñoz has produced the most elaborate account of queer failure to date and he explains the connection between queers and failure in terms of a utopian "rejection of pragmatism," on the one hand, and an equally utopian refusal of social norms on the other. Muñoz, in *Cruising Utopia*, makes some groundbreaking claims about sex, power, and utopian longing. Sometimes gay male cruising practices and anonymous sex take center stage in this genealogy of queer utopian longing but at other moments, sex is conjured in more subtle ways, as it was in *Disidentifications* (1999), as a desiring and melancholic relation between the living and the dead. Often, Muñoz's archive takes center stage and at times he turns to the fabulous failure of queer culture mavens like Jack Smith or Fred Herko but at others he is quite openly working with the success stories (O'Hara, Warhol) in order to propose a whole archaeological strata of forgotten subcultural producers who lie hidden beneath the glittering surface of market valued success. While Muñoz makes queerness absolutely central to cultural narratives of failure, there is a robust literature that marks failure, almost heroically, as a narrative that runs alongside the mainstream. And so, let's begin by looking at a spectacular narrative about failure that does not make the connection between failure and queerness and see what happens. This should foreclose questions about why failure must be located within that range of political affects that we call *queer.*

Punk Failures

Irvine Welch's notorious classic punk novel, *Trainspotting* (1996), is a decidedly unqueer novel about failure, disappointment, addiction, and violence set in the slums of Edinburgh. The novel is made up of obscene rants and violent outbursts from the Scottish working class, but it also contains limpid moments of punk negativity that point, in their own snarling way, to the implicit politics of failure. *Trainspotting* depicts the trials and tribulations of unemployed Scottish youth seeking some escape from Thatcher's Britain with ferocious humor and wit. Renton, the novel's antihero and one of about five narrators in the text, refuses the usual developmental trajectory of narrative progression and spends his time shuttling back and forth between the ecstasy of drugs and the agony of boredom. He undergoes no period of maturation, he makes no progress, neither he nor his mates learn any lessons, no one quits the bad life, and ultimately many of them die from drugs, HIV, violence, and neglect. Renton explicitly acknowledges his refusal of a normative model of self-development and turns this refusal into a bitter critique of the liberal concept of choice:

> Suppose that ah ken aw the pros and cons, know that ah'm gaunnae huv
> a short life, am ay sound mind etcetera, etcetera, but still want tae use
> smack? They won't let ye dae it. They won't let ye dae it, because it's seen as
> a sign of thir ain failure. The fact that ye jist simply choose tae reject whit
> they huv tae offer. Choose us. Choose life. Choose mortgage payments;
> choose washing machines; choose cars; choose sitting oan a couch watch
> ing mind-numbing and spirit-crushing game shows, stuffing fuckin junk
> food intae yir mooth. Choose rotting away, pishing and shiteing yersel in a
> home, a total fuckin embarrassment tae the selfish, fucked-up brats ye've
> produced. Choose life. Well, ah choose not tae choose life. If the cunts
> cannae handle that, it's thair fuckin problem. As Harry Lauder sais, ah jist
> intend tae keep right on to the end of the road. (187)

Renton's choice to not choose "life" situates him in radical opposition to modes of masculine respectability but also gives him space to expose the contradictory logic of health, happiness, and justice within the postwelfare state. In this brilliantly wicked speech he justifies his choice of drugs over health as a choice "not to choose life," where "life" signifies "mortgage payments . . . washing machines . . . cars . . . sitting oan a couch watching mind-numbing and spirit-crushing game shows, stuffing fuckin junk food intae yir mooth," and basically rotting away in domesticity. Society, he tells us, "invents a spurious convoluted logic to absorb people whose behavior is outside its mainstream" (187); within this logic "life," a numbing domestic passivity, constitutes a better moral "choice" than a life of drugs and drink. This same logic offers the armed forces to young men over street gangs and marriage over sexual promiscuity.

The polemic extends also to the structure of colonial rule within the United Kingdom. In a scathing diatribe against the English for colonizing Scotland and the Scots for letting them, Renton rants in defense of his maniacal and violent friend, Begbie: "Begbie and the like are fucking failures in a country ay failures. It's no good blaming it on the English for colonising us. Ah don't hate the English, they're just wankers. We are colonised by wankers. We can't even pick a decent, vibrant, healthy culture to be colonised by. No. We're ruled by effete arseholes. What does that make us? The lowest of the low, the scum of the earth. The most wretched, servile, miserable, pathetic trash that was ever shat into creation. I don't hate the English. They just get on with the shit they've got. I hate the Scots" (78). Renton's diatribe may not win points for its inspirational qualities, but it is a mean and potent critique of British colonialism on the one hand and of the falsely optimistic rhetoric of anticolonial nationalism on the other. In a very different context Lisa Lowe has described writing that refuses the binary of colonialism versus nationalism as "decolonizing writing," which she calls "an ongoing disruption of the colonial mode of production" (1996: 108). *Trainspotting*, a Scottish decolonizing novel, envisions drugs, theft, and violence as the "weapons of the weak" utilized by the colonized and working-class males of Edinburgh's slums.

Renton's critique of the liberal rhetoric of choice and his rejection of hetero-domesticity results in a spewing, foaming negativity that seeks out numerous targets, both dominant and minoritarian. Sometimes his negativity slips easily into racism, sexism, and deep homophobia, but at other times it seems to be in tune with a progressive politics of critique. Indeed Renton's speech finds its echo in recent queer theory that associates negativity with queerness itself. Lee Edelman's book *No Future* recommends, Renton-like, that queers might want to "choose, instead, not to choose the Child, as disciplinary image of the Imaginary past or as a site of a projective identification with an always impossible future" (2005: 31). While Edelman's refusal of the choices offered folds the symbolic order back upon itself in order to question the very construction of political relevance, *Trainspotting*'s refusals cling fast to the status quo because they cannot imagine the downfall of the white male as part of the emergence of a new order. *Trainspotting* ultimately is far too hetero-masculine in its simple reversals of masculine authority, its antifemale fraternity, and its unpredictable bursts of violence. Without an elaborate vision of alternative modes, the novel collapses into the angry and seething language of the male punk from whom a legacy of patriarchal and racial privilege has been withheld. In this example of unqueer failure, failure is the rage of the excluded white male, a rage that promises and delivers punishments for women and people of color.

How else might we imagine failure, and in terms of what kinds of desired political outcomes? How has failure been wielded for different political projects? And what kind of pedagogy, what kind of epistemology lurks behind those activities that have been awarded the term *failure* in Anglo-American culture? The rest of this chapter is an archive of failure, one that is in dialogue with Sandage's "hidden history of pessimism" and Muñoz's "queer utopia" and that explores in the form of notes and anecdotes, theories and examples what happens when failure is productively linked to racial awareness, anticolonial struggle, gender variance, and different formulations of the temporality of success.

Fourth Place: The Art of Losing

The highs and lows of the Olympic games every four years showcase the business of winning and the inevitability, indeed the dignity of losing. The unrelentingly patriotic coverage of the games in many countries, but particularly in North America, gives a beautifully clear image of the contradictions of American politics and more specifically of the desire of white Americans to flex their muscles *and* pose as the underdog all at the same time. While individual American athletes practice plenty of failure at the games, American audiences are generally not permitted to witness those failures; we are instead given wall-to-wall coverage of triumphant Yanks in the pool, in the gym, and on the track. We are given the history of winners all day, every day, and so every four years American viewers miss the larger drama of the games, emerging as it does from unpredictability, tragedy, close defeat, and yes, messy and undignified failure.

In a photography project associated with the Olympic games in Sydney in 2000 the artist Tracy Moffat took profoundly moving pictures of people who came in fourth in major sporting events (see plates 1 and 2). In a catalogue essay associated with a show of these works, Moffat says that she had heard rumors that someone had suggested her as one of the official photographers for the games that year. She comments, "I fantasized that if I really were to be the 'official photographer' for the Sydney 2000 Olympics I would photograph the sporting events with my own take on it all—I would photograph the losers."[1] She says that while everyone else would be directed by the mainstream media to watch the triumphant spectacle of winning, she would focus on "the images of brilliant athletes who didn't make it." Ultimately, however, she settled on the position of fourth for her photo record of losing because coming in fourth was, for her, sadder than losing altogether. By coming in fourth the athlete has just lost, just missed a medal, just found a (non)place outside of recorded history. Moffat notes, "Fourth means that you are almost good. Not the worst (which has its own perverted glamour) but almost. Almost a star!" Fourth place constitutes the antiglamour of losing. As she says, it is not the perverse pleasure of being so bad you are almost good; no, fourth represents a very unique position, beyond the glory but before the infamy.

Moffat tried to capture in her photographs the very moment the athlete realized that he or she had come in fourth: "Most of the time the expression is expressionless, it's a set look, which crosses the human face. It's an awful, beautiful, knowing mask, which says 'Oh shit!'" She photographs swimmers still in the pool, their bitter tears mixed with chlorinated water; her camera finds runners exhausted and exasperated, fighters knocked to the ground, players picking up sports equipment after the event. The whole series is a document of desperate disappointment, dramatic defeat, and the cruelty of competition.

These images remind us that winning is a multivalent event: in order for someone to win, someone else must fail to win, and so this act of losing has its own logic, its own complexity, its own aesthetic, but ultimately, also, its own beauty. Moffat tries to capture the texture of the experience of failure, the outside of success and the statistical standard that determines who loses today by a fraction of a second, a centimeter, an ounce, and who tomorrow is lost to anonymity. Fourth for Moffat also refers to the "fourth" world of Aboriginal culture, and so it references the erased and lost art of a people destroyed by the successful white colonizers.

George W.: The Art of Google-Bombing

A few years ago, if you googled *failure* the first entry to appear was "Biography of George W. Bush." Was this the work of some clever Internet activists? Apparently so. As BBC News reports, Google is fairly easily manipulated by "Google-bombing" to tie certain pages to particular phrases, and so one group of Google-bombers managed to hook up George W.'s page to the phrase *miserable failure*. We would all agree that George W. deserves to enter the annals of history under the category of failure, and yet failure is a lofty word for Bush, since it implies that he had a plan and then failed to execute it. In actual fact what is stunning about Dubya is how far he went on so little. Failure, as the images in the *Fourth* series imply, connotes a certain dignity in the pursuit of greatness, and so while *miserable* might be a good word for the Bush-Cheney era, they were actually horribly successful in terms of dominant understandings of success. George W. Bush of course represents the problems of building an economy and a politics around winners and winning instead of around the combinations of loss and failure that are inevitable to any system. Just so you know, entry number two when you googled *failure* was "Biography of Jimmy Carter" and number three was "Michael Moore." The link for Moore takes you to a picture of him at the Republican National Convention holding up an "L for Loser" hand sign.

The Anti-Aesthetic of the Lesbian

Which of course takes us to other L words. *Lesbian* is irrevocably tied to failure in all kinds of ways. Indeed, according to Heather Love, "same-sex desire is marked by a long history of association with failure, impossibility and loss. . . . Homosexuality and homosexuals serve as scapegoats for the failures and impossibilities of desire itself" (2009: 21). And Guy Hocquenghem notes in "Capitalism, the Family and the Anus," "Capitalism turns its homosexuals into failed normal people, just as it turns its working class into an imitation of the middle class" (1993: 94). For Love, queer bodies function within a psychoanalytic framework as the bearers of the failure of all desire; if, in a Lacanian sense, all desire is impossible, impossible because unsustainable, then the queer body and queer social worlds become the evidence of that failure, while heterosexuality is rooted in a logic of achievement, fulfillment, and succes-s(ion). Hocquenghem repudiates the psychoanalytic frame and instead sees capitalism as the structure that marks the homosexual as somehow failed, as the subject who fails to embody the connections between production and reproduction. Capitalist logic casts the homosexual as inauthentic and unreal, as incapable of proper love and unable to make the appropriate connections between sociality, relationality, family, sex, desire, and consumption. So before queer representation can offer a view of queer culture it must first repudiate the charge of inauthenticity and inappropriateness. For example, the television show The L Word wants to overcome and replace the "backwards history" of lesbians with a sunny and optimistic vision of gay women. The makers of the obnoxious and infectious Showtime soap would love, in other words, to redefine lesbian by associating it with life, love, leisure, liberty, luck, lovelies, longevity, Los Angeles, but we know that L can also stand for losers, labor, lust, lack, loss, lemon, Lesbian. "Same sex, different city," the ads for the show declare cheerily. And it is that "same sex" assurance that represents the heart of The L Word's success, for the loser in the glossy and femme-centric series is of course the butch, who can appear only as a ghostly presence in the fluffy andro character of Shane.

What The L Word must repudiate in order to represent lesbian as successful is the butch. The butch therefore gets cast as anachronistic, as the failure of femininity, as an earlier, melancholic model of queerness that has now been updated and transformed into desirable womanhood, desirable, that is, in a hetero-visual model. But the butch lesbian is a failure not only in contemporary queer renderings of desire; she stands in for failure in consumer culture writ large because her masculinity becomes a block to heteronormative male desire. While feminine lesbians, of the variety imagined within a hetero-pornographic imagination, are deployed in advertising culture to sell everything from beer to insurance policies, the masculine lesbian proves an anathema to consumer culture. And so in The L Word we see that in order to make "lesbians" appealing to men and straight women, the specific features which have stereotypically connoted lesbian in the past—masculine appearance and interests and jobs—must be blotted out to provide a free channel for commodification. Indeed commodification as a process depends completely upon a heteronormative set of visual and erotic expectations. While even feminine gay men can function within this framework (because they still model a desire for hetero-masculinity) the butch lesbian cannot; she threatens the male viewer with the horrifying spectacle of the "uncastrated" woman and challenges the straight female viewer because she refuses to

butch failure

participate in the conventional masquerade of hetero-femininity as weak, unskilled, and unthreatening. The L Word lesbians "succeed" within the specular economy of televisual pleasure precisely by catering to conventional notions of visual pleasure. By including a boyish but not mannish character, Shane, the show reminds the viewer of what has been sacrificed in order to bring the lesbian into the realm of commodification: namely, overt female masculinity. Shane instead occupies the role of the butch while evacuating it at the same time; she dates heterosexual and bisexual women, she gets mistaken (unrealistically) for a man, she dresses in an androgynous way—but she remains recognizably and conventionally female. Shane's success, and the success of The L Word in general, relies upon the excision of the lesbian mark of failure.

The Queer Art of Failure

Gender trouble of the butch variety is very often at the very heart of queer failure. But the queer legend Quentin Crisp transforms the apparent pathos of the gender queer into an asset: "If at first you don't succeed, failure may be your style" (1968: 196). In this witty refusal of the dogged Protestant work ethic Crisp makes the crucial link between failure and style and, in his own effeminate persona, embodies that link as gender trouble, gender deviance, gender variance. For Crisp, failure as a style also involves his "career" as a "naked civil servant," someone who chooses not to work and someone for whom work cannot be life's fulfillment. Indeed his autobiography, The Naked Civil Servant, links his own coming of age, and his moment of coming out into his own particularly flamboyant queerness, with the fall of Wall Street in 1931. He writes, "The sky was dark with millionaires throwing themselves out of windows. So black was the way ahead that my progress consisted of long periods of inert despondency punctuated by spasmodic lurches forward toward any small chink of light I thought I saw. . . . As the years went by, it did not get any lighter, but I became accustomed to the dark" (2). This particular ethos of resignation to failure, to lack of progress and a particular form of darkness, a negativity really (which I discuss in later chapters), can be called a queer aesthetic. For Crisp, as for an artist such as Andy Warhol, failure presents an opportunity rather than a dead end; in true camp fashion, the queer artist works with rather than against failure and inhabits the darkness. Indeed the darkness becomes a crucial part of a queer aesthetic.

In Bodies in Dissent (2006) Daphne Brooks makes a similar claim about the aesthetic of darkness in relation to the theatrical performances of African Americans from the period of antebellum slavery to the early twentieth century. Using an impressive array of primary materials culled from archives in the U.S. and the U.K., she reconstructs not only the con- ~wm~ texts for African American performance but also the reception of these stagings of "embodied insurgency" and the complex meanings of the performers' own bodily histories, biographies, and risky theatrical endeavors. Like Joseph Roach in *Cities of the Dead* (1996), Brooks crafts a critical methodology capable of retrieving lost performance cultures, negotiating their aesthetic complexity and rendering their meaning to both black and white audiences in the U.S. and the U.K. Roach's work forms a backdrop for some of Brooks's energetic re-creations of nineteenth-century African American transatlantic performance, and she takes from him the notion that culture reproduces itself through performance in the mode of "surrogation." I used Roach's notion of surrogation as cultural production in chapter 2 on forgetfulness; here I am interested in the way Brooks uses the term to think about how subcultural performers and images incorporate traditions of performance and activate new sets of political meanings and references. For Brooks, the body of the performer becomes an archive of improvised cultural responses to conventional constructions of gender, race, and sexuality, and the performance articulates powerful modes of dissent and resistance. She reads the theatrical texts in her archive along the axis of propulsive transformation and seeks, through patient historical contextualization and inspired textual analysis, to locate in each text sites of aesthetic and political possibility. For example, she develops a brilliant reading of the aesthetics of opacity and locates textual darkness as a "trope of narrative insurgency, discursive survival, and epistemological resistance" (108). Darkness, Brooks continues, "is an interpretive strategy" and a mode of reading the world from a "particular and dark position" (109). It is this understanding of "textual darkness," or the darkness of a particular reading practice from a particular subject position, that I believe resonates with the queer aesthetics I trace here as a catalogue of resistance through failure.

Following Brooks's aesthetics and Crisp's advice to adjust to less light rather than seek out more, I propose that one form of queer art has made failure its centerpiece and has cast queerness as the dark landscape of confusion, loneliness, alienation, impossibility, and awkwardness. Obviously nothing essentially connects gay and lesbian and trans people to these forms of unbeing and unbecoming, but the social and symbolic systems that tether queerness to loss and failure cannot be wished away; some would say, nor should they be. As Lee Edelman, Heather Love, and others have argued, to simply repudiate the connections between queerness and negativity is to commit to an unbearably positivist and progressive understanding of the queer, one that results in the perky depictions of lesbians in The L Word or the reduction of gay men in film and on TV to impossibly good-looking arbiters of taste.

"Darkness," says Brooks, "is an interpretive strategy," (2006: 109) launched from places of darkness, experiences of hurt or exclusion; darkness is the terrain of the failed and the miserable. The idea of a queer darkness, a strategy of reading as well as a way of being in the world, explains a series of depictions of queer life in photography from the early and mid-twentieth century. Brassai's photographs of lesbian bars in Paris in the 1930s and Diane Arbus's odd photographs of female "friends" both partake in very different ways in these dark images of queers. Brassai's famous and iconic photographs of Paris capture hidden worlds of thieves, pimps, prostitutes, and queers. In the text that introduces his censored collection on their publication in the 1970s, he explains that he had always disliked photography until he was inspired to "translate all the things that enchanted [him] in nocturnal Paris" (1976: n.p.). The photographs collected as The Secret Paris of the 1930's are intended to look back on the sinful and seamy worlds that Brassai documented but could not show at the time the photographs were taken. When the book was finally published in the 1970s it was accompanied by a moralistic text designed to explain the weird images to an imaginary "straight" reader. Brassai calls Le Monocle a singular "temple of Sapphic love" among all the whorehouses in Montparnasse and describes the habitués as exotic masculine creatures who wore their hair short and reeked of "weird scents, more like amber or incense than roses and violets." Despite the judgmental text, the photographs of Le Monocle capture what looks to be a fantastic, dynamic lesbian nightlife, far more interesting than most queer bars that exist in Paris today. That said, the photographs also capture what Heather Love calls "impossible love" or "the impossibility at the heart of desire" (2009: 24). With this concept she means to indicate lines of connection between political exclusion in the past and political exclusion in the present. While liberal histories build triumphant political narratives with progressive stories of improvement and success, radical histories must contend with a less tidy past, one that passes on legacies of failure

8. Brassai, "La Grosse Claude et son amie, au 'Monocle,'"
ca. 1932. © Estate Brassai–RMN.

and loneliness as the consequences of homophobia and racism and xeno-
phobia. As Love puts it, "Backward feelings serve as an index to the ruined
state of the social world; they indicate continuities between the bad gay
past and the present; and they show up the inadequacies of queer narratives of progress" (27). To feel backward is to be able to recognize something in these darker depictions of queer life without needing to redeem
them.

The photographs of Le Monocle are shrouded in darkness, shadowy
even though the scenes they depict are quite upbeat and joyful. In this
way the images are able to capture both the persistence of queer life
and the staging of queer life as impossible. Brassai's narrative speaks
of pathetic inverts longing for unattainable masculinity: "All the women
were dressed as men, and so totally masculine in appearance that at
first glance one thought they were men. A tornado of virility had gusted
through the place and blown away all the finery, all the tricks of feminine
coquetry, changing women into boys, gangsters, policemen. Gone the

trinkets, veils, ruffle! Pleasant colors, frills! Obsessed by their unattainable goal to be men, they wore the most somber uniforms; black tuxedos, as though in mourning for their ideal masculinity."

Of course as even a quick glance at the photos reveals, "all" of the women were not dressed as men; some were dressed in high-femme outfits, and the tuxedos that indicated the butches' state of mourning could as easily be jaunty evening wear or even wedding outfits. And yet there is something dark about the images, something lost, something unattainable. What remains unattainable in the butches' masculinity, we might say, is what remains unattainable in all masculinity: all ideal masculinity by its very nature is just out of reach, but it is only in the butch, the masculine woman, that we notice its impossibility. Brassai's photographs thus capture three things; the darkness of the night worlds within which queer sociability takes place; the failure of ideal masculinity that must be located in the butch in order to make male masculinity seem possible; and a queer femininity that is not merely dark but invisible. Queer femininity in these images disappears as lesbianism when partnered with the more visibly queer butch, and when it does come into visibility it appears inauthentic in relation to both queerness and heterosexuality. In these senses one can say that the photographs represent queer failure and craft a queer aesthetic to do so.

But that was then. As Sontag writes, "The moody, intricately textured Paris of Atget and Brassai is mostly gone" (2001: 16). Reading Brassai now, we can marvel at the queer Paris he saw and can provide new captions, visual and textual, that rewrite and inhabit his narratives of melancholia and masquerade. Brassai located these images in a section in his collection titled "Sodom and Gomorrah" and labeled them "homosexual," thinking, obviously, that he had captured a lost and forbidden world of sinful inversion. The title refers to the biblical myth of orgiastic realms selected for destruction in Genesis. Heather Love uses the myth of Sodom and Gomorrah to think about the backward look that Lot's wife casts while leaving the sinful cities. This look turns her into a pillar of salt: "By refusing the destiny that God has offered her, Lot's wife is cut off from her family and from the future. She becomes a monument to destruction, an emblem of eternal regret" (2009: 5). Brassai, however, thinks back to Proust's "Sodom and Gomorrah." He describes his reaction as he watched the women dancing together in the bar: "I thought of Marcel Proust, of his jealousy, his sick curiosity about the foreign pleasures of Gomorrah. The fact that Albertine had been unfaithful to the narrator with a woman bothered him far less than the kinds of pleasures she had experienced with her partner. 'What can they really be feeling,' he continually wondered" (1976: n.p.).

What indeed? The age-old question of lesbian sex—What do they do and feel together?—emerges here within a visual world that Brassai creates even as it eludes him. The photographs tell more than Brassai can ever narrate: of inventive transgendering, the careful remodeling of the "heterosexual matrix" by butch-femme couples reveling in the possibilities that Paris at night offered them in the 1930s, and of darkness, the shadow world within which the inauthentic, the unreal, and the damned play out their shadow lives. Another photograph from Paris also shrouds the image of the lesbian in shadow and fails to penetrate its façade. Cecil Beaton's portrait of Gertrude Stein from 1935 shows another view of queer Paris, one that has entered into official histories and which seems removed in time and space from Brassai's underworlds. However, as if to hint at the shadow world that haunts the histories for which we have settled, Beaton presents the viewer with two Steins.

In the foreground a large and masculine Stein, dressed in a heavy over-coat and wearing a tight cap on her head, stares grimly into the lens. The only concession to femininity is her collar brooch, a shadow fetish replacing what should be a tie with an image of feminine decoration. The hands are crossed, the lips are pursed, and the face is lined and serious. Behind the large Stein stands a shadow Stein, now without the overcoat; we see her skirt and waistcoat and brooch, and the brooch now makes us look again at the first Stein. This portrait of Stein repeats another image of Stein with her lover, Alice B. Toklas, in which Stein stands in the middle foreground and to the right and Toklas shadows her back and to the left. In both images of the gender-ambiguous body of Stein, her masculinity is measured against another image in which she is doubled but not mirrored. Toklas, who looks defiantly back at the camera as if to deny her placement as Stein's other or dependent, puts Stein's masculinity into perspective. By making us see Stein through Toklas, the photograph forces us to adjust the measurements we usually use to "see" gender; the gender queerness of both Toklas and Stein relays back and forth between them as the viewer's gaze shuttles from one to the other, guided by a strange wire sculpture that hangs between them and throws its own shadow upon the wall. The posing of the queer subject as shadow and

9. Cecil Beaton, "Gertrude Stein." (1935). Bromide print. 8 3/8 in. × 6 3/4 in. (21.4 cm × 17.0 cm). Courtesy of the Cecil Beaton Studio Archive at Sotheby's.

shadowed seems to cast the construction of queerness as secondary to the primacy of heterosexual arrangements of gender and relationality, but in fact it comments upon the disruptive potential of shadow worlds.

Writing about Diane Arbus, another archivist of "sexual underworlds," Sontag claims, "Like Brassai, Arbus wanted her subjects to be as fully conscious as possible, aware of the act in which they were participating. Instead of trying to coax her subjects into a natural or typical position, they are encouraged to be awkward—that is to pose" (2001: 37). The pose, Sontag suggests, makes the subjects look "odder" and, in the case of Arbus's work, "almost deranged." Sontag criticizes Arbus for using her camera to find and create freaks, and she compares her unfavorably to

Brassai, noting that Brassai not only documented "perverts and inverts" but also "did tender cityscapes, portraits of famous artists" (46). Arbus makes "all her subjects equivalent" by refusing to "play the field of subject matter" (47). Her narrowness, in other words, makes her a solipsistic voyeur rather than a talented photographic artist. Indeed Arbus's photographs of transvestites, midgets, and dwarfs do present the world as a freak show and parade queer and ambiguous bodies in front of the camera to illustrate the range and depth of freakish alterity. And while Brassai's photographs were largely shot at night, Arbus presents her subjects in the clear and cold light of day. But Arbus does not limit her freak show to so-called freaks; patriots, families, elderly couples, and teenagers all look strange and distorted through her lens. To use Eve Kosofsky Sedgwick's terms, Arbus "universalizes" freakishness while Brassai "minoritizes" it. Brassai looks at the transgender world as if peering at strange insects under a rock; Arbus finds ambiguity across a range of embodiments and represents it as the human condition. In the portrait "Naked Man Being a Woman, NYC, 1968" she records the representational instability of the body itself, the fact that it cannot function as a foundation for order, coherence, and neat systems of correspondence.

Arbus cited both Weegee and Brassai as influences on her work and said of Brassai, "Brassai taught me something about obscurity, because for years I have been tripped out on clarity. Lately it's been striking me how I really love what I can't see in a photograph. In Brassai, in Bill Brandt, there is the element of actual physical darkness and it's very thrilling to see darkness again" (Bosworth 2006: 307). In Brassai's pictures the darkness actually frames what can be seen; the context for every image is the night itself, and the players in the secret worlds of Paris are illuminated momentarily by the camera's gaze but threaten to fade to black at any moment. For Arbus, the darkness and what cannot be seen are less a function of light and shadow and more a result of psychological complexity. Her image "Two Friends at Home, NYC, 1965" cites Brassai's butch-femme couples but removes them from the unreal night worlds and places them in daylight. Arbus's biographer, Patricia Bosworth, wrote about this image, "[Arbus's] constant journey into the world of transvestites, drag queens, hermaphrodites and transsexuals may have helped define her view of what it means to experience sexual conflict. She once followed 'two friends' from street to apartment, and the resulting portrait suggests an almost sinister sexual power between these mannish females. (The larger, more traditionally feminine figure stands with her arm possessively around the shoulder of her boyish partner. In another shot the couple is seen lying on their rumpled bed; one of them is in the middle of a sneeze—it is both intimate and creepy)" (2006: 226). Notice that it is Bosworth rather than Arbus who assigns the label "creepy" to the image and who represents the photograph of two friends as part of an undifferentiated world of freaks: trannies, intersex people, circus performers, disabled people. Arbus assigns no such values to her subjects; rather she labels these two dykes "friends." One could argue that the term refuses to see the sexual dynamic animating the two, but in fact the rumpled bed and the physical closeness of the two bodies ensure that we acknowledge, in Arbus's terms, what we cannot see.

For Arbus, the photograph itself stands in for a lost world, a context that eludes the viewer who cannot see beyond the spectacle of difference. Arbus in fact inserted herself, almost desperately, into these worlds of difference and tried to use her photographs to force viewers to be aware that they do not see everything or even anything. When a viewer like Bosworth looks at the butch-femme couple in their apartment, a couple whom Arbus has followed home, she sees something she believes she is not supposed to see, and so the image becomes "intimate and creepy." (I could not find the sneeze picture that so disturbs Bosworth.) But when queer viewers see the image nearly forty years after it was taken, we see something intimate and messy: it offers us a visual bridge back to a pre-Stonewall queer world, a world that is both infinitely removed from ours and amazingly close. The butch's open gaze at the camera, at Arbus, and the femme's protective look at her partner and away from the camera create a circuit of vision within which each participant in the image's construction, the artist and her two subjects, both sees and is seen. Arbus can be read through this picture as less a prurient voyeur and more a chronicler of the unseen, the unspoken, and the untold.

Monica Majoli, a contemporary queer artist based in Los Angeles, picks up the theme of darkness in her work (see plates 3 and 4). Majoli takes photographs of her ex-lovers as they appear in a black mirror and then paints from the photographs of the mirror images. Impossibly dark and impenetrable, and brimming with melancholy, these portraits defy the definition of mirror, of portrait, and even of love. A mirror image of course is first of all a self-portrait, and so the images must be read as both a representation of the artist herself and depictions of love affairs and their aftermath (see plates 5 and 6). In most of the portraits Majoli pairs a drawing or painting of a figure with an abstract version, calling attention to the murkiness of all oppositions in a darkened mirror space. While a conventional painting might depend upon some kind of relation between the figure and the ground, in these portraits the background fills out the figure with emotional intensity, with darkness, and asks us to look hard at interiority itself. The abstract versions are no harder or easier to read or to look at than the figures, reminding us that the figures are also abstractions and that the shape of a head or the outline of a breast guarantees nothing in terms of a human presence or connection or intimacy. The portraits are painfully intimate and at the same time refuse intimacy. All attempts to look closer, to make out features, to understand the trajectory of a line end in the same boiling darkness, a black that is not flat because it is a mirrored surface and a mirror that is not deep because it sucks up the light from the image.

The portraits are made after the love affair has ended and represent what we think of as failure—the failure of love to last, the mortality of all connection, the fleeting nature of desire. Obviously desire is present in the very gesture of painting, and yet desire here, like the black mirror, devours rather than generates, obliterates rather than enlightens. Majoli's paintings are technically very difficult (how to sculpt a figure out of darkness, how to draw in the dark, to reflect the emotional and affective issues) but also emotionally wrought (how to narrate the relationship that ends, how to face the end of desire, how to look at one's own failures, mortality, and limitations). She holds up a dark mirror to the viewer and insists that he or she look into the void. Hearkening back to a history of representations of homosexuality as loss and death from Proust to Radclyffe Hall, Majoli's paintings converse with the tradition of imaging begun by Brassai and extended by Arbus.[2]

Failure animates much of the work of another California artist, Judie Bamber. For her the thematics of losing and failure appear within visuality itself as a line or threshold beyond which you cannot see, a horizon that marks the place of the failure of vision and visibility itself. While José E. Muñoz casts queerness as a kind of horizon for political aspiration (Muñoz: 2010), Bamber's horizons remind us that possibility and disappointment often live side by side. Bamber's seascapes, painted over a period of two years, make a record of the subtle but finite shifts in mood, tone, and visuality that "nature" offers to the gaze. In her work the landscape becomes cinematic, not one overwhelming painterly whole but a series of fragments presented montage style within a series that has a beginning and a definite end. When we look at the paintings we are underwhelmed by nature and begin to see nature as technology, as an apparatus (see plates 7 and 8). The viewer is drawn over and over to the horizon, the line between sky and sea that sometimes shocks with its intensity and at other times disappears altogether. The ebb and flow of the horizon in and out of vision is in many ways the theme of the series as a whole. Bamber's depiction of the horizon as limit speaks to a queer temporality and a queer spatiality that resist a notion of art as capable of seeing beyond and in fact makes art about limitation, about the narrowness of the future, the weightiness of the past, and the urgency of the present.

This notion of a limited horizon returns us to Edelman's book No Future (2005), in that both Bamber and Edelman seem to be inscribing queer failure into time and space. While for Bamber the seascapes drain nature of its romance and its sense of eternity, for Edelman the queer is always and inevitably linked to the death drive; indeed death and finitude are the very meaning of queerness, if it has meaning at all, and Edelman uses this sense of the queer in order to propose a relentless form of negativity in place of the forward-looking, reproductive, and heteronormative politics of hope that animates all too many political projects. My attempt to link queerness to an aesthetic project organized around the logic of failure converses with Edelman's effort to detach queerness from the optimistic and humanistic activity of making meaning. The queer subject, he argues, has been bound epistemologically to negativity, to nonsense, to antiproduction, and to unintelligibility, and instead of fighting this characterization by dragging queerness into recognition, he proposes that we embrace the negativity that we anyway structurally represent. Edelman's polemic about futurity ascribes to queerness the function of the limit; while the heteronormative political imagination propels itself forward in time and space through the indisputably positive image of the child, and while it projects itself back on the past through the dignified image of the parent, the queer subject stands between heterosexual optimism and its realization.

At this political moment Edelman's book constitutes a compelling argument against a U.S. imperialist project of hope, or what Barbara Ehrenreich (2009) has called "bright-sidedness," and it remains one of the most powerful statements of queer studies' contribution to an anti-imperialist, queer, counterhegemonic imaginary. And yet I want to engage critically with Edelman's project in order to argue for a more explicitly political framing of the antisocial project, a framing that usefully encloses failure. While Edelman frames his polemic against futurity with epigraphs by Jacques Lacan and Virginia Woolf, he omits the more obvious reference that his title conjures up and that echoes through recent queer antisocial aesthetic production, namely "God Save the Queen" as sung by the Sex Pistols. While the Sex Pistols used the refrain "No future" to reject a formulaic union of nation, monarchy, and fantasy, Edelman tends to cast material political concerns as crude and pedestrian, as already a part of the conjuring of futurity that his project must foreclose. Indeed he turns to the unnervingly tidy and precise theoretical contractions of futurity in Lacan because, like Lacan and Woolf, and unlike the punks, he strives to exert a kind of obsessive control over the reception of his own discourse. Twisting and turning back on itself, reveling in the power of inversion, Edelman's syntax itself closes down the anarchy of signification. In footnotes and chiastic formulations alike he shuts down critique and withholds from the reader the future and fantasies of it. One footnote predicts criticism of his work based on its "elitism," "pretension," whiteness, and style, and projects other objections on the grounds of "apolitical formalism." He professes himself unsympathetic to all such responses and, having foreclosed the future, continues on his way in a self-enclosed world of cleverness and chiasmus. Edelman's polemic opens the door to a ferocious articulation of negativity ("Fuck the social order and the Child in whose name we're collectively terrorized; fuck Annie; fuck the waif from Les Mis; fuck the poor, innocent kid on the Net; fuck Laws both with capital Ls and with small; fuck the whole network of Symbolic relations and the future that serves as its prop" [29]), but ultimately he does not fuck the law, big or little L; he succumbs to the law of grammar, the law of logic, the law of abstraction, the law of apolitical formalism, the law of genres.

So what does or would constitute the politics of "no future" and by implication the politics of negativity? The Sex Pistols made the phrase "No future" into a rallying call for Britain's dispossessed. In their debut song, written as an anticelebratory gesture for the queen's silver jubilee, they turned the National Anthem into a snarling rejection of the tradition of the monarchy, the national investment in its continuation, and the stakes that the whole event betrayed in futurity itself, where futurity signifies the nation, the divisions of class and race upon which the notion of national belonging depends, and the activity of celebrating the ideological system which gives meaning to the nation and takes meaning away from the poor, the unemployed, the promiscuous, the noncitizen, the racialized immigrant, the queer:

God save the queen
She ain't no human being
There is no future
In England's dreaming. . . .
Oh god save history
God save your mad parade
Oh lord god have mercy
All crimes are paid.
When there's no future
How can there be sin
We're the flowers in the dustbin
We're the poison in your human machine
We're the future your future. . . .
God save the queen
We mean it man
And there is no future
In England's dreaming. . . .
No future no future
No future for you
No future no future
No future for me.

No future for Edelman means routing our desires around the eternal sunshine of the spotless child and finding the shady side of political imaginaries in the proudly sterile and antireproductive logics of queer relation. It also seems to mean something (too much) about Lacan's symbolics and not enough about the powerful negativity of punk politics, which, as I pointed out in relation to Trainspotting, have plenty to say about symbolic and literal nihilism. When the Sex Pistols spat in the face of English provincialism and called themselves "the flowers in the dustbin," when they associated themselves with the trash and debris of polite society, they launched their poison into the human. Negativity might well constitute an antipolitics, but it should not register as apolitical.[3]

In chapter 4 I follow the trail of an antisocial feminism made by Jamaica Kincaid, among others. Here I want to turn to an antisocial feminist extraordinaire, who articulated a deeply antisocial politics that casts patriarchy as not just a form of male domination but as the formal production of sense, mastery, and meaning. Valerie Solanas recognized that happiness and despair, futurity and foreclosure have been cast as the foundations of certain forms of subjectivity within patriarchy, and she relentlessly counters the production of "truth" within patriarchy with her own dark and perverted truths about men, masculinity, and violence. For Solanas, patriarchy is a system of meaning that neatly divides positive and negative human traits between men and women. She inverts this process, casting men as "biological accidents" and at the same time refusing to take up the space of positivity. Instead she colonizes the domain of violence and offers, helpfully, to cut men up in order to demolish the hegemonic order. While straight men are "walking dildos," gay men are simply "faggots" and embody all the worst traits of patriarchy because they are men who love other men and have no use for women. In SCUM Manifesto (Solanas 2004) homosociality of all kinds is called "faggotry," and men are supposed to both fear and desire it. For Solanas, men in all forms are the enemy, and there is no such thing as a male rebel. She famously turned theory into practice when she took a gun and shot Andy Warhol for "stealing" a script from her. While we might be horrified by the anarchic violence of her act, we also have to recognize that this kind of violence is precisely what we call upon and imply when we theorize and conjure negativity.

The real problem, to my mind, with the antisocial turn in queer theory as exemplified by the work of Bersani, Edelman, and others has less to do with the meaning of negativity—which, as I am arguing, can be found in an array of political projects, from anticolonialism to punk—and more to do with the excessively small archive that represents queer negativity. On the one hand the gay male archive coincides with the canonical archive, and on the other hand it narrows that archive down to a select group of antisocial queer aesthetes and camp icons and texts. It includes, in no particular order, Tennessee Williams, Virginia Woolf, Bette Midler, Andy Warhol, Henry James, Jean Genet, Broadway musicals, Marcel Proust, Alfred Hitchcock, Oscar Wilde, Jack Smith, Judy Garland, and Kiki and Herb, but it rarely mentions all kinds of other antisocial writers, artists, and texts such as Valerie Solanas, Jamaica Kincaid, Patricia Highsmith, Wallace and Gromit, Johnny Rotten, Nicole Eiseman, Eileen Myles, June Jordan, Linda Besemer, Hothead Paisan, Finding Nemo, Lesbians on Ecstasy, Deborah Cass, SpongeBob, Shulamith Firestone, Marga Gomez, Toni Morrison, and Patti Smith.

Because it sticks to a short list of favored canonical writers, the gay male archive binds itself to a narrow range of affective responses. And so fatigue, ennui, boredom, indifference, ironic distancing, indirect-ness, arch dismissal, insincerity, and camp make up what Ann Cvetkovich (2003) has called "an archive of feelings" associated with this form of antisocial theory. But this canon occludes another suite of affectivities associated with another kind of politics and a different form of nega-tivity. In this other archive we can identify, for example, rage, rudeness, anger, spite, impatience, intensity, mania, sincerity, earnestness, over-investment, incivility, brutal honesty, and disappointment. The first ar-chive is a camp archive, a repertoire of formalized and often formulaic responses to the banality of straight culture and the repetitiveness and unimaginativeness of heteronormativity. The second archive, however, is far more in keeping with the undisciplined kinds of responses that Leo Bersani at least seems to associate with sex and queer culture, and it is here that the promise of self-shattering, loss of mastery and meaning, unregulated speech and desire are unloosed. Dyke anger, anticolonial de-spair, racial rage, counterhegemonic violence, punk pugilism—these are the bleak and angry territories of the antisocial turn; these are the jagged zones within which not only self-shattering (the opposite of narcissism in a way) but other-shattering occurs. If we want to make the antisocial turn in queer theory we must be willing to turn away from the comfort zone of polite exchange in order to embrace a truly political negativity, one that promises, this time, to fail, to make a mess, to fuck shit up, to be loud, unruly, impolite, to breed resentment, to bash back, to speak up and out, to disrupt, assassinate, shock, and annihilate.

"If at first you don't succeed," wrote Quentin Crisp, "failure may be your style." The style of failure is better modeled by my list of antisocial dignitaries. It is quite possibly a lesbian style rather than a gay style (since very often gay style is style writ large), and it lives in the life and works of Patricia Highsmith, for example, who wrote hateful letters to her mother and in her notebooks scribbled of her strong desire to be disinvited to friends' dinner parties.[4] I will return to the archive of antisocial femi-nism later in the book, but for now, in relation to the art of failure, I turn to queer artwork preoccupied with emptiness, a sense of abandonment. The queer collaborative Spanish artists Cabello/Carceller link queerness to a mode of negativity that lays claim to rather than rejects concepts like *emptiness, futility, limitation, ineffectiveness, sterility, unproductiveness*. In this work a queer aesthetic is activated through the function of negation rather than in the mode of positivity; in other words, the works strive to establish queerness as a mode of critique rather than as a new investment in normativity or life or respectability or wholeness or legitimacy. In some of their early work, for example, they portrayed collaboration as a kind of death struggle resulting in the death of the author, the end of individuality, and the impossibility of knowing where one person ends and another begins. In other photographs they abandon the figure altogether and photograph space itself as queer.

In a series of photographs following a research trip to California in 1996–97 Cabello/Carceller document the empty promises of utopia. The images of vacant swimming pools in these works signify the gulf between fantasy and reality, the subjects and the spaces onto which they project their dreams and desires. The empty pools, full of longing and melancholy, ask the viewer to meditate on the form and function of the swimming pool; from there we are drawn to contemplate the meaning and promise of desire. These swimming pools, empty and lifeless, function as the city street does for Benjamin: they work in an allegorical mode and speak of abundance and its costs; they tell of cycles of wealth and the ebb and flow of capital; the pool also functions as a fetish, a saturated symbol of luxury; and like the shop windows in the Parisian arcades described by Benjamin, the water in a swimming pool reflects the body and transforms space into a glittering dream of relaxation, leisure, recreation, and buoyancy. At the same time the empty pools stand like ruins, abandoned and littered with leaves and other signs of disuse, and in this ruined state they represent a perversion of desire, the decay of the commodity, the queerness of the disassociation of use from value. When the pool no longer signifies as a marker of wealth and success it becomes available to queer signification as a symbolic site of failure, loss, rupture, disorder, incipient chaos, and the desire animated by these states nonetheless.

The swimming pool is a place of meditation, an environment within which the body becomes weightless and hovers on the surface of a submerged world; it is a site where the body becomes buoyant, transformed by a new element, and yet must struggle, overcome by the new and potentially hostile environment. Like a tiled Atlantis, the exposed pool, filled now with air rather than water, reveals what lies beneath the sparkling surface of chlorine-enhanced blue. It takes us to a threshold and forces us to contemplate jumping into air and space. Some of Cabello/Carceller's images draw the eye to the threshold and show how the comforting rectangle of the swimming pool can blur into a shapeless mass. These blurred thresholds lend the pool a menacing aspect; in "Sin título (Utopia) #27, 1998–99" we are reminded that the ladders leading into and out of the

10. Cabello/Carceller, "Sin título (Utopia) #27," 1998–99." Color photograph. 70 cm × 50 cm. Printed with permission of Elba Benítez Gallery (Madrid) and Joan Prats Gallery (Barcelona).

11. Cabello/Carceller, "Sin título (Utopia) #29," 1998–99." Color photograph. 70 cm × 50 cm. Printed with permission of Elba Benítez Gallery (Madrid) and Joan Prats Gallery (Barcelona).

pool, placed at the top of the pool and rarely descending to the floor, are useless without water. The empty pool becomes a trap for the human body when the water has been emptied out.

The spaces emptied of bodies rhyme with another series by Cabello/Carceller: empty bars strewn with the debris of human interaction. These photographs, like the photos of the empty swimming pools, record the evidence of presence in the absence of the body. The emptied-out spaces demand that the viewer fill in the blanks; we may feel almost compelled to complete the picture in front of us, to give it meaning and narrative. We people it ourselves by allowing it to reflect back to us, not the missing self, but the unwillingness we feel at the edge of the void. The photographers lead their viewers to the site of dispersal and then leave us there, alone, to contemplate all that has been lost and what remains to be seen. These images of the desolate bars, however, represent, almost heroically, not only queer community, but also what it leaves behind. The bar area in "Alguna Parte #5" looks tawdry and exposed; the bottles of alcohol nestle up to a fire extinguisher, implying the combustibility of the environment. Now fire, not water, is the element that lies in wait. The litter-strewn floor, dotted with disco lights and unruly shadows, speaks not of abandonment, like the empty pools, but of use and materiality. The greasy, sticky, sweaty floor displays the impact of bodies on its surface and counterposes the bar to the clean and hygienic spaces of heteronormative domesticity.

The bar is simultaneously an interior and an exterior space (as is the swimming pool); these are spaces, heterotopic spaces in Foucault's terms (like mirrors), where the surface gives way to depth and the depth is revealed as illusory. Like the pools, these interiors offer up a confusing array of surfaces; their planes are not laid one on top of the other but confuse perspectival vantage points and mix up the relation between the foreground and the background, what is emphasized and what is downplayed. The smoke adds to the blurred vision and intensifies the inverted relations between internal and external, body and space, floor and wall, bench and bar. In the multiplicity of planes the viewer understands the vantage point of the lesbian bar as scattered, constellated, and as we wander through we are shocked, suddenly, to have glimpsed the outside, to have crossed a threshold; the camera takes up a new vantage point in relation to the bar, and as we come close to the sticky floors, as we contemplate the debris before us, we glance up and see the outside beckoning

12. Cabello/Carceller, "Alguna Parte #5," 2000. Color photograph. 125 cm ×
190 cm. Printed with permission of Elba Benítez Gallery (Madrid) and Joan
Prats Gallery (Barcelona).

13. Cabello/Carceller, "Alguna Parte #2," 2000. Color photograph, 125 cm ×
190 cm. Printed with permission of Elba Benítez Gallery (Madrid) and Joan
Prats Gallery (Barcelona).

14. Cabello/Carceller, "Alguna Parte #23," 2000. Color photograph, 150 cm ×
100 cm. Printed with permission of Elba Benítez Gallery (Madrid) and Joan
Prats Gallery (Barcelona).

through the back of the bar. The door is open, it is morning, and the bar stands exposed to the light of day.

The light of day, like the disco lighting in the lesbian bar, comes in many forms and performs different functions for viewers and for those who dwell within it. Returning to Judie Bamber's seascapes, we see how they too are preoccupied with thresholds that cannot be crossed, relationships between light and dark and the dissection of the void. In these paintings of the ocean, set in Malibu, Bamber orchestrates the drama of the relation between sky and sea but without ever succumbing to a romanticization of nature. In fact the series constitutes a kind of critique of nature; by archiving the shifting contrasts between air and water, she actually remarks upon the limits of nature, its finitude, rather than its infinite sublimity. There came a time, Bamber recalls, when she looked out at the ocean from her balcony in Malibu and realized that the view that presented itself was one that she had seen before rather than another unique display of color and natural virtuosity. What Bamber paints, then, is the limit: the limit of vision, the limit of nature, the limit of color itself, the circumscribed imagination, the lack of futurity, or, in other words, the expansion and contraction of all our horizons. As Nayland Blake writes of these paintings in a catalogue essay that accompanied their first showing, "It is important that these are paintings of the Pacific, the terminating point of American westward expansion. From a place of completion we gaze into a haze of potential that arrests our gaze and yet offers nothing back that could orient us. We have come to an end" (2005: 9). Linking the circumscription of sight to the regulating function of the national fantasy of expansion, Blake astutely links the sense of disorientation produced by the paintings to a political project that relentlessly gobbles up land and materials on behalf of its own racialized reading of destiny and completion. Bamber's paintings as "anti-maps," as images of dissolution and disenchantment, force an abrupt halt to fantasies of national expansion.

Bamber's seascapes are melancholy without conveying nostalgia. They also refuse the auratic mode of artistic production and settle into an aesthetic of repetition; each painting repeats the basic set of relations between sea, sky, and horizon, and each situates the drama of liminality very precisely in time and place. As if to cancel out the possibility that we would read the virtuosity of the artist as what replaces the virtuosity and genius of nature, Bamber tries to eliminate her very brush strokes from the canvas to create the illusion of mechanical reproduction. At the same time the paintings perform what Dianne Chisholm, citing Walter Benjamin, describes as "spacing out," or the miming of the "porosity of space" (2005: 109). In this process, Chisholm argues, the narrator allows herself to be absorbed by the city and to become part of its narrative and its memories. In Bamber's paintings the tense interactions between sea and sky, sky and horizon, light and mood, color and liminality, all produce the "porosity" that the viewer sees and even rejects. According to Chisholm, porosity represented to Benjamin the spaces of the city that dramatize shifts in the mode of commerce or the content of the urban street, the flows of exchange and desire. Chisholm writes, "The porosity of the city of queer constellations enables us to see the confluence of history even as it is engulfed in the capital(ism) of post-modernity. The gay village is exceptionally porous. Here gay life is lived out on streets that are conduits to intimate and communal contact and prime arteries of commodity traffic" (45). Bamber's paintings are of the city and yet separate from them; they are images of Los Angeles, a reminder of the city's appeal; the seascapes both reflect and repel—they shine from the sun and absorb all light back into their surfaces. They seem to emit their own light source and, like the stereotype of Los Angeles body culture, they confuse the relationship between natural beauty (the sunset) and technologically enhanced beauty (the spectacular sunset on a smoggy day). Bamber's seascapes remind us that visions of utopia are class-bound; while one group of Los Angelinos look out on the smog-enhanced seascape, another group is trapped within the same toxicity inland. Fantasies of sufficiency and safety are crisscrossed by the sirens and helicopters that maintain the city as an invisible grid of regulated spaces.

Bamber's extreme realism, here and elsewhere in her work, connects painting to other media rather than setting it apart as craft in opposition to technology, and it serves to denaturalize the object of the gaze through intense scrutiny. Most seascapes are discussed in terms of epic time frames. The Japanese photographer Hiroshi Sugimoto, like Bamber, is attracted to the seascape as a minimalist image, but unlike Bamber he sees the seascape as a representation of primal time and describes it as "the oldest vision." He uses a fast exposure to "stop the motion of the waves," but the instance he freezes is supposed to connect back to a memorializing sense of longevity and duration (Sugimoto, 1995: 95). Bamber's seascapes, technological as they may be, are more committed to minimalism than Sugimoto's in that no waves at all appear, and she depicts, not arrested motion, but the end of time and motion forward.

While Sugimoto says that he is amazed by the expansiveness of the seascape, its infinite array of differences, Bamber's queer vision sets her apart from the tradition of the genre; she resists the romance we may have found in a Constable, the theatrics in a Courbet seascape, and she refuses the reverence we see in Sugimoto's photographs. Instead she flirts with the here, the now, and creates stark and disciplined images that are as much about the frame as they are about the subject matter.

Much of Bamber's work, whether a perfectly rendered image of a vagina or a photo-realistic depiction of her father, practices a desentimentalizing method of representation. In her paintings of miniature objects like the dead baby finch in plate 9, the scale of the painting both magnifies the death of the bird by framing it as art and diminishes it by making its smallness into a felt quality. The deployment of scale, here and in the seascapes, makes relevance relational and contingent but also turns the still life into something queer, into a limit, a repudiation of duration, longevity, versatility. Bamber captures the thing in its moment of decline or expiration, documenting not just death but the death of an illusion. The painting's title, *I'll Give You Something to Cry About (Dead Baby Finch)*, marries melancholia (the death of the bird) to extreme realism (other things are more important), and it drains out the potential sentiment of the painting, conjured by the subject matter and the small scale, replacing it with precise depiction. The realism of the depiction of the dead, and ugly, bird introduces the viewer to nature most cruel rather than soft-pedaling the death of a young thing. The juxtaposition of the words *dead* and *baby* unites ends with beginnings and reminds us that sometimes an end is not a new beginning: an end is an end is an end.

Children and Failure

Lee Edelman's critique of heteronormative investments in the child dovetails nicely with Bamber's refusal of the affect associated with premature death. But Edelman always runs the risk of linking heteronormativity in some essential way to women, and, perhaps unwittingly, woman becomes the site of the unqueer: she offers life, while queerness links up with the death drive; she is aligned sentimentally with the child and with "goodness," while the gay man in particular leads the way to "something better" while "promising absolutely nothing." Like Renton in *Trainspotting*, Edelman's negativity has a profoundly apolitical tone to it, and so to conclude this chapter I want to discuss the queerness that circulates quite openly in mainstream children's cinema with clear political commitments.

Mainstream films marketed to children produce, almost accidentally, plenty of perverse narratives of belonging, relating, and evolving, and they often associate these narratives with some sense of the politics of success and failure. Rather than be surprised by the presence of patently queer characters and narratives in mainstream kids' films and by the easy affiliation with failure and disappointment, we should recognize the children's animated feature as a genre that has to engage the attentions of immature desiring subjects and which does so by appealing to a wide range of perverse embodiments and relations. Rather than protesting the presence of queer characters in these films, as one *Village Voice* reviewer did in relation to *Shrek 2*, we should use them to disrupt idealized and saccharine myths about children, sexuality, and innocence and imagine new versions of maturation, *Bildung*, and growth that do not depend upon the logic of succession and success.

Mainstream teen comedies and children's animated features are replete with fantasies of otherness and difference, alternative embodiment, group affiliations, and eccentric desires. In many of these "queer fairy tales" romance gives way to friendship, individuation gives way to collectivity, and "successful" heterosexual coupling is upended, displaced, and challenged by queer contact: princes turn into frogs rather than vice versa, ogres refuse to become beautiful, and characters regularly choose collectivity over domesticity. Almost all of these films foreground temporality itself and favor models of nonlinear and non-Oedipal development and disrupted and often forgotten histories. Repetition is privileged over sequence; fairy tale time (long, long ago) and mythic space (far, far away) form the fantastical backdrop for properly adolescent or childish and very often patently queer ways of life. So while children's films like *Babe*, *Chicken Run*, *Finding Nemo*, and *Shrek* are often hailed as children's fare that adults can enjoy, they are in fact children's films made in full acknowledgment of the unsentimental, amoral, and antiteleological narrative desires of children. *Adults* are the viewers who demand sentiment, progress, and closure; children, these films recognize, could care less. Just to illustrate my point about these queer fairy tales as both exciting ways of staging queer time and radical new imaginings of community and association, I want to point to a few common political themes in these films and to note the abundance of explicitly queer characters within them.

Queer fairy tales are often organized around heroes who are in some way "different" and whose difference is offensive to some larger community: Shrek is an ogre forced to live far away from judgmental villagers; Babe is an orphaned pig who thinks he is a sheepdog; and Nemo is a motherless fish with a deformed fin. Each "disabled" hero has to fight off or compete with a counterpart who represents wealth, health, success, and perfection.[5] While these narratives of difference could easily serve to deliver a tidy moral lesson about learning to accept yourself, each links the struggle of the rejected individual to larger struggles of the dispossessed. In Shrek, for example, the ogre becomes a freedom fighter for the refugee fairy tale figures whom Lord Farquaad ("Fuck wad," a.k.a. Bush) has kicked off his land; in Chicken Run the chickens band together to overthrow the evil Tweedy farmers and to save themselves from exploitation; in Babe the sheep rise up to resist an authoritarian sheepdog; and in Finding Nemo Nemo leads a fish rebellion against the fishermen.

Each film makes explicit the connection between queerness and this joining of the personal and the political: monstrosity in Shrek, disability in Finding Nemo, and species dysphoria in Babe become figurations of the pernicious effects of exclusion, abjection, and displacement in the name of family, home, and nation. The beauty of these films is that they do not fear failure, they do not favor success, and they picture children not as preadults figuring the future but as anarchic beings who partake in strange and inconsistent temporal logics. Children, as Edelman would remind us, have been deployed as part of a hetero-logic of futurity or as a link to positive political imaginings of alternatives. But there are alternative productions of the child that recognize in the image of the nonadult body a propensity to incompetence, a clumsy inability to make sense, a desire for independence from the tyranny of the adult, and a total indifference to adult conceptions of success and failure. Edelman's negative critique strands queerness between two equally unbearable options (futurity and positivity in opposition to nihilism and negation). Can we produce generative models of failure that do not posit two equally bleak alternatives?

Renton, Johnny Rotten, Ginger, Dory, and Babe, like those athletes who finish fourth, remind us that there is something powerful in being wrong, in losing, in failing, and that all our failures combined might just be enough, if we practice them well, to bring down the winner. Let's leave success and its achievement to the Republicans, to the corporate managers of the world, to the winners of reality TV shows, to married couples, to SUV drivers. The concept of practicing failure perhaps prompts us to discover our inner dweeb, to be underachievers, to fall short, to get distracted, to take a detour, to find a limit, to lose our way, to forget, to avoid mastery, and, with Walter Benjamin, to recognize that "empathy with the victor invariably benefits the rulers" (Benjamin, 1969: 256). All losers are the heirs of those who lost before them. Failure loves company.

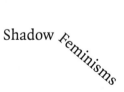
It goes without saying that to be among the callous, the cynical, the un-
believers, is to be among the winners, for those who have lost are never
hardened to their loss; they feel it deeply, always, into eternity.
—Jamaica Kincaid, *Autobiography of My Mother*

Utopias have always entailed disappointments and failures.
—Saidiya Hartman, *Lose Your Mother*

Between patriarchy and imperialism, subject-constitution and object-
formation, the figure of the woman disappears, not into a pristine noth-
ingness, but into a violent shuttling which is the displaced figuration
of the "third-world" woman caught between tradition and modernity.
—Gayatri Chakravorty Spivak, "Can the Subaltern Speak?"

In chapter 2 I proposed forgetfulness as an interruption to generational modes of transmission that ensure the continuity of
ideas, family lines, and normativity itself. While generational
logics and temporalities extend the status quo in a way that favors dominant groups, generationality for oppressed groups can
also indicate a different kind of history, a history associated with
loss and debt. In relation to the lineage of an African America
that begins in slavery, Saidiya Hartman in *Lose Your Mother* suggests, "The only sure inheritance passed from one generation to
the next was this loss and it defined the tribe. A philosopher had
once described it as an identity produced by negation" (2008:
103). Hartman's title indicates a loss that has always already

happened for African Americans, but it also argues against a simple gene-alogical account of history that stretches back in time through the family line. Losing one's mother, as we saw in relation to *Finding Nemo* and *50 First Dates*, is not simply "careless," as Oscar Wilde might say; it actually enables a relation to other models of time, space, place, and connection.

Beginning with the injunction "Lose your mother" and building toward a conclusion that will advocate a complete dismantling of self, I explore a feminist politics that issues not from a doing but from an un-doing, not from a being or becoming women but from a refusal to be or to become woman as she has been defined and imagined within West-ern philosophy. I will trace broken mother-daughter bonds toward an anti-Oedipal feminism that is nonetheless not a Deleuzean body without organs. This feminism, a feminism grounded in negation, refusal, pas-sivity, absence, and silence, offers spaces and modes of unknowing, fail-ing, and forgetting as part of an alternative feminist project, a shadow feminism which has nestled in more positivist accounts and unraveled their logics from within. This shadow feminism speaks in the language of self-destruction, masochism, an antisocial femininity, and a refusal of the essential bond of mother and daughter that ensures that the daughter inhabits the legacy of the mother and in doing so reproduces her relation-ship to patriarchal forms of power.

The tension between memory and forgetting as explored in chapter 3 tends to be distinctly Oedipal, familial, and generational. Are there other models of generation, temporality, and politics available to queer culture and feminism? The Oedipal frame has stifled all kinds of other models for thinking about the evolution of feminist and queer politics. From women's studies professors who think of their students as "daughters" to next wave feminists who see earlier activists as dowdy and antiquated mothers, Oedipal dynamics and their familial metaphors snuff out the potential future of new knowledge formations. Many women's studies departments around the country currently struggle with the messy and even ugly legacy of Oedipal models of generationality. In some of these departments the Oedipal dynamics are also racialized and sexualized, and so an older generation of mostly white women might be simultaneously hiring and holding at bay a younger generation of (often queer) women of color. The whole model of "passing down" knowledge from mother to daughter is quite clearly invested in white, gendered, and hetero nor-mativity; indeed the system inevitably stalls in the face of these racial-ized and heterosexualized scenes of difference. And while the "mothers" become frustrated with the apparent unwillingness of the women they have hired to continue their line of inquiry, the "daughters" struggle to make the older women see that regulatory systems are embedded in the paradigms they so insistently want to pass on. The pervasive model of women's studies as a mother-daughter dynamic ironically resembles patriarchal systems in that it casts the mother as the place of history, tradition, and memory and the daughter as the inheritor of a static system which she must either accept without changing or reject completely.

While Virginia Woolf's famous line about women from A Room of One's Own, "We think back through our mothers if we are women," has been widely interpreted as the founding statement of a new aesthetic lineage that passes through the mother and not the father, the crucial point of the formulation is the conditional phrase (1929: 87). In fact "if we are women" implies that if we do not think back through our mothers, then we are not women, and this broken line of thinking and unbeing of the woman unexpectedly offers a way out of the reproduction of woman as the other to man from one generation to the next. The texts that I examine in this chapter refuse to think back through the mother; they actively and passively lose the mother, abuse the mother, love, hate, and destroy the mother, and in the process they produce a theoretical and imaginative space that is "not woman" or that can be occupied only by unbecoming women.

Psychoanalysis situates the figure of the woman as an incomprehensible, irrational, and even impossible identity. Freud's famous question "What do women want?" is not simply evidence that, as Simone de Beauvoir famously commented, "Freud never showed much interest in the destiny of women" (1989: 39); rather it asks of women why they would want to occupy the place of castration, lack, and otherness from one generation to the next (Jones 1957: 421). Answering the question of what men might want is quite simple in a system that favors male masculinity; what women want and get from the same system is a much more complex question. If, as Freud asserts, the little girl must reconcile herself to the fate of a femininity defined as a failed masculinity, then that failure to be masculine must surely harbor its own productive potential. What do women want? Moreover, how has the desire to be a woman come to be associated definitively with masochism, sacrifice, self-subjugation, and unbecoming? How might we read these avenues of desire and selfhood as something other than failed masculinity and the end of desire?

In this chapter I chart the genealogy of an antisocial, anti-Oedipal, antihumanist, and counterintuitive feminism that arises out of queer, postcolonial, and black feminisms and that thinks in terms of the negation of the subject rather than her formation, the disruption of lineage rather than its continuation, the undoing of self rather than its activation. In this queer feminist genealogy, which could be said to stretch from Spivak's meditations on female suicide in "Can the Subaltern Speak?" (1988) to Saidiya Hartman's idea of a politics that exceeds the social conditions of its enunciation in *Scenes of Subjection* (1997), we might find the narratives of this version of feminism in Toni Morrison's ghosts or among Jamaica Kincaid's antiheroines, and we must track it through territories of silence, stubbornness, self-abnegation, and sacrifice. Ultimately we find no feminist subject but only subjects who cannot speak, who refuse to speak; subjects who unravel, who refuse to cohere; subjects who refuse "being" where being has already been defined in terms of a self-activating, self-knowing, liberal subject. If we refuse to become women, we might ask, what happens to feminism? Or, to pose the question another way: Can we find feminist frameworks capable of recognizing the political project articulated in the form of refusal? The politics of refusal emerges in its most potent form from anticolonial and antiracist texts and challenges colonial authority by absolutely rejecting the role of the colonized within what Walter Mignolo, citing Anibal Quijano, has called "a coloniality of power" (2005: 6).

Postcolonial feminists from Spivak to Saba Mahmood have shown how prescriptive Western feminist theories of agency and power, freedom and resistance tend to be and have proposed alternative ways of thinking about self and action that emerge from contexts often rejected outright by feminism. While Mahmood focuses on Islamic women engaged in religious practices in the women's mosque movement in Egypt to flesh out a critique of feminist theories of agency, in her famous essay "Can the Subaltern Speak?" Spivak uses the example of nineteenth-century bride suicide (after the death of the husband) to demonstrate a mode of being woman that was incomprehensible within a normative feminist framework. Both theorists argue in terms of a "grammar of concepts," to use Mahmood's term, and both consider speech to be something other than the conventional feminist trope of breaking silence. At the heart of Mahmood's book, *The Politics of Piety: The Islamic Revival and the Feminist Subject* is a concept of woman that does not presume the universality of desires for freedom and autonomy and for whom resistance to patriarchal traditions may not be the goal (2005: 180). At the center of Spivak's essay is a notion of womanhood that exceeds the Western feminist formulation of female life. Spivak ends her essay on the perils of intellectual attempts to represent oppressed peoples with an extended meditation on suttee, and Mahmood ends her book with an exploration of the meaning of feminine piety within Islam. Both theorists use patently antifeminist acts and activities to point to the limits of a feminist theory that already presumes the form that agency must take.

Spivak explores the British attempt in 1829 to abolish Hindu widow burning in relation to the self-representation of colonialism as benevolent intervention and places this argument against the claim advanced by nativist Indians that sati must be respected as a practice because these women who lost their husbands actually *wanted* to die. She uses sati to illustrate her claim that colonialism articulates itself as "white men saving brown women from brown men," but also to mark the complicity of Western feminism in this formulation. In a move that echoes Spivak's counterintuitive break from even poststructuralist feminisms, Mahmood explores women in the mosque movement and their commitment to piety in order to ask, "Does the category of resistance impose a teleology of progressive politics on the analytics of power—a teleology that makes it hard for us to see and understand forms of being and action that are not necessarily encapsulated by the narrative of subversion and reinscription of norms?" (2005: 9).

"Can the Subaltern Speak?" sets up a contradiction between different modes of representation within which an intellectual proposes to speak for an oppressed other. Spivak accuses Foucault and Deleuze as well as Western feminism of sneaking a heroic individualism in the back door of discursive critique. "Neither Deleuze nor Foucault," she writes, "seems aware that the intellectual within socialized capital, brandishing concrete experience, can help consolidate the international division of labor" (1988: 275). For Spivak, intellectuals, like poststructuralist feminist theorists for Mahmood, by imagining themselves to be a transparent vector for the exposure of ideological contradictions, cannot account for their own impact on the processes of domination and instead always imagine themselves in the heroic place of the individual who knows better than the oppressed masses about whom they theorize. The very notion of representation, Spivak claims, in terms of both a theory of economic exploitation and an ideological function, depends upon the production of "heroes, paternal proxies and agents of power" (279) and harbors "the possibility that the intellectual is complicit in the persistent constitution of the Other as the self's shadow" (280).

This idea, that intellectuals construct an otherness to "save" in order to fortify a sovereign notion of self, applies also to liberal feminism. In the context of the Hindu widow's suicide, for example, the Western feminist can see only the workings of extraordinary patriarchy, and she also believes in a benevolent British colonialism that steps in to stop a brutal and archaic ritual. For Spivak, feminism is complicit in the project of constructing the subaltern subject it wants to represent and then heroically casting itself as the subaltern's salvation. What if, Spivak seems to ask in her enigmatic final sentence, feminism was actually able to attend to the nativist claim that women who commit suttee actually *want* to die? She writes, "The female intellectual as an intellectual has a circumscribed task which she must not disown with a flourish" (308). Leaving aside the ambiguity of the double negative here ("must not disown"), the meaning of "female," "intellectual," and "circumscribed task" are all up for grabs, especially since Spivak has already contended that suttee makes an essential link between unbeing and femininity. This question clearly informs and influences Mahmood's question about whether we have become willfully blind to forms of agency that do not take the form of resistance. In her Derridean deconstructivist mode, Spivak is calling for a feminism that can claim not to speak for the subaltern or to demand that the subaltern speak in the active voice of Western feminism; instead she imagines a feminism born of a dynamic intellectual struggle with the fact that some women may desire their own destruction for really good political reasons, even if those politics and those reasons lie beyond the purview of the version of feminism for which we have settled. Spivak's call for a "female intellectual" who does not disown another version of womanhood, femininity, and feminism, indeed for any kind of intellectual who can learn how not to know the other, how not to sacrifice the other on behalf of his or her own sovereignty, is a call that has largely gone unanswered. It is this version of feminism that I seek to inhabit, a feminism that fails to save others or to replicate itself, a feminism that finds purpose in its own failure.

A more accessible text makes the very same point. In one of my favorite feminist texts of all time, the epic animated drama *Chicken Run*, the politically active and explicitly feminist bird Ginger is opposed in her struggle to inspire the birds to rise up by two other "feminist subjects." One is

15. Babs and Jane Horrocks, from *Chicken Run*. "Are those the only options?"

the cynic, Bunty, a hard-nosed fighter who rejects utopian dreams out of hand, and the other is Babs, voiced by Jane Horrocks, who sometimes gives voice to feminine naïveté and sometimes points to the absurdity of the political terrain as it has been outlined by the activist Ginger. Ginger says, for example, "We either die free chickens, or we die trying." Babs asks naïvely, "Are those the only choices?" Like Babs, and indeed like Spivak and Mahmood, I am proposing that feminists refuse the choices as offered—freedom in liberal terms or death—in order to think about a shadow archive of resistance, one that does not speak in the language of action and momentum but instead articulates itself in terms of evacuation, refusal, passivity, unbecoming, unbeing. This could be called an *antisocial feminism*, a form of feminism preoccupied with negativity and negation. As Roderick Ferguson puts it in a chapter titled "The Negations of Black Lesbian Feminism" in *Aberrations in Black*, "Negation not only points to the conditions of exploitation. It denotes the circumstances for critique and alternatives as well" (2005: 136–37). Building on the work of Hortense Spillers, Ferguson is trying to circumvent an "American" political grammar that insists upon placing liberation struggles within the same logic as the normative regimes against which they struggle. A different, anarchistic type of struggle requires a new grammar, possibly a new voice, potentially the passive voice.

When feminist freedoms, as Mahmood shows, require a humanistic investment in both the female subject and the fantasy of an active, autonomous, and self-activating individualism, we have to ask who the subjects and objects of feminism might be, and we need to remember that, as Spivak puts it, to speak on behalf of someone is also to "restore the sovereign subject within the theory that seems most to question it" (1988: 278). If speaking for a subject of feminism offers up choices that we, like Babs, are bound to question and refuse, then maybe a homeopathic refusal to speak serves the project of feminism better. Babs's sense that there must be more ways of thinking about political action or nonaction than doing or dying finds full theoretical confirmation in the work of theorists like Saidiya Hartman. Her investigations in Scenes of Subjection into the contradictions of emancipation for the newly freed slaves proposes not only that "liberty" as defined by the white racial state enacts new modes of imprisonment, but also that the very definitions of freedom and humanity within which abolitionists operated severely limited the ability of the former slaves to think social transformation in terms outside of the structure of racial terror. Hartman notes, "The longstanding and intimate affiliation of liberty and bondage made it impossible to envision freedom independent of constraint or personhood and autonomy separate from the sanctity of property and proprietal notions of self" (1997: 115). Accordingly where freedom was offered in terms of being propertied, placed, and productive, the former slave might choose "moving about" or roaming in order to experience the meaning of freedom: "As a practice, moving about accumulated nothing and it did not effect any reversals of power but indefatigably held onto the unrealizable—being free—by temporarily eluding the constraints of order. . . . Like stealing away, it was more symbolically redolent than materially transformative" (128). There are no simple comparisons to be made between former slaves and sexual minorities, but I want to join Hartman's deft revelations about the continuation of slavery by other means to Leo Bersani's, Lynda Hart's, and Heather Love's formulations of queer histories and subjectivities that are better described in terms of masochism, pain, and failure than in terms of mastery, pleasure, and heroic liberation.[1] Like Hartman's model of a freedom which imagines itself in terms of a not yet realized social order, so the maps of desire that render the subject incoherent, disorganized, and passive provide a better escape route than those that lead inexorably to fulfillment, recognition, and achievement.

Bersani names as "masochism" the counternarrative of sexuality that undergirds the propulsive, maturational, and linear story installed by psychoanalysis; he suggests that the heroic, organizing narrative defines sexuality as "an exchange of intensities between individuals," but the masochistic version constitutes a "condition of broken negotiations with the world, a condition in which others merely set off the self-shattering mechanism of masochistic jouissance" (1986: 41). It is this narrative that Heather Love turns to in *Feeling Backward*, when she examines "moments of failed or interrupted connection" or "broken intimacies" in order to take the impossibility of love "as a model for queer historiography" (2009: 24).

In what follows I propose a radical form of masochistic passivity that not only offers up a critique of the organizing logic of agency and subjectivity itself, but that also opts out of certain systems built around a dialectic between colonizer and colonized. Radical forms of passivity and masochism step out of the easy model of a transfer of femininity from mother to daughter and actually seek to destroy the mother-daughter bond altogether. For example, in the work of Jamaica Kincaid the colonized subject literally refuses her role as colonized by refusing to be anything at all. In *Autobiography of My Mother* (1997) the main character removes herself from a colonial order that makes sense of her as a daughter, a wife, and a mother by refusing to be any of these, even refusing the category of womanhood altogether. At the novel's beginning the first-person narrator tells of the coincidence of her birth and her mother's death and suggests that this primal loss means that "there was nothing standing between me and eternity. . . . At my beginning was this woman whose face I had never seen, but at my end there was nothing, no one between me and the black room of the world" (3). Obviously the loss of her mother and the "autobiography" of that mother that ensues is an allegorical tale of the loss of origins within the context of colonialism and the loss of telos that follows. But rather than nostalgically searching for her lost origins or purposefully creating her own telos, the narrator, Xuela Claudette Richardson, surrenders to a form of unbeing for which beginnings and ends have no meaning. With no past to learn from, no future can be imagined, and with a present tense that is entirely occupied by colonial figures, language, logics, and identities, the colonized self has two options: she can become part of the colonial story or she can refuse to be part of any story at all. Xuela chooses the latter: *Autobiography of My Mother* is the unstory of a woman who cannot be anything but the antithesis of the self that is demanded by colonialism. Xuela neither tells her own story of becoming, nor does she tell her mother's story; by appropriating her mother's unstory as her own she suggests that the colonized mind is passed down Oedipally from generation to generation and must be resisted through a certain mode of evacuation.

While Xuela's relationship to her mother is mediated by loss and longing, her relationship with her half-Scots, half-Caribbean policeman father is one of contempt and incomprehension. She despises his capitulation to colonialism, to the law, and to his own mixed heritage, and she tries, through the writing of this narrative, to root out his influence and inhabit completely the space of her absent Carib mother: "And so my mother and father then were a mystery to me; one through death, the other through the maze of living; one I had never seen, one I saw constantly" (41). Choosing death and absence over a colonized life, Xuela avoids becoming a mother herself; aborting a child, she avoids love, family, and intimacy and disconnects herself from all of those things that would define her. In her refusal of identity as such Xuela models a kind of necropolitical relation to colonialism: her refusal to be is also a refusal to perform the role of other within a system that demands her subjugation. "Whatever I was told to hate," she says, "I loved most" (32).

In an interview about *Autobiography of My Mother* Kincaid was told, "Your characters seem to be against most things that are good, yet they have no reason to act this way—they express a kind of negative freedom. Is this the only freedom available to the poor and powerless?"[2] Kincaid answered, "I think in many ways the problem that my writing would have with an American reviewer is that Americans find difficulty very hard to take. They are inevitably looking for a happy ending. Perversely, I will not give the happy ending. I think life is difficult and that's that. I am not at all—absolutely not at all—interested in the pursuit of happiness. I am not interested in the pursuit of positivity. I am interested in pursuing a truth, and the truth often seems to be not happiness but its opposite" (1997: 1). Kincaid's novels do indeed withhold happy endings, and she adds a fine shading to the narrative of colonialism by creating characters who can never thrive, never love, and never create precisely because colonialism has removed the context within which those things would make sense. Kincaid concludes the interview by saying, "I feel it's my business to make everyone a little less happy."

Kincaid's commitment to a kind of negative life, a life lived by a colonized character who refuses purpose and who as a result leaves the reader unsettled, disturbed, and discomforted, represents a Fanonian refusal to blindly persist in the occupation of categories of being that simply round out the colonial project. Where a colonized subject finds happiness, Kincaid, following Fanon, seems to say, he or she confirms the benevolence of the colonial project. Where a colonized woman bears a child and passes on her legacy to that child, Kincaid insists, the colonial project can spread virus-like from one generation to the next. Refusing to operate as the transfer point for transgenerational colonization, Xuela inhabits another kind of feminism, again a feminism that does not resist through an active war on colonialism, but a mode of femininity that self-destructs and in doing so brings the edifice of colonial rule down one brick at a time.

But is this passively political mode of unbecoming reserved for the colonized and the obviously oppressed? What happens if a woman or feminine subject who occupies a privileged relation to dominant culture occupies her own undoing? In Elfride Jelinek's novel *The Piano Teacher* (2009) the refusal to be is played at the other end of the scale of power. Jelinek is an Austrian author who was not very well known in 2004, when she won the Nobel Prize for Literature. Her novels, generally speaking, dissect Austrian national character and depict the inner workings of the family, domesticity, and marriage in postwar Austria as a seething mess of resentments, bitterness, cramped intimacies, and vicious incestuous love in the wake of fascism. In the process of ripping apart the family she implicitly and explicitly takes aim at a nation that is far from done with its Nazi past and with the small-town anti-Semitism and racism that fueled it. Jelinek's father, a Czech Jewish chemist, managed to survive the Holocaust, but many members of his family died. Her mother, a Roman Catholic from an important Viennese family, encouraged her daughter to become a pianist from an early age, but Jelinek instead became a writer of deliberately ugly depictions of an aspirational middle class. Like Kincaid's novel, Jelinek's *The Piano Teacher* documents the destructiveness of the mother-daughter bond. Needless to say, Austrians were not terribly pleased at her selection by the Nobel committee, and her works regularly received poor reviews in both Europe and the U.S. A member of the committee, Knut Ahnlund, even left the Academy in protest, describing Jelinek's work as "whining, unenjoyable public pornography" and "a mass of text shoveled together without artistic structure." He also claimed that her selection for the Nobel Prize "has not only done irreparable damage to all progressive forces, it has also confused the general view of literature as an art."[3] Jelinek did not attend her own Nobel Prize ceremony but sent a video message in her stead. It is widely assumed that she skipped the ceremony on account of her agoraphobia.

In *The Piano Teacher* Erika Kohut, the main character, is an unmarried Austrian woman in her thirties living with her mother in Vienna after the Second World War and giving piano lessons in her spare time at the Vienna Conservatory. She colludes with her mother in a certain fantasy about music, about Austria, about high culture, and about cultural superiority. On many days Erika leaves the house and indeed the bedroom that she shares with her controlling mother and wanders the city, as if searching for some way out of the claustrophobic life of professional boredom and petty quarrels with her mother. On some nights she visits peep shows in the Turkish part of town or follows amorous couples to their cars and furtively watches their sexual struggles. Such is her life until a new student comes to her class, the handsome young Walter Klemmer. Klemmer sees his prim teacher as a potential conquest and begins to romance her, and soon they begin a secret sexual relationship.

When Erika meets Klemmer it seems as if the narrative of incestuous mother-daughter collusion must surely reach its end and cede ground to a more appropriate intergenerational kind of desire, the desire of the young man for his older teacher. Klemmer's courtship of Erika consists of his trying to charm her while she insults him in return. He asks her on a date; she "feels a growing repulsion" (79). He walks her and her mother home; she wishes he would leave them alone. When finally the brash young man does head off into the Vienna evening, Erika returns home to her maternal cocoon and locks herself in the bathroom to cut away at her private flesh with a shaving razor.

When Klemmer and she begin an explicitly sexual relationship, Erika writes him a letter demanding that he sexually abuse and mistreat her, break her down, starve her, and neglect her. She wants to be destroyed and she wants to destroy her own students in the process. From Klemmer, Erika demands sadistic cruelty: "I will writhe like a worm in your cruel bonds, in which you will have me lie for hours on end, and you'll keep me in all sorts of different positions, hitting or kicking me, even whipping me!" (216). Erika's letter says she wants to be dimmed out under him, snuffed out: her well-rooted displays of obedience require greater degrees of intensity. Her letter is, as Klemmer puts it, "an inventory of pain" (217), a catalogue of punishments that he is sure no one could endure. She wants the young man to crush her, torment her, mock her, gag her, threaten her, devour her, piss on her, and ultimately destroy her. Klemmer reads the letter in her presence, refuses outright to meet her demands, and withdraws into the night, only to return later to obey the letter in its direction to dismantle and abuse her.

While the narrator of Kincaid's novel pulls herself and her mother back from the narratives that colonialism would tell about them, Jelinek exposes her mother-daughter duo to intense and violent scrutiny and locks them in a destructive and sterile incestuous dance that will end only with their deaths. The novel ends with the protagonist fighting with and then kissing her aged mother in their shared bed and then wounding a young female student who is preparing for a recital. She then wounds herself with a knife, stabbing herself, not trying to kill herself exactly but to continue to chip away at the part of her that remains Austrian, complicit, fascist, and conforming. Erika's passivity is a way of refusing to be a channel for a persistent strain of fascist nationalism, and her masochism or self-violation indicates her desire to kill within herself the versions of fascism that are folded into being — through taste, through emotional responses, through love of country, love of music, love of her mother.

Cutting

Cutting is a feminist aesthetic proper to the project of female unbecoming. As Erika Kohut walks along the streets of Vienna at the end of The Piano Teacher she drips blood onto the sidewalk. The cut she has made in her shoulder, which repeats a number of other cuts she has applied to her own skin and genitalia at other times, represents her attempt to remake herself as something other than a repository for her mother, her country, and her class, but it also crafts a version of woman that is messy, bloody, porous, violent, and self-loathing, a version that mimics a kind of fascist ethos of womanhood by transferring the terms of Nazi misogyny to the female body in literal and terrifying ways. Erika's masochism turns her loathing for her mother and her Austrianness back onto herself. With the notable exception of work by Lynda Hart in Between the Body and the Flesh: Performing Sadomasochism (1998) and Gayle Rubin's early essays on s/m, power, and feminism, masochism is an underused way of considering the relationship between self and other, self and technology, self and power in queer feminism. This is curious given how often performance art of the 1960s and 1970s presented extreme forms of self-punishment, discipline, and evacuation in order to dramatize new relations between body, self, and power. It may be illustrative to turn to Freud, who refers to masochism as a form of femininity and a kind of flirtation with death; masochism, he says, is a byproduct of the unsuccessful repression of the death instinct to which a libidinal impulse has been attached. While the libido tends to ward off the death drive through a "will to power," a desire for mastery, and an externalization of erotic energy, sometimes libidinal energies are given over to destabilization, unbecoming, and unraveling. This is what Leo Bersani refers to as "self-shattering," a shadowy sexual impulse that most people would rather deny or sublimate. If taken seriously, unbecoming may have its political equivalent in an anarchic refusal of coherence and proscriptive forms of agency.

Following up on the act of cutting as a masochistic will to eradicate the body, I want to use the example of collage, a cut-and-paste genre, to find another realm of aesthetic production dominated by a model of radical passivity and unbeing. Collage precisely references the spaces in between and refuses to respect the boundaries that usually delineate self from other, art object from museum, and the copy from the original. In this respect, as well as in many others, collage (from the French coller, to paste or glue) seems feminist and queer. Collage has been used by many female artists, from Hannah Hoch to Kara Walker, to bind the threat of castration to the menace of feminist violence and both to the promise of transformation, not through a positive production of the image but through a negative destruction of it that nonetheless refuses to relinquish pleasure.

To apprehend the violence implied by collage, one only has to think of the work of Kara Walker, the African American artist who has used cut paper and the silhouette form to convey the atrociously violent landscape of the American racial imagination. By maintaining a constant tension between the elements of the work, the collage asks us to consider the full range of our experience of power—both productive power, power for, but also negative power, or power to unbecome. Hijacking the decorative silhouette form, Walker glues life-size black silhouettes to white gallery walls to produce a puppet show version of the sexual life of slavery. In the black figures and the white spaces in between she manages to convey both the myriad ways that the human body can be opened up, ripped apart, penetrated, turned inside out, hung upside down, split, smashed, fractured, and pulverized and the nearly limitless archive of the human violent imaginary. Despite the flatness of the silhouette form, she creates an illusion of depth, sometimes by projecting light onto the dioramas she creates but also by making the whole gallery a canvas and then gluing cutouts, sketches, and paintings all over its walls. In some pieces she also writes letters to her detractors and enemies and refuses the reading of her work as simply confirming stereotypes.

The array of discourse that chatters from the walls of the museum and that dialogues with the silence of the black characters in the cut pieces implies that institutions of art are themselves catalogues of both racial violence and the erasure of such violence through the theoretical association of art with beauty. The title of one of her shows, "Kara Walker: My Complement, My Enemy, My Oppressor, My Love," names the sadomasochistic terrain of speech and silence and makes clear that in a world engendered by sexual violence and its bastard offspring, a world where the enemy and the oppressor is also the lover, the victim is not choosing between action and passivity, freedom and death, but survival and desire. In such a world sex is the name for war by other means. From the horrified responses to her work (charges mainly of creating a new archive of racist imagery), many of which are pulled into her textual collages, Walker draws out the anxieties that she also represents. Using art as bait and deploying the female body in particular as a site for the negative projection of racial and colonial fantasy is simply a modern technology. But using the same technology to turn racism and sexism back upon themselves like a funhouse mirror is a part of what I am calling feminist negation. In fact in 1964 Yoko Ono used her own body as a battleground to draw out the sadistic impulses that bourgeois audiences harbor toward the notion of woman. Her performance "Cut Piece" is not a collage, but the elements of the performance—cutting, submitting, reversing the relations between figure and ground, audience and performer—do conform to the definition of collage that I am using here. What is more, in the dynamics that Ono explores between stillness and motion, production and reception, body and clothing, gender and violence, she allows for a complex and fascinating discourse on feminism and masochism to emerge at the site of the cut or castration itself. In her nine-minute-long performance she sits on stage while members of the audience come up and cut off pieces of her clothing. The act of cutting is thus assigned to the audience rather than to the artist, and the artist's body becomes the canvas while the authorial gesture is dispersed across the nameless, sadistic gestures that disrobe her and leave her open to and unprotected from the touch of the other. As the performance unfolds, more and more men than women come to the stage, and they become more and more aggressive about cutting her clothing until she is left, seminude, hands over her breasts, her supposed castration, emotional discomfort, vulnerability, and passivity fully on display. How can we think about femininity and feminism in the context of masochism, gender, racialized display, spectatorship, and temporality?

In a brilliant analysis of "Cut Piece" Julia Bryan Wilson acknowledges the reading of Ono's performance within a meditation on female masochism, but, she proposes, most often these readings fix Ono's mute and still female body within a closed system of female submission and male aggression. As she puts it, "There is little possibility in these interpretations that the invitation Ono proffers might be positive—no space for "Cut Piece" to be a gift, a gesture of reparation, or a ritual of remembrance" (2003: 103). Locating Ono's peformative offering of her clothes, her body, and her silence against the backdrop of the bombings of Hiroshima and Nagasaki, Wilson places the piece within a global imaginary. Calling it a "reciprocal ballet" in terms of its gesture of generosity and a "tense pantomime" in terms of the way Ono stages her own vulnerability and brings her flesh close to strangers wielding scissors, Wilson refuses to sever Ono's remarkable performance from either postwar Japanese art or the rest of her oeuvre. Nor is Wilson content to rescue the piece from its own self-destruction or consign it to what she calls "solipsistic masochism" (116). Instead she situates the work firmly within the activity of witnessing and casts Ono as a master of the art of sacrifice. I am absolutely convinced by Wilson's reading of "Cut Piece," and I see this reading as definitive on many levels. And yet, while I want to build upon the situating of Ono's work within the context of photographs of torn clothing taken after the atomic blasts in Japan in 1945, I also want to return to the ambivalent model of female selfhood that the performance inhabits.

Wilson notes the strange temporality of "Cut Piece" and the ambivalent optimism in the gesture of allowing people to cut off pieces of one's clothing as souvenirs; in this performance and in Ono's "Promise Piece" (1992), where a vase is smashed and its shards handed out, Wilson points out, there is always the possibility, indeed the probability that the fragments of the whole will never be reunited. I would emphasize this commitment to the fragment over any fantasy of future wholeness, and I want to locate the smashing gestures and the cutting gestures in Ono's work in relation to this other antisocial feminism that refuses conventional modes of femininity by refusing to remake, rebuild, or reproduce and that dedicates itself completely and ferociously to the destruction of self and other.

Wilson notes the tendency to pair "Cut Piece" with Marina Abramović's Rhythm 0 (1974) and Chris Burden's Shoot (1971), but she quickly dismisses Abramović's performance as unscripted and marked by "complete surrender" and is similarly critical of Burden's work, which she sees as an attempt to "manage and engineer aggression" and as "a far cry from the peaceful wishes of Ono and Lennon" (117). Male masochism certainly stakes out a territory very different from female performances of unraveling. While the male masochist inhabits a kind of heroic antiheroism by refusing social privilege and offering himself up Christ-like as a martyr for the cause, the female masochist's performance is far more complex and offers a critique of the very ground of the human. A remarkable amount of performance art—feminist and otherwise—from the experimental scene of the 1960s and 1970s explored this fertile ground of masochistic collapse. Kathy O'Dell (1998) writes about masochistic performance art of the 1970s as a performed refusal of wholeness and a demonstration of Deleuze's claim that "the masochist's apparent obedience conceals a criticism and a provocation" (Deleuze 1971: 77). O'Dell's psychoanalytic account of masochism provides a nice summary of the genre and places pieces by Burden, Cathy Opie, and others into interesting conversation with one another, but ultimately she wants to make masochism into something from which we can learn, through which we can recognize the invisible contracts we make with violence, and with which we can negotiate relations with others. But there is a problem with trying to bind masochistic critiques of the subject to humanistic renegotiations with selfhood. In many ways this reconfiguring of masochism as a way of grappling with and coming to terms with violence rewrites the dilemma I identified at the start of this chapter in terms of a feminism that needs to rescue other "women" from their own destructive tendencies. Performances like "Cut Piece" and Rhythm 0 but also like Faith Wilding's Waiting (1972) do not necessarily want to rescue the woman; rather they hang her out to dry as woman.

Obviously none of these performances immediately suggests a "feminist" act, but they instead make feminism into an ongoing commentary on fragmentariness, submission, and sacrifice. Ono's dismantling performance presses us to ask about the kind of self that comes undone for an audience in nine minutes. Is such an act, and such a model of self, feminist? Can we think about this refusal of self as an antiliberal act, a revolutionary statement of pure opposition that does not rely upon the liberal gesture of defiance but accesses another lexicon of power and speaks another language of refusal? If we understand radical passivity as an antisocial mode with some connection to the anti-authorial statements made within postcolonial women's theory and fiction, we can begin to glimpse its politics. In a liberal realm where the pursuit of happiness, as Jamaica Kincaid might say, is both desirable and mandatory and where certain formulations of self (as active, voluntaristic, choosing, propulsive) dominate the political sphere, radical passivity may signal another kind of refusal: the refusal quite simply to be. While many feminists, from Simone de Beauvoir to Monique Wittig to Jamaica Kincaid, have cast the project of "becoming woman" as one in which the woman can only be complicit in a patriarchal order, feminist theorists in general have not turned to masochism and passivity as potential alternatives to liberal formulations of womanhood. Carol Clover (1993) famously cast male masochism as one explanation for the popularity of horror films among teenage boys, and we might similarly cast female masochism as the willing giving over of the self to the other, to power; in a performance of radical passivity we witness the willingness of the subject to actually come undone, to dramatize unbecoming for the other so that the viewer does not have to witness unbecoming as a function of her own body. Here Joseph Roach's (1996) formulation of culture as a combination of projection, substitution, and effigy making comes into play. Indeed radical passivity could describe certain versions of lesbian femininity. Queer theory under the influence of Judith Butler's work on the "lesbian phallus" argues for the recognition of the potentiality of masculine power in a female form, but this still leaves the feminine lesbian unexplained and lost to an antiphallic modality.

In fact if one form of phallic queerness has been defined by the representation of the body as hybrid and assembled, then another takes as its object the dis-appearance of the body altogether. In an explicitly queer use of the collage, that tension between the rebellious energy of gender variance and the quiet revolt of queer femininity comes to the fore. J. A. Nicholls's work has mostly involved figuration and has evolved around the production of work in stages, the building of an aesthetic environment through representational strata that become progressively more flat and progressively more painterly at the same time. This movement works precisely against the three-dimensional aspirations of collage which build up from the canvas and transform the dialogue between paint and canvas into a multivocal discourse through the importation of "external" materials. In her process Nicholls first creates, Frankenstein-like, a small collage of myriad parts and materials of the figure she wants to

16. J. A. Nicholls, *all of my days*, 2006. Oil/acrylic on canvas, 145 cm × 110 cm. Printed with permission of J. A. Nicholls.

paint. Next she paints a version of the collage onto large canvases, trying to capture the quality of the pieced-together materials in an assemblage of moving and static parts, anatomically correct limbs and cartoon-like stumps, motion and stillness, identity and facelessness. Some of her figures recline like classical nudes, but many of them, gender-ambiguous figures all, are suspended in time, space, water, or paint. They are glued together, the sum of their parts, and they twist and turn in and out of wholeness, legibility, and sense.

In new work Nicholls turns to landscapes, emptying the landscape of figures altogether, turning from gender variance as assemblage to queer femininity as startling absence. What had been a backdrop becomes a stage; what was ground becomes figure; what had been secondary becomes primary. The landscape emptied of figures, when considered in relation to her paintings of figures, still does speak about figuration. Only here figuration, as in Kara Walker's art, is absence, dis-appearance, and illegibility. In *Here and Now* the landscape is graphic and dramatic, vivid and emotional (see plate 10). The figure's psyche is spread horizontally across the meeting of ocean and land rather than encased vertically in an upright body, and the relationships between inside and outside, the primary drama staged by the collage, are cast here as sky and land, vegetation and waves, blue and green, with a barely transparent fence marking the nonboundary between the two. Time and space themselves collide at this boundary, here and now, and the immediacy and presence of the emotional landscape announce themselves in the startlingly dynamic waves in the middle ground. In *Higher Ground* and *New Story* the canvases are marked more by stillness and fixity, and the landscape becomes much more of a backdrop waiting for a figure (see plates 11 and 12). These new paintings attempt to represent femininity as a blurring of the female form with the natural landscape and as a violent cutting out of the figure altogether. The surreal and often hyperartificial landscapes represent queer femininity as a refusal of conventional womanhood and a disidentification with the logic of gender variance as the other of normativity.

Appropriately, given the new subject matter, Nicholls also uses a new form of collage that challenges the viewer to consider the meaning of collage in the age of digital graphics. She scans a photograph into the computer, where she uses Photoshop to cut and paste different elements and materials onto the photo. She then prints the image and paints from it onto a canvas. The three media—photography, digital imaging, and painting—become sites for elaborate and complex digital collage. Whereas in traditional collage by Picasso and others we might find newspaper pieces pasted onto paint, here we find graphic elements grafted through software onto a photograph and then transformed into a painted canvas.

In a contemporary fifty-five-minute performance piece that picks up where these artists left off, titled "America the Beautiful," Nao Bustamante combines avant-garde performance with burlesque, circus act, and the antics of an escape artist. The solo performance marries banality and the rigors of feminine adornment, to high-wire tension, the trembling and wobbly ascent of the bound body up a ladder, and combines the discipline of physical performance with the spectacle of embodied uncertainty. The audience laughs uncomfortably throughout the performance, watching as Bustamante binds her naked body with clear packing tape and clumsily applies makeup and a raggedy blond wig. Sentimental music wafts smoothly in the background and conflicts noisily with the rough performance of femininity that Bustamante stages. In her blond wig and makeup, with her flesh pulled tight, she displays the demands of racialized feminine beauty; to confirm the danger of such beauty, she bends and sways precariously as she dons high heels atop a small ladder. Finally she ascends a much larger ladder carrying a sparkler and threatening at any moment to fall from her perch.

This performance, along with a number of others in Bustamante's portfolio, confirm her as what José Esteban Muñoz (2006) has called a "vulnerability artist." In his inspired essay on Bustamante's performance practice, Muñoz calls attention to the ways Bustamante "engages and re-imagines what has been a history of violence, degradation and compulsory performance" (2006: 194); her engagement with the dangers attached to the subject position of "woman of color" make her vulnerable and infuse her performances with the frisson of potential failure, collapse, and crisis. At a poignant moment in *America the Beautiful*, for example, while perched precariously atop a large tripod ladder, Bustamante turns her back to the audience and uses the stage lights to create a puppet show with her hands. The flickering shadows that she creates on the backdrop refuse to cohere into another theatrical space and merely mirror her blurry status as puppet, mannequin, and doll. But the moment is compelling because it reveals the mode in which Bustamante becomes her own puppet, ventriloquizes herself, constructs her body as a meeting point for violent discourses of beauty, profit, coherence, race, success.

In an interview with Muñoz, Bustamante addresses the improvisational quality of her work and clearly and brilliantly engages both the thesis that there is no such thing as improvisation in performance and the idea that "fresh space" always exists. Something of the balance between rehearsed improvisation and the unpredictability of "fresh space" marks her work as a rigorous refusal of mastery. Muñoz terms this positively as "amateurism," in relation to the ladder performance in "America the Beautiful" in particular, and Bustamante concurs but elaborates: "The work that I do is about not knowing the equipment, and not knowing that particular balance, and then finding it as I go" (Muñoz and Bustamante 2003: 5). As she says, each night the ladder is positioned slightly differently on the floor, or it is a different ladder; the wobbling is different, it has a different range, and her body must respond on the spot and in the moment of performance to the new configurations of space and uncertainty.

Summary

The antisocial dictates an unbecoming, a cleaving to that which seems to shame or annihilate, and a radical passivity allows for the inhabiting of femininity with a difference. The radical understandings of passivity that emerge within Marina Abramović's and Yoko Ono's work, not to mention Faith Wilding's legendary piece "Waiting," all offer an antisocial way out of the double bind of becoming woman and thereby propping up the dominance of man within a gender binary. Predicting master-slave couples in Kara Walker's work and the disappeared figures in J. A. Nicholls's landscapes, Ono's nonact of evacuation and performance stripping implicates the frame in the aesthetic material, just as Spivak cautioned us to consider the role of the intellectual in all representations of the subaltern. In all of these pieces the frame—globalization, the canvas, the gallery walls, academia—binds the perpetrator to the criminal, the torturer to his victim, the corporate raider to the site of pillaging; collage shows the open mouth, the figure in distress, the scream and its cause; it glues effect to cause and queers the relations between the two. In the end there is no subject, no feminist subject, in these works. There are gaping holes, empty landscapes, split silhouettes—the self unravels, refuses to cohere, it will not speak, it will only be spoken. The passive voice that is the true domain of masochistic fantasy ("a child is being beaten,") might just be a transformative voice for feminism. Freud himself said he could not really understand the final phases of the feminine masochistic fantasy which progressed from "a child is being beaten" to "I am being beaten" and finally to "the boys are being beaten by the schoolteacher." But this final phase of the masochistic fantasy transfers punishments definitively away from the body of the subjugated and onto the body of the oppressor. Masochism, finally, represents a deep disruption of time itself (Freeman, 2010); reconciling the supposedly irreconcilable tension between pleasure and death, the masochist tethers her notion of self to a spiral of pain and hurt. She refuses to cohere, refuses to fortify herself against the knowledge of death and dying, and seeks instead to be out of time altogether, a body suspended in time, space, and desire.

Ono's performance of "Cut Piece," racially inflected in 1965 by her status as an Asian woman within the imperial imagination, asks in terms that Hartman might recognize whether freedom can be imagined separately from the terms upon which it is offered. If freedom, as Hartman shows, was offered to the slave as a kind of contract with capital, then moving about, being restless, refusing to acquire property or wealth flirts with forms of liberty that are unimaginable to those who offer freedom as the freedom to become a master. Here Ono sits still, waits patiently and passively, and refuses to resist in the terms mandated by the structure that interpellates her. To be cut, to be bared, to be violated publicly is a particular kind of resistant performance, and in it Ono inhabits a form of unacting, unbeing, unbecoming. Her stillness, punctuated only by an involuntary flinch seven minutes into the event, like the masochistic cuts in *The Piano Teacher* and the refusals of love in *Autobiography of My Mother*, offers quiet masochistic gestures that invite us to unthink sex as that alluring narrative of connection and liberation and think it anew as the site of failure and unbecoming conduct.

CHAPTER FIVE

"The Killer in Me Is the Killer *In You*"

He who cannot take sides must keep silent.
—Walter Benjamin, "One-Way Street," *Selected Writings 1913–1926*

The Queer Art of Failure is an extended meditation on antidisciplinary forms of knowing specifically tied to queerness; I have made the case for stupidity, failure, and forgetfulness over knowing, mastering, and remembering in terms of contemporary knowledge formations. The social worlds we inhabit, as so many thinkers have reminded us, are not inevitable, they were not always bound to turn out this way, and what's more, in the process of producing this reality, many other realities, fields of knowledge, and ways of being have been discarded and, to use Foucault's (2003) term, "disqualified." Queer studies, like any other area of study that agrees upon principles, modes of historiography, and sites of investigation, also has a tendency to solidify into what Foucault calls a "science," or a regime of knowing that depends absolutely upon commonsense narratives about emergences and suppressions. In some queer theoretical narratives, for example, the psychic abjection of the homosexual must be met by a belated recognition of his or her legitimacy. In other scholarly endeavors the gay or lesbian subject must be excavated from the burial grounds of history or granted a proper place in an account of social movements, globalized in a rights-based project, or written into new social contracts. But in more recent queer theory the positivist projects committed to restoring the gay subject to history and redeeming the gay self from its pathologization have been replaced by emphases on the negative potential of the queer and the possibility of rethinking the meaning of the political through queerness precisely by embracing the incoherent, the lonely, the defeated, and the melancholic formulations of selfhood that it sets in motion.

It is conventional to describe early narratives of gay and lesbian life as "hidden from history"; this notion, taken from the title of a well-known anthology edited by George Chauncey and others, constitutes gay and lesbian history as a repressed archive and the historian as an intrepid archaeologist digging through homophobic erasure to find the truth. But as much as we have to excavate some histories that have been rendered invisible, we also bury others, and sometimes we do both at the same time. You could say that gay and lesbian scholars have also hidden history, unsavory histories, and have a tendency to select from historical archives only the narratives that please. So new formulations of queer history have emerged from scholars like Heather Love, who argue for a contradictory archive filled with loss and longing, abjection and ugliness, as well as love, intimacy, and survival. An example of a history from which gay and lesbian scholarship has hidden is the history of relations between homosexuality and fascism. This is the topic of this chapter as I push toward a model of queer history that is less committed to finding heroic models from the past and more resigned to the contradictory and complicit narratives that, in the past as in the present, connect sexuality to politics.

When I say that scholarship has hidden from this at times overlapping history, I do not mean that no one has discussed homosexuality and fascism; in fact there is a large body of work on the topic. But because the role of homosexuality in fascism is very ambiguous and complicated and has been subject to all kinds of homophobic projection, we often prefer to talk about the persecution of gays by the Nazis, leaving aside the question of their collaboration in the regime. So, from the outset, I think it is important to say that there is no single way of describing the relationship between Nazism and male homosexuality, but also that we should not shy away from investigating the participation of gay men in the regime even if we fear homophobic fallout from doing so. Finally, the purpose of any such investigation should not be to *settle* the question of homosexuality in the Nazi Party, but to raise questions about relations between sex and politics, the erotics of history and the ethics of complicity.

As Gayle Rubin succinctly stated in "Thinking Sex," "Sex is always political" (1984: 4). This is indisputable, and yet as work by Leo Bersani, Lee

Edelman, Heather Love, and others has suggested, there is no guarantee as to what form the political will take when it comes to sex. Rubin's work asks us to "think sex" in every context, and Foucault prods us to examine our own investments in cozy narratives of sexual freedom and rebellion. So "queer negativity" here might refer to a project within which one remains committed to not only scrambling dominant logics of desire but also to contesting homogeneous models of gay identity within which a queer victim stands up to his or her oppressors and emerges a hero. Bersani has widely been credited for first questioning the desire to attribute an ethical project to every kind of gay sex. In "Is the Rectum a Grave?" he commented astutely, "While it is indisputably true that sexuality is always being politicized, the ways in which having sex politicizes are highly problematical. Right-wing politics can, for example, emerge quite easily from a sentimentalizing of the armed forces or of blue-collar workers, a sentimentalizing which can itself prolong and sublimate a marked sexual preference for sailors and telephone linemen" (2009: 206). As Bersani says, the erotic is an equal opportunity archive; it borrows just as easily, possibly more easily from politically problematic imagery than from politically palatable material. This leaves open the question of the relationship between sex and politics. Bersani, generally speaking, in a move that is later stretched into a theoretical polemic by Lee Edelman, wants to resist and refuse the desire to make sex into the raw material for a rational political position. Instead he sees a tyranny of selfhood and a glorification of one understanding of the political in most claims for democratic plurality, social diversity, or utopian potential that get written into sex: we clean sex up, he seems to imply, by making it about self-fashioning instead of self-shattering.

The model of "coming to power," a model that Foucault called a "reverse discourse," still provides in many instances the dominant framework for thinking about sex. Many works in queer studies end with a bang by imagining and describing the new social forms that supposedly emerge from gay male orgies or cruising escapades or gender-queer erotics or sodomitic sadism or at any rate queer jouissance of some form or another. Samuel Delany (2001) reads a harmonious narrative of social contact into anonymous sexual contacts in porn theaters; Tim Dean (2009) finds a new model of ethical conduct in barebacking between strangers; and even Lee Edelman's (2005) notoriously cranky theories of the queerness of the death drive seem to harbor some tiny opening for the possibility of an antisocial jouissance. In all three instances, as well as in

Bersani's (2009) work, the utopian jouissance seems primarily available only in relation to male-male anal sex between strangers. But, as I stated earlier, while I am sympathetic to this project of not tidying up sex, I am less than enthusiastic about the archives upon which these authors draw and the resolutely masculinist and white utopias they imagine through the magic portals of tricking.

Perhaps it is always better, *pace* T. S. Eliot, to work toward the whimper rather than the bang, if only because "bang" narratives are almost always, even when describing self-shattering, to use Foucault's cliché-resistant phrase, "to the speaker's benefit." Such narratives, Foucault suggests, are those that we tell ourselves in order to sustain a "repressive hypothesis" that locates the plucky queer as a heroic freedom fighter in a world of puritans. This narrative, Foucault argues forcefully in *The History of Sexuality, Volume 1* (1998), is appealing, compelling, convincing—and utterly wrong. While it is very much "to the speaker's benefit," as Foucault cheekily puts it, to tell this kind of story about the remarkable emergence of sexual minorities from the tyranny of repressive regimes, it is also a way of ignoring the actual mechanics of the history of sexuality within which marginalized subjects participate in and endorse the very systems that marginalize them. But also it ignores the system by which socially transgressive behaviors take on the allure of danger precisely because we are so endlessly seduced by the idea that sexual expression is in and of itself a revolutionary act. That which seems off-limits becomes sexy, and in indulging our interest in the taboo we feel naughty.

While Foucault replaces the romantic narrative of gay and lesbian resistance with the concept of the "reverse discourse," Bersani pushes aside romantic narratives of sexual freedom fighters in favor of an anticommunitarian strand of queer practice. The power of the anticommunitarian position, though Bersani does not characterize it in exactly these terms, is that it counters the tendency for both homosocial and homoerotic bonds between men to form a support network for patriarchal systems by supplanting such bonds with nonrelationality, solitude, masochism. In other words, while the gay man might be a support for the patriarchal state while he is engaged in the business of male bonding and gay community formation, he may become a threat to the political status quo when he refuses masculine mastery, rejects relation altogether, and settles for a "non-suicidal disappearance of the subject." (Bersani, 1996: 99) It is this kind of gay male subjectivity that Bersani traces through the work of Genet, Proust, and others and that he posits as the meaning of homosexuality: homosexuality, he says, by way of Genet, "is congenial to betrayal" (1996: 153). I will not explore Bersani's reading of Genet further, other than to note that betrayal here constitutes a provocative refusal to identify with other gay men as a group; suffice it to say that queer negativity for gay white men depends heavily upon a strangely heroic notion of unbecoming within which a male surrenders to a higher phallic power. This trope of unbecoming can be traced through the archive of avant-garde male modernism. Indeed the self-shattering that occupies the center of Bersani's notion of male masculine unraveling indicates a willingness to be penetrated and to model a masculinity that is not consistent with heterosexual manhood but that is absolutely *not* reducible to being "unmanned" or made into a "woman."

Since, as Bersani makes clear, sexual acts cannot guarantee any particular political stance, progressive or conservative, it is odd that we want to continue to connect gay sex, wherever we may find it, to political radicalism. While Bersani's default position is to shrug off the political context altogether (as in his readings of the French Legion soldiers in Claire Denis's film *Chocolat*), we might instead look to the places where perverse sexuality seems to be tethered to a conservative or right-wing political project. In my book *Female Masculinity* (Halberstam 1998), for example, I noted (without really reckoning with) the participation of Radclyffe Hall and other masculine women in early British fascist movements. Hall was a known anti-Semite, and many of her aristocratic friends were both sympathetic to fascism and fetishistically invested in military uniforms; some formed volunteer police brigades, others joined the army.[1] The meaning of their masculinities at times dovetailed with nationalist and racist projects.

What happens when we find multiple examples of gays or lesbians who collaborate with rather than oppose politically conservative and objectionable regimes? As I have suggested, one tactic has been to ignore the signs of collaboration in favor of a narrative of victimization. Debates over the use of the Pink Triangle from the 1970s on as a universal symbol of the oppression of sexual minorities are a good example of the preference for a narrative of victimization to one of participation. Erik Jensen has traced these debates in an essay titled "The Pink Triangle and Political Consciousness: Gays, Lesbians and the Memory of Nazi Persecution" (2002), showing how activists in Germany and the U.S. in the 1970s overlooked evidence of the participation of gay men in the Nazi regime while inflating the numbers of gay men killed in concentration camps. In a well-known example of this, Harvey Milk, a gay member of the San

Francisco Board of Supervisors, once said, "We are not going to sit back in silence as 300,000 of our gay brothers and sisters did in Nazi Germany. We are not going to allow our rights to be taken away and then march with bowed heads into the gas chambers."[2] But gays were not selected for the gas chambers by the Nazis; they were imprisoned and abused in camps, but not gassed. Jensen remarks, "Activists in the U.S., more so than in West Germany, tended to direct the memory of Nazi persecution outward in order to secure the support of the broader society" (2002: 329).

In an essay written to accompany his film *Desire* and published in the landmark volume *How Do I Look? Queer Film and Video*, Stuart Marshall strenuously objected to any and all uses of the Pink Triangle in contemporary contexts generally and in AIDS activism in particular. Arguing that the Pink Triangle forges a highly debatable connection between homosexuals persecuted by the Nazis under the provision of Paragraph 175 of the German Criminal Code and gay men oppressed in the 1980s by homophobic responses to the AIDS crisis, Marshall writes, "Lost in the analogy are all those aspects of difference and subjectivity that identity politics subordinates and suppresses precisely to ensure political solidarity and action. This has, on a subtle level, far-reaching and possibly reactionary consequences" (1991: 87). This is a powerful criticism of identity politics, made in terms that are different from many contemporary critiques of identity; here the presumption of stable and ethical identity in the present blocks out all evidence of contradictory and possibly politically objectionable identities in the past. Hence gays today identify through the Pink Triangle with the victims of the Third Reich, and not, ever, with their persecutors. In the documentary film *Paragraph 175* (directed by Rob Epstein and Jeffrey Friedman, 2000), for example, many of the men interviewed were imprisoned and tortured by the Nazis in the 1940s, but some spoke nostalgically of their days in the German army, days filled with male comradeship and male bonding. The film cannot imagine any model of history that would tie a modern viewer with the German male soldier rather than with his victim. That historical connection is what I want to explore.

Gay Nazis?

While in Sweden giving a seminar on queer theory, I got into a heated discussion at lunch with a Swedish queer studies scholar about the relationship of the artwork of Tom of Finland to a fascist imaginary. In my typically subtle and diplomatic way, I proposed that any reading of Tom of Finland's über-masculine leather daddies that made a detour around a discussion of fascism was skirting a central component of the work. My Swedish colleague became irritated. Nonsense, he shot back. Tom of Finland was pure eros and had little if anything to do with fascism, imaginary or real. But, I persisted in my gently persuasive way, wasn't the artist in the Finnish army? Didn't the Finns collaborate with the Germans? Wasn't Tom of Finland's imagery born of this fateful encounter with the German soldier males? My Swedish colleague became exasperated: Didn't I know that the Finns were forced to fight for Germany, and that they were not necessarily signing on for fascism? And anyway, he proposed, the historical context cannot fix the meaning of the erotic material! The more my colleague resisted my reading of the intersection of a homoerotics with fascism, the more insistent on it I became. The more insistent I became, the more he resisted and emphasized a separation between erotic imagery and political ideology. Why can't you enjoy the imagery *and* admit that it partakes in a fascist imaginary of homosexuality, I wanted to know. Why can't you separate out representation and reality, historicity and contemporary meanings, fascist masculinities and homosex, he wanted to know.

The encounter was uncomfortable, unsettling, and all the more engaging for being so. Was I being a crudely literal feminist and reading the historical context of the production of Tom of Finland's erotic drawings as definitive in terms of their meaning? Or was my Swedish friend being stubbornly defensive in refusing to read any historical context at all into an archive he found arousing? If we allow for the possibility that Tom of Finland both partakes in a fascist imaginary and resists being reduced to that imaginary, what kind of relationship between politics and the erotic have we engaged? At stake here is not the true political status of Tom of Finland's fantasy world, nor the actual history of the production of the imagery; the real struggle is about the context of contemporary claims that people want to make about the political rightness of their desires. A gay man, or anyone, who finds Tom of Finland's erotic archive appealing does not want to be accused of a furtive investment in fascism, an investment that sneaks in through the backdoor of desire; by the same token we cannot be sure that all of our interests in erotic material are politically innocent. This is not to make a Catherine Mackinnon–type argument that sees power-laden sexual representations as inherently bad. Rather I want to understand why we cannot tolerate the linking of our desires to politics that disturb us.

In an essay published in a special issue of the *Journal of the History of Sexuality* dedicated to German fascism and sexuality, Dagmar Herzog, perhaps the most audacious and original scholar working on this topic, begins by asking a now familiar question: "What is the relationship between sexual and other kinds of politics?" She continues:

> Few cultures have posed this puzzle as urgently, or as disturbingly, as Nazi Germany. The answers are multiple and as yet unresolved; each emerging answer raises further questions. What exactly were Nazism's sexual politics? Were they repressive for everyone, or were some individuals and groups given special license while others were persecuted, tormented or killed? . . . What do we make of the fact that scholars from the 1960's to the present have repeatedly assumed that the Third Reich was "sex-hostile," "pleasureless," and characterized by "official German prudery," while in films and popular culture there has been a countervailing tendency to offer lurid and salacious anecdotes as a substitute for the serious engagement with the complexities of life under German fascism? (2002: 3–4)

Herzog's great contribution to the literature has been to show that, contrary to popular belief, the Nazis were not simply sexually repressive or upholders of a rigid sexual moral order; they deployed homophobia and sexual morality only when and where it was politically expedient to do so, and at other times they turned a blind eye so long as the participants in the sexual activity under scrutiny were "racially pure." In this essay Herzog combines Foucault and Freud to expose the contradictory and uneven sexual politics of the Nazis. One of her most potent insights is that "we simply cannot understand why Nazism was so attractive to so many people" without examining the *production* as well as the repression of sexuality under the regime. The rest of the essay, however, tends to apply this insight only to the politics of heterosexuality. Herzog describes a seemingly unified policy in the Third Reich in relation to homosexuality: homophobia, she notes, was part of a more general racial system dedicated to the promotion of Aryan reproduction and the suppression of all Jewish influence. But when it comes to dominant masculinities, as the Tom of Finland material suggests, the politics of homosexuality in Nazi Germany look as complicated and contradictory as those of heterosexuality.

A number of queer theorists have tried their hand at unraveling the connections between homosexuality and Nazism. For example, Eve Kosofsky Sedgwick both acknowledges the relations between homoeroticism and fascism and pushes against this association: "It should be unnecessary to say that the fantasy of Nazi homosexuality is flatly false; according to any definition of homosexuality current in our culture, only one Nazi leader, Ernst Roehm, was homosexual, and he was murdered by the ss on Hitler's direct orders in 1934. What seems more precisely to be true is that at any rate German fascism (like in less exacerbated form twentieth century culture at large) emerged on a social ground in which 'the homosexual question' had been made highly salient" (1994: 49). Sedgwick is responding to what she perceives to be both a popular and a feminist tendency to conflate the Nazis with homosexual community, a tendency that can be found in the work of theorists such as Luce Irigaray as well as in popular form in films like Luchino Visconti's *The Damned* (1969) and Bernado Bertolucci's *The Conformist* (1970). I have no wish to occupy the offensive and potentially homophobic position of the feminist who misreads fascist masculinism as the very definition of male homosexuality, but I do want to challenge Sedgwick's blanket statement about the complete and total lack of any connection between Nazism and homosexuality. To state so baldly that only one Nazi leader was *homosexual* sounds defensive given that we know there were actually groups of men who did indeed associate erotic bonds between men with the kind of classical myth making that the Nazis were known for. It is also a way of avoiding the charge that there is some kind of structural relationship between male homosexuality and Nazism by simply saying that we know of only a single homosexual Nazi. In fact Roehm was known to preside over a stable of homosexual storm troopers. While I agree with Sedgwick that the presence of homosexual men in fascist groups does not make Nazism homosexual (any more than the fact that the vast majority of Nazis were heterosexual would make the phenomenon of Nazism heterosexual), I also think that the overt persecution of homosexual men does not remove the possibility that there were indeed disquieting overlaps at times between Nazism and homosexuality.

The history of this overlap can be found in even a casual survey of the intergenerational *Männerbund*, or men's group, from the 1920s and 1930s. There were at least two strands to the homosexual emancipation movements in Germany in the early twentieth century. One, associated with Max Hirschfeld's institute and with theories of intermediate- or third-sexers, is well known; the other strand, homosexual masculinism, is less well known. This strand included men like Hans Blüher and John Henry Mackay, who promoted the Männerbund in the 1930s, as well as Adolf Brand (founder of the Gemeinschaft der Eigenen) and even the Nazi storm trooper Ernst Roehm. They resisted the biologistic theories of inversion favored by Hirschfeld's institute in favor of "culturalist" notions of male homosexuality that functioned in terms of the erotic connection between two conventionally masculine men. This brand of masculinism coincided with a nationalist and conservative emphasis on the superiority of male community and with a racialized rejection of femininity. Indeed among these early homosexual activists, male Jews were seen as men who had been made effeminate by their investments in family and home—a realm that should be left to women—and who, like effeminate homosexuals, did not live up to their virile duty to remain committed to other masculine men and to a masculinist state and public sphere. There is even a word in German for the disgust generated by the feminine gay man: *Tuntenhass*. In their desire for other masculine men the masculinists crafted an individualistic ideology of sexual love that actually dovetailed nicely with certain aspects of the fascist state in its production of and securing of bonds between Aryan men. As the German historian Geoffrey Giles puts it, "The male bonding that the Nazis vigorously encouraged in the name of comradeship was not easily distinguishable from the Wandervogel movement and there must have been millions of young German men who did not have a clear idea of the difference" (Giles, 2002: 260).

The connections between homosexuality, fascism, and modernism have been carefully excavated and theorized by a number of historians and theorists. George L. Mosse, for example, devoted a chapter of his book *The Fascist Revolution: Toward a General Theory of Fascism* (1999) to "homosexuality and French fascism." Mosse notes the complex nature of the actual and discursive relations between fascism and homosexuality: all at once homosexuals were persecuted under fascism in order to maintain the normativity of fascist masculinism, but at the same time fascists continued to be accused of being homosexual, and homosexuals were regularly accused in France and elsewhere of collaborating with the Nazis. Like others, Mosse suggests that a Nazi preoccupation with manliness and virility and a preference for distance from women and domesticity pull Nazism strongly into the vexed area, documented so well by Sedgwick, within which political and sexual bonds between men become confused and entwined. Mosse ends his chapter "On Homosexuality and French Fascism" with a call for "further investigation" (181) into the relations between and among male friendship, homoeroticism, and nationalism.

Andrew Hewitt has theorized the connections illuminated by Mosse in a book titled *Political Inversions* (1996). Taking aim both at the crude, homophobic, and cartoonish characterizations of gay Nazis in film and the more complex and theoretical links made by Adorno and others between totalitarianism and homosexuality, Hewitt outlines an "imaginary fascism," one that makes ahistorical connections between the gay man and the fascist. Hewitt carefully tracks the actual involvement of homosexual men within proto-fascist movements as well as in the Nazi Party, but he also looks at the structural manipulations of language, power, and the imagination that make it easy to conflate homosexuality and fascism; for example, building on Ernst Bloch's essay on the unrepresentability of fascism, he suggests that both homosexuality and fascism share the trope of unspeakability: "If homosexuality dare not speak its own name, it will nevertheless serve as the 'name' of something else that cannot be spoken—fascism" (9). Another reason for the easy association between homosexuality and fascism resides in the popular characterizations of proletarianism as masculine and virile and elitist vanguardist movements as effeminate. A third reason, one that Hewitt discusses in detail in relation to Adorno's contention that "totalitarianism and homosexuality belong together," relies upon the identification of both totalitarianism and homosexuality with the desire for sameness that colors the "authoritarian personality" and threatens dominant or Oedipal logics of desire.

Having demonstrated that the popular and the radical associations of homosexuality and fascism turn on a few shared structural features that become part of a larger homophobic imaginary, Hewitt then turns to the actual history of masculinist gay men in Germany in the 1930s and shows that the narrow scrutiny within queer historiography of the influence of Magnus Hirschfeld and the "third sex" proponents obscures this more complex history of early homosexual emancipation movements. The differences between Hirschfeld's version of homosexual emancipation (the recognition of sexual minorities by the state) and the masculinist version (the elevation of male friendship to a principle of state power) prompts Hewitt to offer up a new set of questions about homosexuality: "We must therefore be sensitive to the strategic function of an emerging homosexuality. Rather than asking What was homosexuality? (or, in Foucauldian terms, When and how was homosexuality?), we need to understand what homosexuality was (and is) for. What political options did it provide, what ways out of an aporetic heterosexism in politics and philosophy? What function did it serve within its contemporary political and philosophical framework?" (1996: 81). In other words, while the Hirsch-

feld institute and the particular biography of Magnus Hirschfeld as a victim of Nazi aggression well suits contemporary formulations of the long
history of the persecution of homosexuals in Euro-American society, the
parallel history of homosexual men who identified strongly with fascist
principles and who participated openly and freely in the Nazi Party is far
less frequently invoked. By asking what homosexuality might be for, what
its function was, Hewitt moves the emphasis away from an uninterrupted
account of homosexual struggle and allows for a much more variegated
history of sexuality within which sexual otherness serves both dominant
and subordinate regimes, sometimes at the same time. Unlike Sedgwick,
though he relies heavily on her work, Hewitt is not denying the connections between homosexuality and fascism; rather his purpose is to say
that something radical can be extracted from the gay masculinists despite
their unsavory political associations.

In his chapter on the early politics of masculinism Hewitt provides the
history of male homophile movements that emerged in response to the
encouragement of homoerotic bonds within Weimar Germany and early
Nazism. He questions what he characterizes as "the omission of masculinism from even more recent queer historiography" (82). Like Hewitt, I
want to question this omission, but our reasons for doing so are somewhat different. For Hewitt, the detour that gay history takes around German masculinism forecloses a set of questions about the relations between the political and the libidinal and allows for the dismissal of the
masculinists as both politically embarrassing and sexually repressed.
Hewitt returns to the masculinists — men like Han Blüher and John Henry
Mackay, as well as (by implication) sinister figures like Adolf Brand and
even Ernst Roehm — in order to prevent versions of male homosexuality
that function in terms of the erotic connection between two conventionally masculine men from being reduced to or caricatured as repressed,
sexphobic, closeted, or simply part and parcel of a patriarchal order.
In fact he claims, "We must confront the reality that both fascism and
homosexual masculinism were real and radical attacks on that order —
even though their historical and empirical instantiations were anything
but liberatory in any accepted sense" (85). But I believe that the erasure
of the masculinist gay movement indicates an unwillingness to grapple
with difficult historical antecedents and a desire to impose a certain kind
of identity politics on history; in other words, the notion of a unified gay
identity produces a universalizing and racially specific history of homosexuality stretching back through twentieth-century Europe and in-

scribed in avant-garde male modernism, but not in fascist sensibilities. It also allows for AIDS activists in the 1990s, many of whom were white and middle class, to don a pink triangle and imagine their struggle in relation to the men targeted by the Nazi regime.

Hewitt, as I have suggested, does not agree with Sedgwick that there is no evidence of an overlap between Nazism and homosexuality. He actually gravitates to the shared ground and tries instead to see when and where the claims that gay masculinists were making about their desires strike a radical note in terms of a critique of the heteronormative presumptions about Oedipalized desire. Predictably this is where Hewitt and I part ways. While I understand very well the argument that queer theory has favored gender-opposed couples (butch-femme, for example) and gender-inverted subjects (Wilde, Hall) and has in the process ignored gender-conforming subjects, or what Biddy Martin referred to in a lesbian context as "femininity played straight," this does not seem like the right reason to rehabilitate men's groups invested in "masculinity played straight." While for Martin the seemingly obvious privileging of the gender queer over the gender normative sets up a troubling erasure of the lesbian femme, for Hewitt the focus on gender inversion in the early twentieth century sets up a detour around the gay masculine man. But while the erasure of the queer femme smacks of an antifeminist preference for transgressive masculinity over transgressive femininity, the erasure of the masculine gay man indicates an unwillingness to grapple with difficult historical antecedents.

Queer male and female cross-gender identification, in other words, like queer male and female gender normativity, have had different relations to gender politics, masculinism, and domesticity. In fact we can trace some contemporary feminist mistrust of female-to-male gender variance back to the early twentieth century, when female masculinity was cast by Otto Weininger and others as, simultaneously, a sign of the collapse of gender distinctions and, by implication, of civilized society, and a marker of female genius. Early feminists had to fight against social constructions of femininity as passive and weak while guarding against the notion that when they were active and strong, they were masculine or manly. So while the masculine woman might be cast as socially deviant and possibly criminal in some circles, in others she was accepted as superior to her feminine and weak sisters; Gertrude Stein, for example, eagerly embraced Weininger's ideas because they gave her a rationale for her genius and its relationship to her masculinity.[3] Weininger's

(2009) basic idea was that all people are made up of a mix of maleness and femaleness and that partners should be drawn to each other on the basis of complementarity: extreme masculinity should seek out extreme femininity, for example, and androgynous masculinity should seek out androgynous femininity. He works toward a totalizing theory of desire within which the couple, like some Platonic ideal, together forms a whole. These gendered positions moreover are racialized, and the difference between male and female is also characterized in terms of the difference between Aryan and Jew; while the Aryan male, for Weininger and other masculinists, idealizes the relations between action, state, and self, the Jew, in his essentially feminized condition, embodies the conditions of a feminized statelessness. The Jew is feminized because he is embedded in the family, without any possibility of greatness or genius.

Stein's attraction to the work of Weininger becomes more understandable in the context of Janet Malcolm's remarkable book *Two Lives* (2008), which asks how Gertrude and Alice, two very public Jewish lesbians, managed to survive the Second World War in Europe. The short answer is that both women dis-identified as Jews and had no problem with the idea of finding a German collaborator, a gay man named Bernard Fay, to protect them during this treacherous time. Malcolm characterizes both women as conservative and reactionary; she finds evidence of Stein's support of the Spanish fascist leader Franco and shows how Toklas supported Fay after the war and tried to help free him from jail.

So much for the masculine woman and her potential political attachments. As for the effeminate man, he was viewed by Weininger and others as a traitor to a politics of virility and as someone who had betrayed patriarchal fraternity. Weininger makes an essential connection between Jews and women: he reads Jews as hopelessly effeminate and women as completely without political capabilities. Both lack distinct egos and are consequently unable to rule, unable to achieve individual greatness and, in the case of the Jews, are unable to achieve citizenship. In early twentieth-century Germany, where the patriarchal state, male bonding, and homoerotic fraternity were cast as continuous with one another, the effeminate or cross-identified man was vilified by all sides. As I have already noted, this does not mean that the Nazis condemned homosexuality tout court; indeed the masculine homosexual was in complete concordance with the state's anti-Semitic and misogynistic conceptions of masculinity and femininity. Furthermore the Nazi state, as Herzog argues in *Sex after Fascism*, was opportunistic in its official relation to sexuality—not at all the repressive regime that it was later depicted as, says Herzog: "Many Nazi 'experts' advanced a social constructionist view of sexuality that insisted that sexual identity was variable and vulnerable" (2007: 34). Accordingly homosexuality could be viewed as both congenital and culturally specific, and as both a lack of virility and a surplus of masculinity. So while the Nazis' position on male sexuality in particular was very tolerant, it was in relation to feminization that they expressed moral outrage. The effeminate homosexual was persecuted in Nazi Germany both for his rejection of the heterosexual family and for his embrace of the feminine. Some German homosexuals also set themselves up in opposition to gender "deviants" and saw the effeminate man as someone who disrupted the Gemeinschaft der Eigenen, or the Community of the Special, a fraternity of masculine homosexuals.

Like Bersani's elaboration of a nonredemptive politics in *Homos*, Hewitt is interested in refuting a wholly liberal tradition of reading homosexuality back through radical social movements. He wants to remember a far *less liberal tradition of homophilia* from the early twentieth century, and from Germany in particular, in order to analyze the relationship between eros and politics and to see that eros is not always and everywhere a force for good that has been met by negative and repressive power. Hewitt's question about the function of homosexuality is echoed in Bersani's commentary on the negative force of a male homosexuality that seeks to unbecome. I am building on their complex insights and trying to use them both to uncover the long history of gay masculinism but also to try to use that history to understand contemporary politics: in recent years in Europe we have witnessed the emergence of a particular form of homonationalism among right-wing leaders who also happen to be gay. Jörg Haider, for example, the leader of the Austrian Freedom Party and later the founder of the Alliance for the Future of Austria, was exposed as a gay man after he died suddenly in a car crash in 2008. Haider's party was strongly right wing, nationalistic, and driven by anti-Semitic and anti-immigrant sentiments; his parents had been members of the Nazi Party. After his death he was exposed as a gay man who had been involved with another man for years, despite being publicly married to a woman. Like the Dutch gay politician Pim Fortuyn, Haider was considered a "far-right populist," and neither man saw any conflict between their sexual identity and their intolerant views of "outsiders," foreigners, Jews, and Muslims. Anti-immigrant gay politics arises out of clumsy characterizations of Islam as deeply homophobic and assumes a relationship between gay tolerance and liberal democracy. As scholars such as Joseph Massad, Fatima El-Tayib, and Jasbir Puar have shown, these characterizations of Islam misread the sexual economies of Islamic countries on the one hand and join gay and lesbian respectability to neoliberalism on the other. They also allow for strange political couplings of right-wing populism and gay rights.

I have argued that the desire to completely separate homosexuality from Nazism and to cast as homophobic all attempts to connect them misunderstands the multiplicity of gay history and simplifies the function of homosexuality. For Sedgwick, homosexuality constitutes a vital part of a new way of knowing that instantiated new regimes of the person, the social, and the body. For Hewitt, homosexuality constitutes a logic of association that at times lines up with and at other times opposes emancipatory regimes, but not in any predictable way. For both theorists, homosexuality is not so much an identity stretching across time as a shifting set of relations between politics, eros, and power. I have argued that in order to capture the complexity of these shifting relations we cannot afford to settle on linear connections between radical desires and radical politics; instead we have to be prepared to be unsettled by the politically problematic connections history throws our way.

The Killer in Me Is the Killer in You

By way of conclusion I want to consider some images by two contemporary artists who both, in their own way, deal with the complex relations between homo-masculinities and fascism. The painter Attila Richard Lukacs and the photographer and curator Collier Schorr both fuse fascistic imagery with homoeroticism, and both are unafraid to confront the historical, aesthetic, and sexual consequences of the violent collision between these two systems of representation. While for Lukacs the gay skinhead represents a kind of apex of heroic, sacrificial, and romantic masculinity, for Schorr the Nazi soldier male represents the place of a kind of ruined masculinity, a site of betrayal (as her photograph "Traitor" makes clear). These images emerge as a question passed on from one generation to another: What does your masculinity mean now?

Crystal Parikh (2009) has recently articulated an "ethics of betrayal" within what she calls "emergent U.S. literatures and cultures"; she defines betrayal as a critical perspective on the conditions of "belonging, assimilation and exclusion" within the racial state. Betrayal, whether

17. Collier Schorr, "Traitor," 2001–4. Black and white photograph, 103.5 cm × 80.6 cm. CS 388. Courtesy of 303 Gallery, New York.

understood in psychoanalytic terms as a kind of truth-telling that defies repression or in deconstructive terms as an inevitable duplicity, names a mode of being that is both demanded and rejected by the moral systems we inhabit. Marginalized subjects in particular tend to be situated in an active relationship with the dilemma of betrayal, if only because normative models of citizenship situate the minoritarian subject as a kind of double agent, one who must be loyal to the nation but cannot fail to betray it. The queer and feminist dimensions of disloyalty and betrayal open onto a different kind of politics, a politics which, at various times in this

18. Collier Schorr, "Night Porter (Matthias)," 2001. Black and white photograph, 47 cm × 38.1 cm. CS 542. Courtesy of 303 Gallery, New York.

book, comes to be associated with masochism, unbecoming, and negativity. But at a time when loyalty to the nation often means unquestioned acquiescence to both the brutalities of unchecked U.S. military aggression and the ideologies of freedom and democracy used to justify such political violence, betrayal and disloyalty are part of the arsenal of a vital and dynamic oppositional discourse.

Another of Schorr's images, "Night Porter (Matthias)," invoking not only the highly problematic film by Liliana Cavani produced in 1974 but also Sontag's essay on "fascinating fascism," provides a startling reperformance of an image of betrayal; here Matthias dresses up as Charlotte Rampling dressing up as an SS office in *The Night Porter*. While for Sontag, Cavani illustrated the emergence of fascism in the postwar period as a style, as moreover a set of aesthetic preferences for symmetry and order and as a gay erotic interest in sadomasochism, Schorr has a much more subtle understanding of fascism, power, queerness, and masculinity as they are cycled through a visual aesthetic. Here it is not that an s/m dynamic has replaced intimacy with theater or that people, especially women, desire their own subjugation; instead Schorr's image illustrates that fascism cannot easily be projected onto the other. "The killer in you is the killer in me," the title for Schorr's own meditation on performance and politics in *Freeway Balconies* (2008), suggests that the micropolitics of fascism live on in the self as much as in the other, in the perverse as well as the healthful, in the doing as much as in the being.

A "fascinating fascism" lives on in the heroic portraits of skinheads by Attila Richard Lukacs: skinheads alone, together, in groups, fucking, standing, fighting. Lukacs refuses to turn away from the potent transhistorical pull that Nazi imagery has upon a gay male imaginary. Instead he confronts the possibility that identification can take lurid and negative forms: "I have this recurring dream where I am a serial killer," he told Richard Goldstein in *The Village Voice*. Goldstein comments, "Lukacs has made his mark by representing acts that verge on murder—brutal beatings and ritual humiliation as well as rhapsodic sex between tough young men. His adoring portraits of skinheads and thugs have made him the official bad boy of his native Canada."[4] For Lukacs, the soldier male, whether in military uniform or in the uniform of the skinhead, becomes a potent switch point for desire and death. His portraits pay attention to the ways politics speaks through desire, though not in any literal way (see plate 13).

Lukacs explores the erotic charge of fascism in multiple forms; in some of his works he paints his skinheads in the shadow of a swastika, both embracing and rejecting the symbol through their coupled form; in others he leaves the swastika to the imagination, and in a few he actively draws and then paints out the symbol, as if to paint it as an erased origin for certain forms of homosexual masculinist desire. In this way Lukacs crafts gay mythologies out of fetishistic combinations of nationalism, violence, and sex and allows pornography to compete with classical imagery.

The heroicized image of the white skinhead, here an English variety,

19. Attila Richard Lukacs, *True North*, 1989. Oil on canvas. Courtesy of the artist.

remains constant throughout as Lukacs switches between styles and national variations (Persian or Indian miniatures, high realism, kitsch). But these appropriations of other modes of painting do not influence his take on masculinity; instead his figures occupy and colonize the forms themselves and adapt them to the needs of a very Christian utopia. As Goldstein describes it, "Here is Fight Club set in an even more idyllic world, where women don't even exist—an Eden without Eve." To be crude about it, German gay masculinism finds ample expression here, and many of the models from Lukacs's paintings are from his time spent in Berlin. While Lukacs and his commentators tend to want to situate his work in the realm of the fetishistic, the "uncensored," the apolitical, we can certainly find a politics at work here: unfettered masculinism—seductive, raw, and terrible; appropriative, dangerous, and antireproductive. Like Bersani, Lukacs seems to want to say that wherever desire may wander, perversely we must follow, and in the process we will find new intersections of desire and the political. But do we?

What if we are less seduced by the potent and fetishistic archive of masculine imagery that fascism offers to the contemporary gay imagination? What if we still want to question the particular links between politics and sex that fascism produces? Collier Schorr, a Jewish and queer photographer, is well known for a series of photo images that she made while living in southern Germany and staying with a family in a small town there. Her project "Neue Soldaten (New Soldiers), 1998" features photographs of young men playing at being soldiers. In some scenes the soldiers are dressed in Swedish uniforms, in others they are in U.S. military fatigues, in a few they appear as Israeli soldiers, and in others they wear Nazi uniforms. Schorr discusses how different it was for the boys to put on the Nazi uniform. Whereas they felt it was possible to play the "good guy" while wearing the other uniforms they were uncomfortable in the German uniform, unsure, afraid to be the bad guy, afraid not to be. The photographs stood in for an unrepresentable past; Schorr comments, "I brought a piece of history to them to which they didn't have access before."[5] This past was embedded in the landscape, the family, the village, the nation, but could not be inhabited or shown. Schorr goes on to say, "I make the work that Germans would make about Germany if they were American." She was also, however, trying to change the meaning of her Jewishness by confronting the large, Aryan male, the specter of terror from her youth, the enemy. But in this highly antinarcissistic project she realized that "talking about your enemies is another form of narcissism."

Her work tries hard to reckon, not with the self and its travails, but with the neighbor, the neighboring other, the proximate self that is nonetheless not you.

Schorr considers her work to be an ongoing investigation into the meaning of German masculinity in the long wake of the Holocaust (a context wholly absent from Lukacs's work), and by implication, her photographs also situate American white masculinity in that same shadow and Israeli militarism alongside both (Schorr 2003). Dressing up young German men in a variety of military outfits and shooting images of them in nature, she reflects upon the long history of the construction of German masculinity in the context of a relation to an idealized concept of unspoiled nature and deconstructs it at the same time. As Brett Ashley Kaplan says of Schorr's work, "By inserting her models into a German landscape riddled with traumatic memory, Schorr recoups the fascist tainting of the landscape tradition and appropriates it for a Jewish, antifascist sensibility" (2010: 128).

Unlike the Tom of Finland images and the Lukacs skinheads which partake in the reproduction of Nazi fetishism, Schorr's images acknowledge the frank sexual appeal of the military imagery, but they also capture the discomforting reality of that appeal. Her work in general is about memory and forgetting, cultural identity and appropriations, masquerade and revelation, and cross-identification as a queer mode of gender that can be deployed across other surfaces of identification. Schorr says of her Deutsche Guggenheim show, "Freeway Balconies," a collaborative meditation on performance, national identity, and unbelonging, "My own work involves asking people to perform my ideas of their history and identity." Referring to her portrait series of Bavarian youths in military gear she says, "I took off on that idea of what we 'recognize' in others, how we posit ourselves next to them. Each artist in the show is in some way asking the audience to reflect on that reflection" (Latimer 2008).

Schorr spent extended time in that small town in southern Germany trying to fulfill the role of an artist, archivist, and historian of German culture and imaging the kind of work that a German artist might make on masculinity were the material from the Nazi past not so off-limits. As a Jew and an American, not to mention as a queer person, Schorr was able to engage in a kind of counterintuitive modality of identification and disidentification that leads to some startling imagery: "I'm an artist with a persona," Schorr explains. "My work is about forging an identification with a place that I'm not from."[6] Of the relationship she created with the

20. Collier Schorr, "Andreas, POW (Every Good Soldier Was a Prisoner of War)," Germany, 2001. C-Print, 99.1 cm × 72.4 cm. CS 303. Courtesy of 303 Gallery, New York.

small Bavarian town where she crafted these images of German soldiers, she comments, "I consider it my town, but one that only half exists between what I see and what I imagine happened there, sort of like a retelling of German history in an American voice."

Schorr is also deeply interested in space, in the landscape against which her German boys play. The land that earlier took on such meaning for the pre-Nazi youth groups now hides the debris of that past in the form of what Schorr calls "relics and memories." These relics may take the form of a button pressed into the earth, a piece of a uniform. When asked what the family with whom she was staying thought about her dressing up their boys in Nazi uniforms, Schorr had this to say: "I think that when you take out a Nazi uniform in Germany a couple things happen really quickly. People are scared and somewhat excited. It's like this kind of forbidden thing. I remember unpacking the uniforms and the grandmother of the family, I asked her, 'Oh, does this shirt look like it's from that time period?' Because I wasn't sure if I was holding a reproduction or not. And she said, 'Oh, I haven't seen that since the '40s.' And I said, 'Well there you go . . .' Clearly, these were things that she recognized from when she was like eight years old or nine years old" (Schorr 2003). What does it mean to have an affective reaction to a piece of clothing that now stands in for genocide?

When you show them a Nazi uniform, says Schorr, "people are scared and somewhat excited." Again the combination of terror and eros, the forgotten and the forbidden is what allows for Nazi imagery to be recycled endlessly as sexual fetish. Schorr could almost be quoting Sontag's comments on the fascination exerted by fascism. In her denouncement in 1975 of the work of Leni Riefenstahl Sontag wrote, "Photographs of uniforms are erotic material, and particularly photographs of SS uniforms. Why the SS? Because the SS seems to be the most perfect incarnation of fascism in its overt assertion of the righteousness of violence, the right to have total power over others and to treat them as absolutely inferior. It was in the SS that this assertion seemed most complete, because they acted it out in a singularly brutal and efficient manner; and because they dramatized it by linking themselves to a certain aesthetic standard" (Sontag, 1975: 4). Schorr seems to want to resist the simplistic equation of Nazism with S/M, but she is also trying not to fetishize or at least refetishize the material and instead seems to want to use it to think through the fatal webs of masculinity into which young men are thrown. She sees her soldiers as certainly something much less than heroes, and yet they are something more than victims or martyrs. In one image a white German boy dresses up as an African American soldier in an attempt to reroute his masculinity away from Germanness and through an identification with an otherness that must always elude him. Schorr says of her model, "His refusal to be German is pointless — he blasts Southern music from his car like a scream against a German sky that takes no notice." She is less interested in the (failed) performance of blackness than in the potent desire to be someone else, particularly the desire for the white German to be a "figure he sees as persecuted, misunderstood, or underestimated" (Schorr 2003).

In an early study for the portrait "Traitor," an image that she used in her curated show "Freeway Balconies" in the Deutsche Guggenheim in 2008, Schorr has painted the young man's lips, censored the swastika on his arm and the ss insignia on his lapels, and blacked out his eyes (see plate 14). Beneath the image the chapter title "Booby Trap" appears, along with handwritten text: "talking about your enemies is another form of narcissism." The show as a whole addresses the project of identifying not simply with other people but with roles, performances, situations; it also addresses the project I have sketched out here, in which one is forced to identify with or at least acknowledge unheroic pasts. Acknowledging the contingency of selfhood, "Freeway Balconies" and Schorr's contribution to the show in particular asks, and I quote Schorr, "Could everything be different if one's image of oneself was that of another?" (Schorr, 2008: 15). This image of a rouged "Traitor" provides one answer to this question. We cannot reduce Schorr's "Night Porter (Matthias)" to a reclamation of an offensive image or to a repudiation of the fascination of fascism; it is in fact an inscrutable image, a visual contradiction, irreducible, seductive, terrifying, and sexy all at once. If it says anything, it says "The killer in you is the killer in me" and lets no one off the hook.

Conclusion

Using the provocative example of the imagined and real relationship between homosexuality and Nazism, I have argued in traitorous terms (traitorous to a politically pure history of homosexuality) that the desire to completely separate homosexuality from Nazism and to cast as homophobic all attempts to connect them misunderstands the multiplicity of gay history and simplifies the function of homosexuality. In a disloyal historiography homosexuality is not so much an identity stretching across time as a shifting set of relations between politics, eros, and power. To capture the complexity of these shifting relations we cannot afford to settle on linear connections between radical desires and radical politics; we have to be prepared to be unsettled by the politically problematic connections that history throws our way. Hence this book has engaged stupidity, countered hegemonic memory modes with queer forgetfulness, and looked to female masochism and gay betrayal to think through the meaning of failure as a way of life.

CHAPTER SIX

Animating *Failure*

Who am I? Why a fox? Why not a horse, or a beetle, or a bald eagle? I'm saying this more as, like, existentialism, you know? Who am I? And how can a fox ever be happy without, you'll forgive the expression, a chicken in its teeth?
—*Fantastic Mr. Fox*

On the topic of animation, as on so many other topics, I disagree with Slavoj Žižek (2009), who, in an article on the link between capitalism and new forms of authoritarianism, offers up the animated film *Kung Fu Panda* (2008) as an example of the kind of ideological sleight of hand that he sees as characteristic of both representative democracy and films for children. For Žižek, the fat and ungainly panda who accidently becomes a kung fu master is a figure that evokes George W. Bush or Silvio Berlusconi: by rising to the status of world champion without either talent or training, he masquerades as the little man who tries hard and succeeds, when in fact he is still a big man who is lazy but succeeds anyway because the system is tipped in his favor. By embedding this narrative in a fluffy, cuddly panda bear film, Žižek implies, what looks like entertainment is actually propaganda. Žižek has managed to get a lot of mileage out of his reading of this film precisely because his "big" critiques of economy and world politics seem so hilarious when personified by a text supposedly as inconsequential as *Kung Fu Panda*. I do not totally disagree with his analysis of an emergent form of authoritarian capitalism, but I strenuously object to his reading of *Kung Fu Panda*. Like so many animated films for children, *Kung Fu Panda* joins new forms of animation to new conceptions of the human-animal divide to offer a very different political landscape than the one we inhabit or at least the one Žižek imagines we inhabit.

Žižek also tackles the subject of failure in a book appropriately titled *In Defense of Lost Causes* (2008), but rather than take failure apart, as I have tried to do in this book, as a category levied by the winners against the losers and as a set of standards that ensure that all future radical ventures will be measured as cost-ineffective, he situates failure as a stopping point on the way to success. As in his other books, he pillories postmodernism, queers, and feminism, ignores critical ethnic studies altogether, and uses popular culture with high theory not to unravel difficult arguments or to practice a nonelite pedagogy but only to keep insisting that we are all dupes of culture, misreaders of history, and brainwashed by contemporary politics. Žižek does not defend lost causes; he just keeps trying to resurrect a model of political insurgency that depends upon the wisdom, the intellectual virtuosity, and the radical insight of, well, people like him.

Whereas Žižek uses popular culture and film in particular only to keep proving his Lacanian take on everything as good and true and to accuse others of being bamboozled by the shiny candy wrappers of Hollywood cinema, I have proposed in this book that animated cinema, far from being a pure form of ideology, and hegemonic ideology at that, as Žižek claims, is in fact a rich technological field for rethinking collectivities, transformation, identification, animality, and posthumanity. The genre of animation, particularly animation for children, has been used by both the right and the left to argue about the indoctrination of youth through seductive and seemingly harmless imagery. While Ariel Dorfman's classic book *How to Read Donald Duck* (1994) positioned Disney in the 1970s as a vehicle for U.S. imperialism, Sergei Eisenstein in the 1940s saw Disney cartoons in particular as a form of revolt: "Disney's film are a revolt against partitioning and legislating, against spiritual stagnation and greyness. But the revolt is lyrical. The revolt is a daydream" (1988: 4). In this daydream, says Eisenstein, we are able to see the world differently through a series of absurd oppositions that shuffle the coordinates of reality just enough to deliver Americans from the standardized monotony of life under capitalism. As I mentioned in the introduction, Walter Benjamin also invested hope in the magical opportunities afforded by the loopy figures of animation; before Walt Disney began meeting with Nazi officials in the 1930s Benjamin glimpsed the utopic possibilities of the riotous representational qualities of the colorful worlds of Mickey Mouse and friends. The combination of text and image, the layering of mechanisms of identification through animal avatars, and the magical mixture of color and craziness definitely allow for cartoons to serve as attractive tools for the easy transmission of dense ideologies. And yet the reduction of the animated image into pure symbol and the simplification of animated narratives into pure allegory do an injustice to the complexity of the magical surrealism that we find in animated cinema. While animation tends to be read as all form or all content, as pure message or pure image, it is in fact a heady mix of science, math, biology, and, in the case of stop-motion animation, alchemy, engineering, and puppetry.

In the first few CGI features to come out of Pixar and other animation studios, films like Finding Nemo, Monsters, Inc., and A Bug's Life, animators broke away from two-dimensional animation by creating logarithms for motion in water (Finding Nemo), by animating hair to make it move in realistic ways (Monsters, Inc.), and by using swarm technology to animate crowds (A Bug's Life). John Lasseter, chief creative office at Pixar and director of many of the first Pixar films, has said of A Bug's Life, for example, "The living organism is the entire ant colony, it's not the individual ant. It's such an important thing, and it became the theme of the story. . . . Individually the ants could be defeated, but if they stand up together and work together, there's nothing they cannot do" (quoted in Sarafian 2003: 217). The combination of attention to the specificity of ant life and the development of a computer technology capable of generating crowds or swarms creates depth at the level of both narrative and form. Katherine Sarafian studied the production of the multitude in A Bug's Life and learned that the crowd of insects was not created by replication of one animal into many; the crowd was actually treated as a character in the film by a "crowd team" which modeled crowd behavior, motion, waves of activity, and individual responses within the crowd to create "crowdness"— a visual read on the crowd that was believable precisely because it was flexible and plastic and not rigid and homogeneous. Crowd scenes such as those in A Bug's Life were unthinkable before CGI and became standard fare after its introduction; once the technology is in place (very expensive technology at that) animators want to put it to good use—hence more films on social insects like bees and more ants, films with schools of fish, huddles of penguins, and packs of rats. And more narrative drifts into

21. A *Bug's Life*, directed by John Lasseter, 1998. "The men behind the bugs."

the territory of the multitude, the people, the power of the many and the tyranny of the few. Two-dimensional cartoons often dealt with individual forms in linear sequences—a cat chasing a mouse, a cat chasing a bird, a wolf chasing a roadrunner, a dog chasing a cat. But CGI introduced numbers, groups, the multitude. Once you have an animation technique for the crowd, you need narratives about crowds, you need to animate the story line of the many and downplay the story line of the exception. Obviously, as I said in chapter 1, not all animated features of recent years play on revolutionary or anarchistic themes. So what allows some animated worlds to be transformative and returns others to the mindless repetition of the same?

In a very complicated article titled "A Theory of Animation: Cells, L-Theory and Film," Christopher Kelty and Hannah Landecker (2004) try to account for the emergence of animation from scientific attempts to record cellular life and death. In the process they link animation to a form of intelligent imaging, a mode within which images begin to think for themselves. They describe one particularly memorable animated sequence from *Fight Club* that simulates a journey through the protagonist's brain. The sequence is remarkable for being a simulation of the brain (created using L-systems or algorithms that can model plant development) that, on account of its internal logic and inner complexity, comes close to being a brain. Kelty and Landecker write, "Contemporary film, art, and architecture are replete with biologically inflected forms: L-systems, cellular automata, and genetic algorithms are used to create (among other things) the complex forests, photorealistic skin and hair, and lively and deadly animated crowds that are now regular features of software packages such as Alias Wavefront's 'Maya' or Softimage's 'Behavior'" (32). Animation, Kelty and Landecker show, merges mathematical modeling with biological systems of growth and development and then uses both to "grow" an image. In this way animation is much more than the setting in motion of a nonhuman image; it is a site where image and biology meet and develop into another form of life. Kelty's and Landecker's very useful "media archaeology" links early twentieth-century micro-cinematography, used to capture the processes of cell life and death, to computer graphic animations in the late twentieth century, used to create lively art. At stake for Kelty and Landecker is a more thorough understanding of the dynamic relations between scientific and philosophical theory and a less pronounced separation between reality and representation.

I am primarily interested in Kelty's and Landecker's work for their insight into the science of contemporary animation and CGI's seemingly magical originality. Animated worlds, they seem to imply, are more than an enhanced view of reality or even an imaginative alternative to the real; they are in fact living and breathing systems with their own internal logics, with growing and living matter. As Deleuze argues for cinema in general, animated images are disruptions to habitual methods of thought. Kelty and Landecker also remind us that life is movement; the early still photography that scientists tried to use to capture cellular transformation was useless precisely because it suspended the very processes that the camera needed to capture in motion. The dynamic between motion and stillness is the dynamic between life and death that is nowhere more dramatically captured than in stop-motion animation.

Stop-motion animation has been around in one form or another since the late nineteenth century. Historians tend to credit Albert Smith and J. Stuart Blackton for the first use of the medium in *The Humpty Dumpty Circus* (1898); predictably in this film, as in so many that followed, toys come to life, transformed from wooden to animated. This theme is common to all kinds of Gothic literatures and is one of the definitions of the uncanny that Freud considers in his famous essay of 1925 but ultimately rejects in favor of a psychoanalytic understanding of the uncanny as something that has been repressed and returns to consciousness. This return can certainly take the form of a reanimation, but the uncanniness is not the animated creature so much as the repressed feeling that has come back to life. Freud wrote, "if psycho-analytic theory is correct in maintaining that every emotional effect, whatever its quality, is transformed from repression into morbid anxiety, then among such cases of anxiety there must be a class in which the anxiety can be shown to be come from something repressed which recurs. This class of morbid anxiety would then be no other than what is uncanny, irrespective of whether it originally aroused dread or some other affect" (1958: 148). Building on Freud's notion of the uncanny we can think about animated objects as embodying a repetition, a recurrence, an uncanny replay of repressed activity. There is no question that stop-motion lends animation a spooky and uncanny quality; it conveys life where we expect stillness, and stillness where we expect liveliness.

Stop-motion animation is a time-consuming, technically challenging, precise activity. After each shot, a figure or puppet or prop is moved slightly; thus a stop-motion or claymation feature is made one frame at a time. Motion is implied by the relation of one shot to another rather than recorded by a camera traveling alongside moving objects. As the name suggests, stop-motion depends not on continuous action but on the relations between stillness and motion, cuts and takes, action and passivity. Unlike classical cinema, in which the action attempts to appear seamless and suture consists of the erasure of all marks of editing and human presence, stop-motion animation is uncanny precisely because it depends on the manipulation of the figures in front of the camera by those behind it. These relations of dependency, of submission even, are precisely the ones that we go to the cinema to forget. So the ghostly shifts that stop-motion animation records and incorporates, the shifts between action and direction, intention and script, desire and constraint, force upon the viewer a darker reality about the human and about representation in general.

In stop-motion animation the themes of remote control, manipula-

22. Wallace and Gromit in *The Curse of the Were-Rabbit*,
directed by Steve Box and Nick Park, 2005.

tion, entrapment, and imprisonment are everywhere. Even in the rela-
tively cheerful British classic *Wallace and Gromit*, man and dog are constantly manipulated by the machines they invent to make life easier. For
example, in *Wrong Trousers* (1993, directed by Nick Park) Wallace, under
the burden of financial problems, takes in a penguin as a lodger to make
some extra money. Gromit suspects that the penguin is a shady character,
and he follows him closely to see what he is up to. The penguin, Feathers
McGraw, disguises himself as a chicken and commits crimes. When he
finds the techno trousers that Wallace invented to walk Gromit without
human assistance, he uses them to remotely control Wallace to steal a
large diamond from a museum. After a long chase that concludes with a
raucous ride on a model railway, Gromit captures the penguin and turns
him in. Wallace throws the techno trousers in the dustbin, and he and
Gromit return to their domestic routine. In the meantime the trousers
walk off by themselves. In *A Close Shave*, the culprit is a robo-dog, and in
The Curse of the Were-Rabbit Wallace accidentally creates a Frankensteinian
monstrous rabbit in his Mind Manipulation O-Matic Machine, a unit designed to brainwash rabbits not to eat the town's vegetable gardens.

While the *Wallace and Gromit* series uses relations between and among
humans, animals, and machines to scramble conventional assumptions

about control, manipulation, and free will, in Nick Park's other stop-motion film, Chicken Run, the idea of entrapment and imprisonment is front and center. The claymation birds, as I discussed in chapter 1, hatch a plot to escape from the confines of the chicken farm and use Wallace-like contraptions to fly the coop. Park's films in general are cheerful, whimsical, funny, and not exactly dark, but at the same time they deal squarely with questions of exploitation, servitude, entrapment, and forced labor. Some recent American stop-motion features use the genre for distinctly dark purposes.

Coraline (2009), for example, is an incredibly dark and moody feature by Henry Selick that explores the loneliness of a young girl with busy parents who longs for a different kind of life, full of color, excitement, extraordinary events and people. Her wish comes true when she finds a secret passageway in the new apartment into which she and her parents have just moved. The passageway leads to another world, a mirror image of the one she left behind, but with seemingly loving parents, colorful and outlandish characters, and sweets and toys galore. Predictably the new world, entertaining as it is, turns out to be a monstrous land of lost souls, and Coraline has to figure out how to escape back to her own world, avoid the devouring love of her "Other Mother," and restore the lost souls of the ghostly children she finds there. In Coraline the symbol of the other world is the button eye, the mark of the loss of the soul and the transformation of child into doll. While many animation films and children's stories fantasize about a toy world that is a great improvement on the human world, this one paints a toy dystopia in blinding colors and hip design motifs. It merges at times with the circus, the theater, and the botanical garden, and it aligns the artificial with the monstrous and the real and true with the good.

In fact Coraline is a deeply conservative narrative about the dangers of a world that is crafted in opposition to the natural world of family and the ordinary. The most obvious symptom of the film's conservative commitments is the spidery Other Mother, a Black Widow who governs her mute husband with an iron claw and eats her young. Like some bad Freudian horror film, Coraline uses stop-motion not to revel in the glory of invention and originality, as the Wallace and Gromit series does; nor does Coraline use its uncanny stop-start jerky motions to draw attention to the mechanisms of capital, as Chicken Run does. In Coraline stop-motion is the marker of the unreal, the queer, the monstrously different, and animation opposes the natural. Coraline transforms over the course of the film from a proto-feminist critic of the family, boys, and normativity into a submissive girl and dutiful daughter, committed not to production but to reproduction.

Obviously there is no guarantee that animation, and stop-motion animation in particular, will produce politically progressive narratives. As in the horror genre in general, monsters can offer pointed critiques of normativity and a queer alternative, or they can phobically encase the fears of the culture in queer, racialized, and female bodies. Ultimately, however, animation allows the viewer to enter into other worlds and other formulations of this world. By refusing to see animated films as simply flat allegorical statements, we can begin to understand why Žižek is so wrong about *Kung Fu Panda*. If, as Kelty and Landecker propose, cinema is not simply image or image masquerading as reality, but, as David Rodowick puts it in his reading of Deleuze, an "image of thought, a visual and acoustic rendering of thought in relation to time and movement" (Rodowick, 1997: 6), then animated cinema cannot be the staging of this or that unified set of ideological commitments. It must also always be the image of ideologically committed thought. It is also the image of change and transformation itself, so we should not be surprised to find that in animated cinema transformation is one of the most dominant themes.

The media archaeology provided by Kelty and Landecker for animation reminds us to look for the meaning of animation at the level of form as well as content. We cannot just take a film like *Kung Fu Panda*, shake it up with a little dose of contemporary politics, and pour its contents out onto the counter to look at how well it has absorbed and blended with one political message. Nor, for that matter, are young spectators simply empty vessels, SpongeBobs waiting to be saturated with adult morality. In fact *SpongeBob SquarePants* more than most animated series for children reminds us that children resist ready-made meaning, ignore heavy-handed morality, and pay careful attention to details in a film that most adults might pass over. Most animated films for children are antihumanist, antinormative, multigendered, and full of wild forms of sociality. Their antihumanism springs from both the predominance of nonhuman creatures and the refusal of individualism that is inscribed into the collective form of art making that goes on at an animation campus like DreamWorks and Pixar. The antinormative nature of animated film, as I suggested earlier, arises out of the wacky juxtapositions found in animated worlds between bodies, groups, and environments. And the multigendered forms sprout from the strangeness of voice-body combinations, the imaginative rendering of character, and the permeability of the relation between background and foreground in any given animated scene.

To bring this meditation on stop-motion animation, darkness, and failure to an (in)appropriate conclusion, I want to turn now to *Fantastic Mr. Fox* to consider how stop-motion might bring out the queer and radical potential of a genre populated by wild animals and committed to a form of antihumanism. While *Coraline* used the antihuman in order to confirm the goodness and rightness of the world as it is, *Fantastic Mr. Fox* uses wild animals to expose the brutality and narrow-mindedness of the human. Based on a Roald Dahl novel, *Fantastic Mr. Fox* (2009, directed by Wes Anderson) tells the story of an aspiring fox (voiced by George Clooney) who gives up his wild ways of chicken hunting to settle down with his foxy lady (voiced by Meryl Streep) in a burrow. As the film begins, we find Mr. Fox striving for something more, looking for excitement in his life, wanting to move above ground and out of the sedate world of journalism and into the wild world of chasing chickens. From his new home in a tree, Mr. Fox can see the three farms of Boggis, Bunce, and Bean, which present him with a challenge he cannot refuse. "Who am I?" he asks his friend Kylie, an eager but not gifted possum. "Why a fox? Why not a horse, or a beetle, or a bald eagle? I'm saying this more as, like, existentialism, you know? Who am I? And how can a fox ever be happy without, you'll forgive the expression, a chicken in its teeth?" How indeed?

Of course Mr. Fox cannot be happy without that chicken in his teeth; the difference between a fox in the hole and a fox in the wild is just one hunting trip away. The symbols of wildness in the film have much to do with stop-motion animation technology; for example, when the foxes sit down to eat, they serve up food on tables with table cloths and observe good manners until the food is in front of them, at which point the motion speeds up and we hear sounds not of polite eating but of the foxes tearing their food apart. The jerkiness of the stop-and-go animation replaces the smoothness of the mannered movements associated with civility and humanness and aligns stop-motion with a relay between wild and domestic, destruction and consumption.

One scene in particular captures this tension between wildness and domestication, stillness and motion, survival and death. In the much debated "wolf scene" of *Fantastic Mr. Fox*, the animated creatures enter the in between realm theorized by Kelty and Landecker as intelligent imaging and by Freud as "the uncanny." In this scene, Mr. Fox and his friends zoom homeward after escaping from the farmers' traps. In a whimsical set up typical of this film, Mr. Fox is driving a motorcycle with a side-car. The wind (a hair dryer probably) ruffles the animals' fur and they bump along towards their underground hideout. Suddenly Kylie the Possum looks back and warns the other animals: "Don't turn around!" Of course, all the animals immediately turn their heads around! For a moment, the animals peer out through the camera at the audience and then we cut to a long shot and see the motorcycle screech to a halt. What follows is a shot reverse-shot sequence within which Mr. Fox looks off toward the woods and sees a lone wolf, a black wolf, standing proudly on a rock and peering back at Mr. Fox and friends. Mr. Fox hails the wolf in English, French, and Latin ("canin lupus" says Mr. Fox pointing at the wolf and then "vulpes vulpes" pointing to himself). "I have a phobia of wolves," says Mr. Fox and then, when language doesn't work, Mr. Fox retreats to gesture. He looks long and hard at the wolf, his eyes welling with tears before throwing up a fist in salute and receiving a fist back.

This scene has been questioned in the blogosphere for its odd racial references—the wolf is black and the salute exchanged between the wolf and Mr. Fox is a Black Power salute making it seem as if the wolf represents some kind of racial other as well as otherness itself. While the racial overtones are definitely there, and there could be an implication that otherness and wildness are the properties of Blackness, the scene can also be taken as a nod to the liveliness of the wild, the wildness of animation itself and the animatedness of life in general. The wolf also represents the outside of the fox/farmer dyad and the utopian possibility of an elsewhere; and in his aloneness, the wolf signifies singularity, isolation, uniqueness but also death. The emotion that wells up in Mr. Fox as he confronts his fears ("I have a phobia of wolves") brims with all these possibilities and brings us back to the Freudian theory of the uncanny— something that has been repressed recurs, the repressed instinct. The uncanny here is represented by the wolf and as he confronts the wolf, repressed feelings flood Mr. Fox and he turns to face his dread, his anxiety, his other and in doing so, he reconciles to the wild in a way that instructs the humans watching the film to reconcile to wildness, to animatedness, to life and to death.

As for the gender politics of wildness and domesticity, while this stop-motion animation marvel seems ultimately to reinforce the same old narrative of female domesticity and male wildness, in fact it tells a tall tale of masculine derring-do in order to offer up some very different forms of masculinity, collectivity, and family. Just to touch on the highlights of the film: Mr. Fox has a sissy son, Ash, who desperately wants his father's approval but who also wears dresses and lipstick; Mr. Fox loses his tail in an encounter with the farmers but does not miss a beat in his masculine confidence as a result; the wild animals are chased underground by the farmers, where they forge new cross-species alliances, alliances that break with the human-like functions they previously performed and instead revel in the sheer animality of precariousness and survival.

Ultimately all of the radical animations I have catalogued in this book are films not simply *about* globalization or neoliberalism, individuality or conformity; they are also about what has been animated and how, what technology has been crafted, and what stories arise from the contact between that technology and the many animation engineers who use it collaboratively to craft a new narrative. Accordingly *Kung Fu Panda* is not about unworthy leaders or success; it is a story of awkward grace and odd connections between seemingly unrelated species (the panda's father is a crane, for example). A *Bug's Life* is not just about bravery in the face of tyranny; it showcases the ability to think in multiples, to move as a crowd, to identify as many. *Finding Nemo* is not about searching or the father-son relationship; it is not even about survival. It is a film about oceanic consciousness, underworld alliances, and, to quote the title of a book by Samuel Delany, the motion of light on water (Delany, 2004).

Likewise *Fantastic Mr. Fox* is not only about fighting the law and the farmers; it is also about stopping and going, moving and halting, inertia and dynamism; it is about survival and its component parts and the costs of survival for those who remain. One of the very best moments in *Fantastic Mr. Fox*, and the moment most memorable in terms of stop-motion animation and survival, comes in the form of a speech that Mr. Fox makes to his woodland friends who have outlived the farmers' attempt to starve them all out of their burrows. The sturdy group of survivors dig their way out of a trap laid for them by Boggis, Bunce, and Bean and find themselves burrowing straight up into a closed supermarket stocked with all the supplies they need. Mr. Fox, buoyed by this lucky turn of events, addresses his clan for the last time: "They say all foxes are slightly allergic to linoleum, but it's cool to the paw—try it. They say my tail needs to be dry cleaned twice a month, but now it's fully detachable—see? They say our tree may never grow back, but one day, something will. Yes, these crackles are made of synthetic goose and these giblets come from artificial squab

23. *Where the Wild Things Are*, directed by Spike Jonz, 2009.
"Happiness is not always the best way to be happy."

and even these apples look fake—but at least they've got stars on them.
I guess my point is, we'll eat tonight, and we'll eat together. And even in
this not particularly flattering light, you are without a doubt the five and
a half most wonderful wild animals I've ever met in my life. So let's raise
our boxes—to our survival."

Not quite a credo, something short of a toast, a little less than a speech,
but Mr. Fox gives here one of the best and most moving—both emotionally and in stop-motion terms—addresses in the history of cinema. Unlike *Coraline*, where survival is predicated upon a rejection of the theatrical, the queer, and the improvised, and like *Where the Wild Things Are*, where
the disappointment of deliverance must be leavened with the pragmatism of possibility, *Fantastic Mr. Fox* is a queerly animated classic in that
it teaches us, as *Finding Nemo*, *Chicken Run*, and so many other revolting
animations before it, to believe in detachable tails, fake apples, eating
together, adapting to the lighting, risk, sissy sons, and the sheer importance of survival for all those wild souls that the farmers, the teachers,
the preachers, and the politicians would like to bury alive.

I opened this book with an appropriately peppy engagement with
SpongeBob SquarePants; in chapter 5 I offered a less bouncy articulation of
homosexual fascism precisely in order not to let queerness off the hook
as a place where the commitment to fail and to, in the words of Samuel
Beckett (1938), "fail again, fail better" tends to give way to a desire for

oddly normative markers of success and achievement. Queerness offers the promise of failure as a way of life (and here I am obviously amending Foucault's formulation of homosexuality as "friendship as a way of life"), but it is up to us whether we choose to make good on that promise in a way that makes a detour around the usual markers of accomplishment and satisfaction. Indeed while Jamaica Kincaid reminds us that happiness and truth are not at all the same thing, and while numerous anti-heroes, many of them animated, quoted in these pages have articulated a version of being predicated upon awkwardness, clumsiness, disorientation, bewilderment, ignorance, disappointment, disenchantment, silence, disloyalty, and immobility, perhaps Judith in the movie version of *Where the Wild Things Are* says it best: "Happiness is not always the best way to be happy."

I have turned repeatedly (but not exclusively) in this book to the "silly" archives of animated film. While many readers may object to the idea that we can locate alternatives in a genre engineered by huge corporations for massive profits and with multiple product tie-ins, I have claimed that new forms of animation, computer-generated imagery in particular, have opened up new narrative opportunities and have led to unexpected encounters between the childish, the transformative, and the queer. In this last chapter, and by way of conclusion, I have looked at the dark side of animation, the ways animation, and stop-motion animation in particular, takes us not simply through the looking glass but into some negative spaces of representation, dark places where animals return to the wild, humans flirt with their own extinction, and worlds end. Of course in animation for children they never do quite end, and there is usually a happy conclusion even to the most crooked of animated narratives. In *Coraline*, for example, the young girl who has escaped through the walls of her apartment to a bizarre universe with an "Other Mother" and "Other Father" returns home and is finally happy to be there. In *Fantastic Mr. Fox* the hunted and haunted animals that have been driven from their homes by the farmers rejoice in their sheer survival. In *Where the Wild Things Are*— part animation, part magical puppetry—Max leaves the sad, haunted beasts with whom he has built and destroyed habitats and submits to the strong pull of the Oedipal home. But along the way to these "happy" endings, bad things happen to good animals, monsters, and children, and failure nestles in every dusty corner, reminding the child viewer that this too is what it means to live in a world created by mean, petty, greedy, and violent adults. To live is to fail, to bungle, to disappoint, and ultimately to die; rather than searching for ways around death and disappointment, the queer art of failure involves the acceptance of the finite, the embrace of the absurd, the silly, and the hopelessly goofy. Rather than resisting endings and limits, let us instead revel in and cleave to all of our own inevitable fantastic failures.

Introduction

1. Benjamin Wallace-Wells, "Surfing the University: An Academic Dropout and the Search for a Theory of Everything," *New Yorker*, 21 July 2008, 33.

2. See David A. Price, *The Pixar Touch* (New York: Alfred A. Knopf, 2008).

3. David Graeber also discusses "low theory" in his book on anarchism. He writes: "Even more than High Theory, what anarchism needs is what might be called Low Theory: a way of grappling with those real, immediate questions that emerge from a transformative project" (9). I think Graeber and I are thinking along the same lines here.

CHAPTER ONE. *Animating Revolt*

1. Amy Sutherland, "What Shamu Taught Me about a Happy Marriage," *New York Times*, 25 June 2006, Style section.

2. See, for example, Roger Ebert, "March of the Penguins," *Chicago Sun-Times*, 8 July 2005; Stephen Holden, "The Lives and Loves (Perhaps) of Emperor Penguins," *New York Times*, 24 June 2005. Holden writes, "Although 'March of the Penguins' stops mercifully short of trying to make us identify with the hardships overcome by a single penguin family, it conveys an intimate sense of the life of the emperor penguin. But love? I don't think so."

3. Jon Mooallem, "The Love That Dare Not Squawk Its Name: Can Animals Be Gay," *New York Times*, 31 March 2010, Magazine section.

4. Natalie Angier, "In Hollywood Hives, the Males Rule," *New York Times*, 13 November 2007, Science section.

1. For more on queerness as "disorientation," see Ahmed 2007.

2. Bruce LaBruce, "Dudes' Smooch Leads the Way," *Eye Weekly*, 1 February 2001, online.

3. A similar argument motivates Macarena Gomez-Barris's meditations on the politics of remembering in the wake of state terror in *Where Memory Dwells* (2009).

4. Lisa Duggan and Richard Kim, "Beyond Gay Marriage," *The Nation*, 18 July 2005, 25.

5. See Newton 1996; Weston 1998; Rubin 1975; Eng 2003; Butler 2002.

6. This film is just one of a whole slew of "forgetting" films, including *Memento* (2000, directed by Christopher Nolan) and *The Eternal Sunshine of the Spotless Mind* (2004, directed by Michel Gondry). But the earnest films on forgetting are too quick to make forgetting into the loss of individuality. I am interested in what forgetting enables, not what it blocks.

7. See Muñoz's *Crusing Utopia* and Freeman's *Time Binds*. These very important books on queer temporality came out as I was finishing my book and therefore I have engaged with them less than I should have. Muñoz also writes extensively on failure in *Cruising Utopia*.

CHAPTER THREE. *The Queer Art of Failure*

1. See Rosyln Oxley9 Gallery, www.roslynoxley9.com.

2. For details on Patricia Highsmith's troubled relationship with her mother, her anti-social tendencies, and her propensity for lists, see Joan Schenkar, *The Talented Miss Highsmith* (2009).

3. Hearkening back to a history of representations of homosexuality as loss and death from Proust to Radclyffe Hall, Majoli's work also converses with that of artists painting from dark rather than light—sometimes called the "tenebrists," painters like Caravaggio (famously rendered as queer by Derek Jarman in a film of the same name), and Rembrandt, who painted out of the darkness while refusing to make it recede and give way to the light. The eighteenth-century Spanish painter Goya is most often associated with Black paintings, and his works combine horrific subject matter with gloomy perspectives on the human conditions. Art from the dark side refuses humanist narratives about enlightenment, progress, and happiness, and it reminds us of the violence, the density, of human experience. This is what we forget when we insist upon positive images in popular representation and when we focus only on political recognition and acceptance in our politics. For further information on the black mirror and the politics of painting in the dark, see Lasch 2010 and English 2010.

4. Tavir Nyong'o makes a similar argument in relation to Lee Edelman's polemic and the missing reference to punk (Nyong'o 2008).

5. Robert McRuer has theorized the multiple relations between queerness and disability in his landmark book, *Crip Theory* (McRuer, 2006).

CHAPTER FOUR. *Shadow Feminisms*

1. Elizabeth Freeman tackles a similar reconsideration of s/m in relation to feminism and queer temporalities in a chapter titled: "Turn the Beat Around: Sadomasochism, Temporality, History" in *Time Binds: Queer Temporalities, Queer Histories* (2010: 137–70).

2. Jamaica Kincaid interviewed by Marilyn Snell, "Jamaica Kincaid Hates Happy Endings," *Mother Jones*, September–October 1997.

3. Jeffrey Fleishman, "Member's abrupt resignation rocks Nobel Prize community," *Boston Globe*, 12 October 2005.

CHAPTER FIVE. *Homosexuality and Fascism*

1. For an informative account of the women who formed Britain's Volunteer Police Force see Laura Doan, *Fashioning Sapphism* (2001).

2. Harvey Milk, speech on 25 June 1978, quoted in Randy Shilts, *The Mayor of Castro Street: The Life and Times of Harvey Milk* (New York: St. Martin's Press, 1982), 364.

3. For more on Stein's interest in Weininger, see Harrowitz and Hyams 1995.

4. Richard Goldstein, "Culturati: Skin Deep" in *Village Voice*, February 9–15, 2000.

5. Edith Newhall, "Out of the Past," *New York Magazine*, 3 December 2001, 5.

6. Collier Schorr, "'Racing the Dead' by Howard Halle," *Time Out New York*, 13–17 September 2007.

Agamben, Giorgio. 1998. *Homo Sacer: Sovereign Power and Bare Life*. Palo Alto, Calif.: Stanford University Press.

Ahmed, Sarah. 2007. *Queer Phenomenology*. Durham: Duke University Press.

Althusser, Louis. 2001. *Lenin and Philosophy and Other Essays*. New York: Monthly Review Press.

Beauvoir, Simone de. 1989. *The Second Sex*. New York: Vintage.

Beckett, Samuel. 1938. *Murphy*. 12th edition. New York: Grove Press.

Benjamin, Walter. 1969. "Theses on the Philosophy of History," in *Illuminations: Essays and Reflections*. New York: HBJ: 253–65.

———. 1996. *Selected Writings 1913–1926*, vol. 1, ed. Marcus Bullock and Michael Jennings. Cambridge: Harvard University Press.

Berlant, Lauren. 1997. *The Queen of America Goes to Washington City: Essays on Sex and Citizenship*. Durham: Duke University Press.

Bersani, Leo. 1986. *The Freudian Body: Psychoanalysis and Art*. New York: Columbia University Press.

———. 1996. *Homos*. Cambridge: Harvard University Press.

———. 2009. *Is the Rectum a Grave and Other Essays*. Chicago: University of Chicago Press.

Bishop, Elizabeth. 2008. *Poems, Prose, and Letters*. New York: Library of America.

Blake, Nayland. 2005. "Further Horizons," in *Judie Bamber: Further Horizons*. Claremont, Calif.: Pomona College Museum of Art: 5–9.

Bosworth, Patricia. 2006. *Diane Arbus: A Biography*. New York: W. W. Norton.

Brassai, Gyula Halasz. 1976. *The Secret Paris of the 1930's*. New York: Pantheon.

Brooks, Daphne. 2006. *Bodies in Dissent: Spectacular Performances of Race and Freedom, 1850–1910*. Durham: Duke University Press.

Butler, Judith. 1990. *Gender Trouble: Feminism and the Subversion of Identity*. New York: Routledge.

————. 2002. *Anitgones' Claim: Kinship between Life and Death*. New York: Columbia University Press.

Chisholm, Dianne. 2005. *Queer Constellations: Subcultural Space in the Wake of the City*. Minneapolis: University of Minnesota Press.

Clover, Carol. 1993. *Men, Women, and Chainsaws: Gender in the Modern Horror Film*. Princeton: Princeton University Press.

Crisp, Quentin. 1968. *The Naked Civil Servant*. New York: Plume.

Cvetkovich, Ann. 2003. *An Archive of Feelings: Trauma, Sexuality, and Lesbian Public Cultures*. Durham: Duke University Press.

Dean, Tim. 2009. *Unlimited Intimacy: Reflections on the Subculture of Barebacking*. Chicago: University of Chicago Press.

Delany, Samuel. 2001. *Times Square Red, Times Square Blue*. New York: New York University Press.

————. 2004. *The Motion of Light in Water: Sex and Science Fiction in the East Village*. Minneapolis: University of Minnesota Press.

Deleuze, Gilles. 1971. *Masochism: An Interpretation of Coldness and Cruelty*, trans. Jean McNeil. New York: Braziller.

Derrida, Jacques. 1998. *Archive Fever: A Freudian Impression*, trans. Eric Prenowitz. Chicago: University of Chicago Press.

Doan, Laura. 2001. *Fashioning Sapphism: The Origins of a Modern English Lesbian Culture*. New York: Columbia University Press.

Dorfman, Ariel. 1994. *How to Read Donald Duck: Imperialist Ideology in the Disney Comic*. New York: International General.

Duggan, Lisa. 2004. *The Twilight of Equality?: Neoliberalism, Cultural Politics, and the Attack on Democracy*. Boston: Beacon Press.

Duggan, Lisa, and Richard Kim. 2005. "Beyond Gay Marriage." *The Nation*. 18 July, 25.

Edelman, Lee. 2005. *No Future: Queer Theory and the Death Drive*. Durham: Duke University Press.

Ehrenreich, Barbara. 2009. *Bright-Sided: How the Relentless Pursuit of Positive Thinking Has Undermined America*. New York: Metropolitan Books.

Eisenstein, Sergei. 1988. *Eisenstein 3: Eisenstein on Disney*, trans. Alan Upchurch. New York: Methuen.

El-Tayeb, Fatima. 2011. *Queering Ethnicity: Minority Activism in Postnational Europe*. Minneapolis: University of Minnesota Press.

Eng, David. 2003. "Transnational Adoption and Queer Diaspora." *Social Text* 21, no. 3, 1–37.

English, Darby. 2007. *How to See a Work of Art in Total Darkness*. Cambridge: MIT Press.

Ferguson, Roderick. 2005. *Aberrations in Black: Toward a Queer of Color Critique*. Minneapolis: University of Minnesota Press.

Foucault, Michel. 1995. *Discipline and Punish: The Birth of the Prison*, trans. Alan Sheridan. New York: Vintage.

———. 1998. *The History of Sexuality Volume 1: An Introduction*. New York: Vintage.

———. 2003. *Society Must Be Defended: Lectures at the College De France, 1975–1976*, trans. David Macey. New York: Picador.

Franklin, Sarah. 2006. "The Cyborg Embryo: Our Path to Transbiology." *Theory, Culture and Society Annual Review* 1, no. 1.

Freeman, Elizabeth. 2005. "Monsters, Inc.: Notes on the Neoliberal Arts Education." *New Literary History* 36, no. 1, 83–95.

———. 2010. *Time Binds: Queer Temporalities, Queer Histories*. Durham: Duke University Press.

Freire, Paulo. 2000. *Pedagogy of the Oppressed*, trans. Myra Bergman Ramos. New York: Contiuum.

Freud, Sigmund. 1963. "A Child Is Being Beaten" (1919), in *Sexuality and the Psychology of Love*, ed. Philip Rieff. New York: Simon and Schuster.

———. 1958. "The Uncanny" in *On Creativity and the Unconscious*. New York: Harper & Row: 122–61.

Frichtl, Ben. 2005. "Concerned Women for America." cwfa.org, 13 December (accessed July 6, 2010).

Gibson-Graham, J. K. 1996. *The End of Capitalism (As We Knew It): A Feminist Critique of Political Economy*. London: Blackwell.

Giles, Geoffrey. 2002. "The Denial of Homosexuality: Same-Sex Incidents in Himmler's ss and Police." *Journal of the History of Sexuality* 11, nos. 1–2, January–April, 256–90.

Gomez-Barris, Macarena. 2009. *Where Memory Dwells: Culture and Violence in Chile*. Berkeley: University of California Press.

Gopinath, Gayatri. 2005. *Impossible Desires: Queer Disapora and South Asian Public Cultures*. Durham: Duke University Press.

Gordon, Avery. 1996. *Ghostly Matters: Haunting and the Sociological Imagination*. Minneapolis: University of Minnesota Press.

Graeber, David. *Fragments of an Anarchist Anthropology*. Chicago: Prickly Paradigm.

Gramsci, Antonio. 2000. "Hegemony, Relations of Force, Historical Bloc," in *The Gramsci Reader: Selected writings, 1916–1935*, ed. David Forgasc. New York: New York University Press.

Grandin, Temple. 2010. *Animals Make Us Human: Creating the Best Life for Animals*. New York: Mariner.

Halberstam, Judith. 1998. *Female Masculinity*. Durham: Duke University Press.

Hall, Stuart. 1990. "Gramsci's Relevance for the Study of Race and Ethnicity." *Stuart Hall: Critical Dialogues in Cultural Studies*, ed. Kuan-Hsing and David Morley Chen. New York: Routledge.

———. 1991. "Old and New Identities, Old and New Ethnicities," in *Culture, Globalization and the World System*, ed. Anthony D. King. London: Macmillan: 42–69.

————. 1997. "The Global and the Local: Globalization and Ethnicity," in *Dangerous Liasons: Gender, Nation, and Postcolonial Perspectives*, ed. Anne McClintock, Aamir Mufti, and Ella Shohat. Minneapolis: University of Minnesota Press: 173–87.

Haraway, Donna. 1990. *Primate Visions: Gender, Race, and Nature in the World of Modern Science*. New York: Routledge.

————. 2003. *The Companion Species Manifesto: Dogs, People, and Significant Otherness*. Chicago: Prickly Paradigm Press.

————. 2007. *When Species Meet (Posthumanities)*. Minneapolis: University of Minnesota Press.

Hardt, Michael, and Antonio Negri. 2005. *Multitude: War and Democracy in the Age of Empire*. London: Penguin.

Harrowitz, Nancy A., and Barbara Hyams. 1995. *Jews and Gender: Responses to Otto Weininger*. Philadelphia: Temple University Press.

Hart, Lynda. 1998. *Between the Body and the Flesh: Performing Sadomasochism*. New York: Columbia University Press.

Hartman, Saidiya. 1997. *Scenes of Subjection: Terror, Slavery, and Self-Making in Nineteenth Century America*. Oxford: Oxford University Press.

————. 2008. *Lose Your Mother: A Journey along the Atlantic Slave Route*. New York: Farrah, Strauss and Giroux.

Herzog, Dagmar. 2002. "Hubris and Hypocrisy, Incitement and Disavowal: Sexuality and German Fascism." *Journal of the History of Sexuality* 11, nos. 1–2, January–April, 3–21.

————. 2007. *Sex after Fascism: Memory and Morality in Twentieth Century Germany*. Princeton: Princeton University Press.

Hewitt, Andrew. 1996. *Political Inversions: Homosexuality, Fascism, and the Modernist Imaginary*. Palo Alto, Calif.: Stanford University Press.

Hocquenghem, Guy. 1993. "Capitalism, the Family, and the Anus," in *Homosexual Desire*, trans. Daniella Dangoor. Durham: Duke University Press.

Jelinek, Elfride. 2009. *The Piano Teacher*, trans. Joachim Neugroschel. New York: Grove.

Jensen, Erik. 2002. "The Pink Triangle and Political Consciousness: Gays, Lesbians, and the Memory of Nazi Persecution." *Journal of the History of Sexuality* 11, nos. 1–2, January–April, 319–49.

Jones, Ernest. 1957. *The Life and Work of Sigmund Freud*. Vol. 2. New York: Basic Books.

Kaplan, Brett Ashley. 2010. *Landscapes of Holocaust Postmemory*. New York: Routledge.

Kelty, Christopher, and Hannah Landecker. 2004. "A Theory of Animation: Cells, L-systems, and Film." *Grey Room*, September, 30–63.

Kincaid, Jamaica. 1997. *Autobiography of My Mother*. New York: Plume.

Kipnis, Laura. 2004. *Against Love: A Polemic*. New York: Vintage, 2004.

Klein, Norman. 1997. *The History of Forgetting: Los Angeles and the Erasure of Memory*. London: Verso.

Lacan, Jacques. 1977. *Ecrits*, trans. Alan Sheridan. London: Tavistock.

Lasch, Pedro, ed. 2010. *Black Mirror/Espejo Negra*. Durham: Duke University Press.

Latimer, Quinn. 2008. "Collier Schorr on Brooke Shields and the 'Fall of America.'" Artinfo.com, 1 July (accessed 24 July 2010).

Leslie, Esther. 2004. *Hollywood Flatlands: Animation, Critical Theory, and the Avant-Garde*. New York: Verso.

Linebaugh, Peter, and Marcus Rediker. 2001. *The Many-Headed Hydra: The Hidden History of the Revolutionary Atlantic*. Boston: Beacon.

Love, Heather. 2009. *Feeling Backwards: Loss and the Politics of Queer History*. Cambridge: Harvard University Press.

Lowe, Lisa. 1996. *Immigrant Acts: On Asian American Cultural Politics*. Durham: Duke University Press.

Mahmood, Saba. 2005. *The Politics of Piety: The Islamic Revival and the Feminist Subject*. Princteon: Princeton University Press.

Malcom, Janet. 2008. *Two Lives: Gertrude and Alice*. New Haven: Yale University Press.

Marks, Laura. 2002. *Touch: Sensuous Theory and Multisensory Media*. Minneapolis: University of Minnesota Press.

Marshall, Stuart. 1991. "The Contemporary Political Use of Gay History: The Third Reich," in *How Do I Look? Queer Film and Video*, ed. Bad Object Choices. Seattle: Bay Press.

Martin, Biddy. 1997. *Femininity Played Straight: The Significance of Being Lesbian*. New York: Routledge.

Massad, Joseph A. 2008. *Desiring Arabs*. Chicago: University of Chicago Press.

McRuer, Robert. 2006. *Crip Theory: Cultural Signs of Queerness and Disability*. New York: New York University Press.

Mignolo, Walter. 2005. *Local Histories/Global Designs: Coloniality, Subaltern Knowledges, and Border Thinking*. Princeton: Princeton University Press.

Morrison, Toni. 1987. *Beloved*. New York: Alfred A. Knopf.

Mosse, George L. 1999. *The Fascist Revolution: Toward a General Theory of Fascism*. New York: Howard Fertig.

Moten, Fred, and Stefano Harney. 2004. "The University and the Undercommons: Seven Theses." *Social Text* 79 22, no. 2, 101–15.

Muñoz, José Esteban. 1999. *Disidentifications: Queers of Color and the Performance of Politics*. Minneapolis: University of Minnesota.

———. 2006. "The Vulnerability Artist: Nao Bustamante and the Sad Beauty of Reparation." *Women and Performance: A Journal of Feminist Theory* 16, no. 2, 191–200.

———. 2010. *Cruising Utopia: The Then and There of Queer Futurity*. New York: New York University Press.

Muñoz, José Esteban, and Nao Bustamante. 2003. "Risk/Riesgo: An Interview with Nao Bustamante." *Felix* 2, no. 32, 5.

Nast, Heidi. 2006. "Critical Pet Studies?" *Antipode* 38, no. 5, 894–906.

Newton, Esther. 1996. "My Best Informant's Dress: The Erotic Equation in Fieldwork," in *Out in the Field: Reflections of Lesbian and Gay Anthropologists*, ed. Ellen

Lewin and William L. Leap. Urbana and Chicago: University of Illinois Press, 212–35.

Ngai, Sianne. 2005. "Animatedness," in *Ugly Feelings*. Cambridge: Harvard University Press.

Nietzsche, Friedrich. 1969. "Second Essay: Guilt, Bad Conscience, and the Like" in *On the Genealogy of Morals: A Polemic*. New York: Vintage: 57–96.

Nyong'o, Tavia. 2008. "Do You Want Queer Theory (or Do You Want the Truth)? Intersections of Punk and Queer in the 1970s." *Radical History Review* 100, Winter, 102–19.

O'Dell, Kathy. 1998. *Contract with the Skin: Masochism, Performance Art, and the 1970's*. Minneapolis: University of Minnesota Press.

Parikh, Crystal. 2009. *An Ethics of Betrayal: The Politics of Otherness in Emergent U.S. Literatures and Cultures*. New York: Fordham University Press.

Phelan, Peggy. 1993. *Unmarked: The Politics of Performance*. New York: Routledge.

Preston, Claire. 2005. *Bee*. London: Reaktion Books.

Price, David A. 2008. *The Pixar Touch*. New York: Alfred A. Knopf.

Puar, Jasbir. 2007. *Terrorist Assemblages: Homonationalism in Queer Times*. Durham: Duke University Press.

Ranciére, Jacques. 1991. *The Ignorant Schoolmaster: Five Lessons in Intellectual Emancipation*, trans. Kirsten Ross. Palo Alto, Calif.: Stanford University Press.

Readings, Bill. 1997. *The University in Ruins*. Cambridge: Harvard University Press.

Roach, Joseph. 1996. *Cities of the Dead: Circum-Atlantic Performance*. New York: Columbia University Press.

Rodowick, D. N. 1997. *Gilles Deleuze's Time Machine*. Durham: Duke University Press.

Ronell, Avital. 2002. *Stupidity*. Champaign: University of Illinois Press.

Roughgarden, Joan. 2004. *Evolution's Rainbow: Diversity, Gender, and Sexuality in Nature and People*. Berkeley: University of California Press.

Rubin, Gayle. 1975. "The Traffic in Women: Notes on the 'Political Economy' of Sex," in *Toward an Anthropology of Women*, ed. Rayna Reiter. New York: Monthly Review Press: 157–210.

———. 1984. "Thinking Sex: Notes for a Radical Theory of Sexuality," in *Pleasure and Danger: Exploring Female Sexuality*, ed. Carole Vance. Boston: Routledge.

Sandage, Scott. 2005. *Born Losers: A History of Failure in America*. Cambridge: Harvard University Press.

Sarafian, Katherine. 2003. "Pixar's Digital Aesthetic," in *New Media: Theories and Practices of Digitextuality*, ed. Anna Everett and John T. Caldwell. New York: Routledge.

Schenkar, Joan. 2009. *The Talented Miss Highsmith: The Secret Life and Serious Art of Patricia Highsmith*. New York: St. Martin's Press.

Schorr, Collier. 2003. "German Brutality and Roman Sensuality: Pictures of Soldiers in the Landscape." Interview. PBS, 1 January. Available at pbs.org.

————. 2008. *Freeway Balconies*. New York: Guggenheim Museum.

Scott, James C. 1987. *Weapons of the Weak: Everyday Forms of Peasant Resistance*. New Haven and London: Yale University Press.

————. 1999. *Seeing Like a State: How Certain Schemes to Improve the Human Condition Have Failed*. New Haven: Yale University Press.

Sebald, W. G. 2002. *Austerlitz*. London: Modern Library.

Sedgwick, Eve Kosofsky. 1990. *Epistemology of the Closet*. Los Angeles: University of California Press.

————. 1994. *Tendencies*. New York: Routledge.

————. 2003. "Paranoid Reading, Reparative Reading." *Touching, Feeling: Affect, Pedagogy, Performativity*. Durham: Duke University Press.

Silva, Noenoe. 2004. *Aloha Betrayed: Native Hawaiian Resistance to American Colonialism*. Durham: Duke University Press.

Smith, Zadie. 2006. *On Beauty*. London: Penguin.

Solanas, Valerie. 2004. scum *Manifesto*. Introduction by Avital Ronell. New York: Verso.

Sontag, Susan. 1975. "Fascinating Fascism." *New York Review of Books*, 6 February.

————. 2001. *On Photography*. New York: Picador.

Spade, Dean. 2008. "Documenting Gender." *Hastings Law Journal* 59, 731–842.

Spivak, Gayatri Chakravorty. 1988. "Can the Subaltern Speak?," in *Marxism and the Interpretation of Culture*, ed. Cary Nelson and Larry Grossberg. Champaign: University of Illinois Press.

Sugimoto, Hiroshi. 1995. *Hiroshi Sugimoto: Time Exposed*, ed. Hiroshi Sugimoto and Thomas Kellein. Basel: Kunsthalle, published by H. Mayer, 91–96.

Weininger, Otto. 2009. *Sex and Character*. New York: BiblioLife.

Welch, Irvine. 1996. *Trainspotting*. London: Norton.

Weston, Kath. 1998. "Forever Is a Long Time: Romancing the Real in Gay Kinship Ideologies," in *Long Slow Burn: Sexuality and Social Science*. New York: Routledge.

Williams, Raymond. 1977. *Marxism and Literature*. Oxford: Oxford University Press.

Wilson, Julia Bryan. 2003. "Remembering Yoko Ono's 'Cut Piece.'" *Oxford Art Journal* 26, no. 1, 99–123.

Wittig, Monique. 1992. *The Straight Mind and Other Essays*. Boston: Beacon Press.

Woolf, Virginia. 1929. *A Room of One's Own*. London: Harcourt Brace Jovanovitch.

Žižek, Slavoj. 2008. *In Defense of Lost Causes*. London: Verso.

————. 2009. "Berlusconi in Tehran." *London Review of Books*, 23 July, 3–7.

Page numbers in boldface refer to illustrations.

tiques of, 18–21, 44–45, 49–52; failure and, 87–88
"Capitalism, the Family, and the
Anus" (Hocquenghem), 94–95
Carceller, Ana, and Helena Cabello,
110–16, **112**, 113, **114**, **115**
Carey, Jim, 58
Cavani, Lillian, 164–65
Chauncey, George, 148
Chicken Run (2000), 21, 27–32, **28**, 49,
120, 128–29, **129**; exploitation in,
180; feminist texts in, 48; individualism vs. collectivity in, 44; narratives of revolution in, 79; queerness
of, 119, 185; use of humans in, 45
childhood narratives, 27–28, 30–31,
47–48, 72–74, 118–21; alternative formations and, 52; animated
cinema and, 73, 186; heterofuturity
and, 106–8; monstrous narratives
and, 44–45
Chisholm, Dianne, 117
Chocolat (2000), 151
Cities of the Dead (Roach), 61, 65, 73, 97,
140
Class, The/Entre Les Murs (2008), 13
claymation, 178. See also Chicken Run
Close Shave (1995), 179
Clover, Carol, 140
Code 46 (2003), 74
Colbert, Stephen, 39
collectivity: animality and, 25, 41–48,
51–52; animated cinema and, 22,
45, 174–76, 181–82; individualism
vs., 31–32; masculinity and, 184–85;
queerness and, 29, 70, 110–11
Common, 37
Companion Species Manifesto (Haraway),
36
computer-generated imagery (CGI), 7,
19–20, 22, 29–31, 78, 175–77

Conformist, The (1970), 155
Coraline (2009), 30, 180–81, 182, 185,
186
Crisp, Quentin, 3, 87, 96, 110
cross-species alliances, 79, 80, 184–85
Cruising Utopia (Muñoz), 87, 89, 190 n.7
Curse of the Were-Rabbit (2005), **179**
"Cut Piece" (Ono), 137–39, 144–45
Cvetkovich, Ann, 110
cyborgs, 33–34, 36, 46. See also
transbiology

Damned, The (1969), 155
Deadly Swarm (2003), 52
death drive, 86, 106, 110–11, 135–36,
149–50, 186–87
de Beauvoir, Simone, 125, 140
Delaney, Samuel, 149
Deleuze, Gilles, 124, 127, 129, 139,
177, 181
Denis, Claire, 151
Derrida, Jacques, 86
Desire (1989), 152
disciplinarity, 6, 7, 9–12, 13–15, 25;
antidisciplinarity, 147–48; family as
disciplinary matrix, 72; generational
logics and, 124–25; negativity and,
23–24; pedagogical approaches and,
16–17, 92, 174; Pixar and, 181–82;
subversive intellectuals and, 8, 11
Disidentifications (Muñoz), 89
Disney, Walt, 21, 22, 174–75
Dorfman, Ariel, 174
DreamWorks, 181–82
Dude, Where's My Car? (2000), 21, 58–69
Duggan, Lisa, 71–72
Dumb and Dumber (1994), 58

Ebert, Roger, 49
Edelman, Lee, 73, 98, 106–8, 118, 120,
148–49

Eisenstein, Sergei, 174
Eliot, T. S., 150
El-Tayib, Fatima, 162
Eng, David, 72
Eternal Sunshine of the Spotless Mind
(2004), 74, 190 n.6
Evolution's Rainbow (Roughgarden), 39,
40, 81

failure, 3–5, 7, 24–25, 87–89, 147; as
anticolonialism, 126–28, 131–33,
135; antidisciplinarity as, 9–15, 148;
Bush as, 94; capitalism and, 2–4;
gay betrayal and, 150–51, 162–64,
165, 171; lesbianism as, 95–96; love
and, 104–5, 130–31; low theory
and, 23; potential of, 118–21; queerness and, 90–92; as refusal, 2,
11–12; success vs., 174; survival and,
184–87. See also queer art of failure
familial narratives, 41–43, 46–48,
71–75, 80–82; anticolonialism and,
14–15; father-son dynamics in, 30,
69–70, 73, 79, 184; forgetting and,
76–81; generational logics in, 30,
69–71, 79, 119; kinship discourses
in, 33; kinship networks vs., 33;
masculinity and, 184–85; mother-
daughter bonds in, 30, 123–24,
131–35; of nuclear family, 37, 76,
78; transgender narratives vs.,
78–79
Fanon, Franz, 14, 132–33
Fantastic Mr. Fox (2009), 182–85, 186
Farce of the Penguins (2006), 42
"fascinating fascism" (Sontag), 164
fascism, 165–68; homoerotics of,
152–62, 164, 170–71; roles of homosexuality in, 148. See also Nazis,
Nazism
Fascist Revolution (Mosse), 156

Fay, Bernard, 160
Feeling Backwards (Love), 87, 99, 131
"Female Couple, 1932" (Brassai), 99
Female Masculinity (Halberstam), 151
femininity: failed masculinism as, 125;
Jewish people and, 156, 160; lesbians and, 94–96, 99–100; racialized feminine beauty and, 142–44;
radical passivity and, 136, 139–40,
144–45
feminisms, 124–30, 136, 139–40, 144;
alternative formations and, 140,
145; antisocial feminism, 110, 129;
failure as lesbianism, 4–5; feminist utopias, 21, 32, 48–49; gender
identification and, 159; politics of
refusal and, 131–33
Ferguson, Roderick, 74, 129
50 First Dates (2004), 74–78
Fight Club (1999), 177
Finding Nemo (2003), 53–54, 54;
computer-generated imagery and,
175; cross-species alliances in, 79,
80, 184; familial narratives within,
78–82; gender in, 49; individualism
vs. collectivity in, 44; memory and,
43, 74–75; plans for revolution in,
21; time-loop narrative structures
in, 58
forgetting, 15, 69–86; childhood narratives and, 27–28; freedom and,
63; gender and, 58; knowledge formations and, 147; loss of individuality and, 190 n.6; as power, 58–59,
61–66, 82; stupidity vs., 53–54;
time-loop narrative structures as,
59–61, 68; whiteness and, 61–65.
See also remembering
Fortuyn, Pim, 161
Foucault, Michel, 147, 149–50; on disciplinarity and knowledge, 7–8, 9,

10–11; on failure as a way of life, 3; heterotopic spaces and, 113; knowledge from below and, 11, 23; memory as power and, 15; reverse discourse and, 10–11, 127–28

"Fourth #2" (Moffat), **plate 1**

"Fourth #3" (Moffat), **plate 2**

Franklin, Sarah, 33

freedom: in childhood captivity and adult freedom narratives, 30–31; emancipatory knowledge and, 14–15; feminisms and, 127–30; forgetting and, 63, 80–81; narratives of sexual freedom, 147, 149–50; negative freedom, 132–33

Freeman, Elizabeth, 20, 21, 83, 144, 190 n.7, 191 n.1 (chap. 4)

Freeway Balconies show (2008), 165, 168, 171

Freire, Paolo, 14

Freud, Sigmund, 125, 135–36, 144, 178, 182–83

futurity, 44, 73, 106–8, 118, 120

gender, 51–52, 99–104, 183–84; collectivity and, 184–85; feminism and, 21, 32, 128–29, 159; forgetting and, 58, 69–70; gender identification and, 159–61; gender-opposed couples and, 94–96, 159; generational logics and, 70–74; lesbian masculinity and, 94–96; male stupidity and, 56–59, 61–65, 68–69; multigendered forms in animated cinema and, 181–82; Pixarvolt film genre and, 45–50; radical passivity and, 136, 139–40, 144–45; stupidity and, 54–59; time-loop narrative structures and, 69–70; transgender narratives, 74–75, 78–79, 81–82

generational logics, 30; disciplinarity

and, 124–25; in familial narratives, 69–71, 79–80, 82, 119; of forgetting and remembering, 70–74; loss and, 123–24

Genet, Jean, 151

"Gertrude Stein" (1935), **102**

Ghostly Matters (Gordon), 15

Giles, Geoffrey, 156

Goldstein, Richard, 165, 167

Gondry, Michael, 74, 190 n.6

Gordon, Avery, 15

Grammar of the Multitude (Virno), 31

Gramsci, Antonio, 16–18, 32, 80, 88–89

Haider, Jörg, 161

Hall, Radclyffe, 151

Hall, Stuart, 15–18

happiness, 3–5, **23**, 83–84, 90–91, 106–9, 132–33, 140, 147–48, 186

Happy Feet (2006), 42, 47, 48

Haraway, Donna, 33, 35–37, 46, 67

Hardt, Michael, 32, 51

Hart, Lynda, 130, 135

Hartman, Saidiya, 15, 85–88, 123–26, 130, 145

Harvey, Stefano, and Fred Moten, 8, 11–15

hegemony, 11–12, 16–18, 60–61; counter-, 32, 171; low theory and, 2; pedagogical approaches and, 13–14, 92, 174

"Here and Now" (Nicholls), 142, **plate 10**

Herzog, Dagmar, 154

heterofuturity, 73, 106–8, 118

Hewitt, Andrew, 156–57

"Higher Ground" (Nicholls), **plate 11**

Highsmith, Patricia, 109, 110

Hirschfeld, Max, 155–56, 157

History of Forgetting (Klein), 83

volt genre, 49; racialized feminine beauty, 142–44; white male stupidity and, 55–57, 61–65

radical passivity, 136, 139–40, 144

Ranciére, Jacques, 13–14, 16–17, 20

Readings, Bill, 20

Rediker, Marcus, 18–19, 51

refusal, politics of, 11–12, 126–28, 130–33; failure as, 2, 88–89; feminisms and, 124, 136; individualism and, 181–82; masochism as, 139; mastery and, 143; queer femininity and, 142

remembering, 15, 82–86; forgetting and, 15, 74–75; mythic stability through, 82; nostalgic narratives and, 30, 82, 116–17, 131–32, 152; place-bound memories and, 65–66; as resistance, 77–78. See also forgetting; memory

resistance, 77–86, 118–21, 149–50; anthropomorphism and, 51–52; counterhegemony and, 11–12, 17–18, 32, 171; forgetting as, 70–71; mainstream films for children and, 118–21; negation and negativity as, 127–28; pirate cultures and, 18–23; queerness as assemblage of, 29; reverse discourse and, 10–11

revolutionary narratives, 29–32; in mainstream film, 22–23. See also Chicken Run; Finding Nemo

Rhythm 0 (Abramovic), 138–39

Riefenstahl, Leni, 170

Roach, Joseph, 61, 65, 73, 97, 140

Robots (2005), 45–47, **46**

Rodowick, David, 181

Roehm, Ernst, 155–56, 158

Ronell, Avital, 53, 62

Room of One's Own, A (Woolf), 125

Roughgarden, Joan, 39, 40, 81

Rubin, Gayle, 37, 72, 135, 148–49

Sandage, Scott, 88, 92

Sandler, Adam, 57, 58, 75. See also 50 First Dates

Scenes of Subjection (Hartman), 126, 130

Schorr, Collier, 162, **163**, **164**, 164–68, **168**, 171, **plate 14**

Scott, James C., 6, 9–10, 88

SCUM Manifesto (Solanas), 4, 51, 108–9

Secret Paris of the 1930's (Brassai), 98–103, **99**

Sedgwick, Eve Kosofsky, 12, 65, 73–74, 103, 154–59, 162

Seeing Like a State (Scott), 9–10

"Seven Theses" (Moten and Harvey), 8, 11–15

Sex after Fascism (Herzog), 160–61

sexualities, 33–42, 162–64; animality and, 49–52; betrayal and, 150–51; feminine men and, 155–56; gender-opposed couples and, 159; homonationalism, 161; homosexual emancipation movements, 155–56; homosexuality as shifting set of relations, 171; transgender narratives, 74–75, 78–79, 81–82; white male stupidity about, 66–67

Shoah (1985), 83–84

Shoot (Burden), 139

Shrek (2001), 48, 119, 120

Sideways (2004), 58

Silva, Noenoe, 77

"Sin título (Utopia) #27" (Cabello/Carcellar), 111, **112**, 113

"Sin título (Utopia) #29" (Cabello/Carcellar), **112**

skinheads, 165–68

Smith, Albert, 178

Judith Halberstam is professor of English,
American studies and ethnicity, and gender studies
at the University of Southern California. She is the
author of several books, including *In a Queer Time
and Place: Transgender Bodies, Subcultural Lives* (2005)
and *Female Masculinity* (1998).

Library of Congress Cataloging-in-Publication Data
Halberstam, Judith, 1961–
The queer art of failure / Judith Halberstam.
p. cm.
"A John Hope Franklin Center Book."
Includes bibliographical references and index.
ISBN 978-0-8223-5028-6 (cloth : alk. paper)
ISBN 978-0-8223-5045-3 (pbk. : alk. paper)
1. Social epistemology. 2. Failure (Psychology)
3. Stupidity. 4. Queer theory. I. Title.
BD175.H33 2011
121—dc22   2011010762